PAT MUELLER is Associate Professor and Chairman of the Department of Intramurals for Men at the University of Minnesota. Mr. Mueller is President of the National Intramural Association, National President of Sigma Delta Psi, and Secretary-Treasurer of the National College Physical Education Association for Men. He is Co-editor of the *Directory of Intramural References,* published by the American Association for Health, Physical Education, and Recreation, and Editor of the *National College Physical Education Association for Men Annual Proceedings.*

INTRAMURALS: PROGRAMMING AND ADMINISTRATION

PAT MUELLER
UNIVERSITY OF MINNESOTA

FOURTH EDITION

THE RONALD PRESS COMPANY · NEW YORK

Library of Congress Catalog Card Number: 70–155210
PRINTED IN THE UNITED STATES OF AMERICA

Dedicated to

DR. ELMER D. MITCHELL

The Father of Intramurals in America,
who, in 1925, wrote the original edition
of this book.

Preface

Intramurals: Programming and Administration, in keeping with today's ever-expanding intramural patterns and programs, presents expanded intramural concepts, identifying these programs not only with educational institutions but military, industrial, and community organizations as well. It clearly relates intramurals to recreation and physical education as dictated by modern trends. The book emphasizes essential programming ingredients and concepts which, if understood and implemented, will enable directors or supervisors to administer successful intramural programs for boys or girls, men or women, at all levels, and under any circumstances.

Chapters are sequentially arranged to present logically the many facets of programming, making it ideal for intramural courses. A suggested course outline is included in the Appendix. The subject arrangement plus the practical information and workable ideas also make it valuable for directors charged with establishing new programs and for those who administer existing ones.

The book first discusses the meaning and purpose of intramurals, and then the past, present, and future of these programs. It takes up administrative patterns and personnel selection. A new chapter establishes the relationship of ideas to solving program problems and specifies procedures for producing new ideas. Additionally, ideas for intramurals appear throughout the text to remind the reader of the value of ideation. Also covered are finances, facilities, and equipment; units which serve as a basis for participation; numerous program activities; scheduling techniques; point systems; game and eligibility rules; publicity; and awards.

Two major items of concern today are extramurals and sports clubs. An enlarged chapter unravels some of the knotty problems and encourages administrators to utilize these programs as a means of providing valuable success-and-failure sports experiences for the participants. Increased attention is given to co-recreation, and the new term *co-intramurals* is introduced.

This volume covers the methods of structuring tournament participation. It explains how to manage various kinds of meets; how to adapt tournaments to the activity and number of participants; how to organize leagues; how to design elimination, challenge, and informal-type tournaments; and how to incorporate classification and equalization methods. Several new concepts are introduced, including the Mueller-Anderson playback tournament.

Throughout, numerous forms, charts, tables, and diagrams have been included. Some provide instant short-cut methods for making up schedules; determining the number of rounds, byes, and games; placing byes and seeded players; constructing draw sheets; figuring handicaps and percentages; and assigning point totals for groups and individuals.

The author wishes to express his sincerest appreciation to Sally Jean Blass who sacrificed many extra hours and personal privileges while typing the manuscript; to fellow intramuralists Bruce Anderson, Roy Tutt, and Mike Stevenson, for their ideas, patience, and understanding during its preparation; to Marilyn Miller and Fred Carlson, for interpreting concepts through their illustrative artwork; and to his wife and children for assistance in preparing the manuscript and for enduring the endless hours of absence while it was written.

PAT MUELLER

Minneapolis, Minnesota
August, 1971

Contents

INTRAMURALS: PROGRAMMING AND ADMINISTRATION

1

Intramurals: What and Why

The word "intramural" is derived from the Latin words *intra*, meaning within, and *murus*, meaning wall. Intramural means within the walls or refers to something that operates within some type of framework or limitation. Another way of expressing it is that intramural refers to "anything that is inside of something."

The term is usually paired with other words such as sports, athletics, and activities and, when so combined, implies a program of sports and other activities conducted "within the walls" or imaginary boundaries of some organization or institution. These programs are found in educational institutions at all levels—elementary schools, junior high schools, senior high schools, colleges and universities; and in military, industrial, and community organizations.

EVOLUTION OF INTRAMURAL TERMINOLOGY

Words used to describe these programs have changed from "athletics" to "sports" to "activities." In early days, the intramural program was composed primarily of athletics which were intercollegiate or varsity in nature. Therefore, the term "intramural athletics" was used to title the program. As different types of activities were introduced, the term "sports," because of its more inclusive connotation, replaced athletics. More recently, as programs encompassed not only sports but card games, music, dramatics, crafts, and other events of a nonphysical nature, the expression "intramural activities" has been adopted.

In some programs, all three terms have been dropped, and only the word "intramurals" is used. This shortened title appeals to program su-

3

pervisors and participants because it is concise and all-inclusive. The term is frequently abbreviated with the letters I-M to identify the activities and functions of an intramural program.

Related Terminology

The prefix "intra," as noted, means within; the prefix "extra" means without or beyond; and the prefix "inter" means between or among. While an intramural program exists inside of some established boundaries, extramural or intermural programs are those that function outside of certain limitations. The establishment of boundaries clearly identifies whether a program is intramural or extramural, and changing these boundaries may cause what was once extramural to become intramural and vice versa. For example, in a military program, intramural competition may take place within a regiment, but if it is between regiments, the competition may be called extramural or varsity, depending on how the boundaries are established and the program is defined. A realignment of boundaries could alter the complexion and title of the program.

Although in common practice these activity programs are labeled intramural, extramural, interscholastic, and intercollegiate, logic would permit use of such terms as intrainstitutional, intradivision, extraboundary, extracollegiate, intercommand, and interorganization.

SCOPE OF INTRAMURALS

There are two basic program participation phases of intramurals. The one most commonly accepted by intramural personnel and sometimes thought to be the only aspect, is the highly organized, competitive leagues and tournament games leading to championships. The second phase, equally important, includes the self-directed, impromptu, informal activities. The latter provides the opportunity, voluntarily and informally, to recreate in some form of exercise such as swimming, playing tennis, golf, or handball, bowling, or shooting baskets. A specific effort should be made to build this type of participation into the facilities schedule.

An intramural program should be free to everyone and participation should be elective or voluntary. A well organized and administered program provides opportunities for individuals of all levels of ability to take part in one or both of the above-mentioned phases. Everyone means boys and girls, men and women, the strong and weak, tall and short, the physically handicapped, and those with below average, average, and above average ability. For the intramural program, the basic prerequisite is the desire to participate; the degree of skill is of lesser importance. A balanced program consists of team games, individual and dual sports, co-recreation or co-intramural activities, sports clubs, and special events.

In addition to playing in the program, participants can share in its planning and supervision. Individuals may be involved as players, coaches, managers, supervisors, and officials. They receive not only the benefits from activity participation but also valuable leadership experience while aiding program administration.

Recreation and Physical Education

Intramurals have the unique distinction of being both recreation and physical education. Traditionally, most intramural programs have been aligned with physical education departments. However, recently some programs in newly established institutions and others, as a result of reorganization, have affiliated with recreation.

Where intramurals are located in a particular institution depends largely on the philosophy of those who are in a position to establish these programs. In some situations, intramurals may switch from physical education to recreation, depending on the financial and moral support received from the administrators of the respective programs. The most influential factor in many instances will undoubtedly be which group can provide the most adequate source of funds. Whether intramurals are physical education or recreation is somewhat unimportant except as it relates to the ability of a particular institution to provide sufficient opportunities for meaningful sports experiences.

Intramurals as Recreation. Individuals take part in intramural programs as a result of their own desires and during unincumbered time periods. Therefore, if recreation is defined as "voluntary participation in leisure time activities," the terms intramural and recreation are synonymous. In this concept, intramurals are a phase of the very large recreation movement that has such a prominent place in the culture of the entire world. This recreation movement has grown in the present century to the extent that it is an accepted institution in our way of life, and it promises to grow even more with increasing automation and the accompanying increased leisure time.

This movement includes all forms of active play and sports as well as social activities, art, music, dramatics, dance, nature lore, hobbies, camping, social service, and the quieter forms of recreation such as reading, listening to the radio, and watching television. The intramural phase, however, is primarily concerned with active, recreational activities including organized team play, individual competition, and informal exercise.

When intramural programs have been developed under this philosophy, they are usually organized within some department other than physical education. For example, they may be under the jurisdiction of a Dean or Vice President of Student Affairs, a Student Union, a Student Activities Bureau, or a large institutional organization directed by a recreation coordinator. In some community schools, an intramural or recreation supervisor is employed to administer the school and community recreation program, using school and municipal facilities for all phases of the program.

Some intramural departments and handbooks use the term "intramural and recreation." When this phrase is used, it is an admission that intramurals are something other than recreation. It would undoubtedly be more appropriate to use the term "intramural recreation" with the word "intramural" serving as an adjective to describe a type of recreation. If the philosophy is accepted that intramurals are a part of recreation, then it would seem advisable to use the expression "intramural recreation" and not "intramural and recreation."

Intramurals As Physical Education. If physical education is defined as "education through physical activities," intramurals are a part of physical education because the program provides educational experiences primarily through physical activities. Modern education attempts to structure experiences which are beneficial to the total growth and development of the individual. Through the use of physical activities, physical education, and intramurals as one phase of it, have the same objectives.

Traditionally, the broad physical education program consists of three phases: (1) instructional class activities, (2) varsity athletics, and (3) intramurals. All three use the medium of physical activities to educate individuals. If one of the three is missing, the total physical education program operates at a 33⅓ per cent deficiency.

A wide variety of skills is learned in physical education activity classes. Intramural personnel are well aware of the importance of instruction to the participants. They realize that students may not enter the program unless they are reasonably certain some degree of success will be achieved. If skills are not learned in physical education classes, they must be acquired through sports clubs, community recreation programs, or friends on the sand lots. An intramural program is easier to administer if a school has required physical education or a well organized elective program.

To this extent, the intramural program serves as a laboratory offering students the opportunity to develop further the skills previously learned in physical education activity classes. Many of these activities have "carry-over" value which means the student may continue to utilize these skills in his life after graduation. The combined physical education class instruction and intramural laboratory program provides pleasant experiences that help to shape the individual's attitudes toward physical activities, attitudes that will be beneficial during and after his school career.

Intramurals and Varsity Sports

The intercollegiate and interscholastic varsity programs are organized for the highly skilled specialists. Thus, only a few reap the benefits of this phase of the physical education program. The majority of students need other athletic outlets and a broad, properly administered I-M program fills this need. Sometimes students participating in intramurals develop sufficient skill to enable them to join a varsity squad. However, development of varsity material is generally considered to be incidental.

Some student athletes are not encouraged to try out for varsity teams because of the high degree of selectivity involved in athletic scholarship recruiting. Others do not try out because of a lack of confidence in their own ability, insufficient desire to pay the price of practice and conditioning, heavy class schedules, or the need to work. In intramurals, these individuals have the opportunity to maintain their athletic interests in a less intensified manner.

The intramural program also serves athletes who quit or are dropped from the varsity and freshmen squads. Coaches and intramural directors should assist athletes in making the transition to some intramural activity. Some of the athletes may have an opportunity to return to the varsity after participating on intramural teams. Because some individuals develop late and at different rates, coaches should encourage broad programs of intramurals and physical education, particularly at the elementary, junior high, and senior high school levels.

Ideal Physical Activity Programs

The well-balanced physical education program at all levels is the answer to achieving a goal of "sports for everyone." At the elementary level, pupils should learn physical skills such as running, throwing, climbing, and rhythms. In elementary and junior high school grades, there should be a definite progression of games, contests, relays, and rhythms in order to develop beginning and intermediate skills. This sequential progression should also include competition in team sports with emphasis on participation rather than winning. The elementary and junior high school period is the most opportune time to develop not only activity skills, but also desirable attitudes of the need for participation in physical recreation activities.

At the senior high school level, students should be permitted to elect physical education class activities and to take part in voluntary intramural and varsity athletic programs. At this stage they should further learn the values of physical education, and spend class time learning new skills and perfecting those previously learned.

In the college physical education program, there should be an opportunity to elect an even wider range of sports offered in physical education activity classes, the intramural program, and the intercollegiate program. Ideally, if proper appreciation for participation in physical activities has been taught in the formative years, it will not be necessary to have required classes, but rather the entire physical education system can be elective and without credits or grades.

VALUES OF INTRAMURAL PARTICIPATION

The purpose of intramural programs is very simply and fundamentally to provide human beings with experiences that will assist them in achieving a better state of being. All of these experiences should be directed toward the individual's total development: physical, social, emotional, spiritual, and intellectual.

If an engineer designs and builds a computer, he does so with a specific purpose in mind. The computer performs specific functions to fulfill a need. In other words, it is created for a purpose, designed to accomplish that purpose in the most efficient manner, and constructed according to that design which best accomplishes the successful completion of the intended mission.

It may be assumed that human beings, too, are structured according to a design which fulfills the reasons for their existence.

Intramural participation provides opportunities for individuals to act in and react to sports experiences which will help them achieve purposeful living. The experience reactions permit them to discover goals, to relate to other people in their environment, and to become more fully aware of themselves and their design.

Through the ages, great philosophers and educators have emphasized the values of sports participation and have identified the relationship of the intellectual to the physical. Some of these expressions are presented to substantiate these values.

Socrates (420 B.C.)   Our children from their earliest years must take part in all the more lawful forms of play, for if they are not surrounded with such an atmosphere, they can never grow up to be well conducted and virtuous citizens.

Plato (380 B.C.)   There will be need of sports for the habits of the soul, even at six years of age.

Aristotle (350 B.C.)   The principal aim of gymnastics is education of all youth and not simply that minority of people highly favored by nature.

Comenius (A.D. 1650)   Intellectual progress is conditioned at every step by bodily vigor. To attain the best results, physical exercise must accompany and condition mental training.

Froebel (A.D. 1830)   It is by no means, however, only the physical power that is fed and strengthened in these games; intellectual and moral power, too, is definitely and steadily gained and brought under control.

Hall (A.D. 1902)   For the young, motor education is cardinal, and is now coming in due recognition, and for all, education is incomplete without a motor side. For muscle culture develops brain centers as nothing else yet demonstrably does.

Dewey (A.D. 1919)   Experience has shown that when children have a chance at physical activities which bring their natural impulses into play, going to school is a joy, management is less of a burden, and learning is easier.

Menninger (A.D. 1967)   Too many people do not know how to play. Others limit their recreation to passive observation of the activity of others. Some people harbor the belief of our early forefathers that to play is sinful. Others feel that play is only for children and believe that "as I became a man I put away childish things." Some regard play as simply a waste of time as well as energy. Some consider play a reward for good behavior. Finally, some individuals have had such severe and rugged lives as children that they have never learned to play. The psychiatrist is strongly in disagreement with all of these attitudes. There is considerable scientific evidence that the healthy personality is one who not only plays but who takes his play seriously. And there is also evidence that the inability and unwillingness to play reveals an insecure or disordered aspect of personality.

Success and Failure Experiences

One of the most important values of sports participation is the opportunity for individuals to respond to numerous success and failure experiences. A measure of success encourages a person to do all things in a successful manner, and a degree of failure causes him to try to improve subsequent performances. The mental adjustments to success and failure in sports provide excellent training for similar experiences in other phases of life.

If a person's life is examined, it can be easily observed that he succeeds or fails to a degree in everything he does. For example, classroom performances are graded on an A, B, C, D, and F basis, some salesmen receive bonuses for their performances while others are fired, and generally, everyone is categorized as being better or not as good as someone else.

In analyzing a sporting activity, it is evident that success and failure are constantly present. For example, every time a pitcher throws the ball over the strike zone, it is an element of success for him, but a degree of failure to the batter. If the batter hits the ball, it is success for him, and the pitcher has a feeling of failure. All of these degrees are relative. If the batter hits a single, double, triple, or home run, he has correspondingly elated feelings of success while the pitcher has concurrently deeper feelings of failure.

In further analyzing play, if the ball is hit to the shortstop and the batter is thrown out, it is success for the shortstop and failure for the batter. If the shortstop makes an error, he experiences failure and the base runner succeeds although not to the same degree as if he had hit a single. Every phase of sport can be analyzed to determine the corresponding opposites of success and failure.

Not only are there individual situations to which a player reacts, but team roles as well. If a team wins a ball game, everybody on that team shares in the success. Regardless of the fact that some of the players may not have contributed to the victory, there is still a shared success feeling. For the losing team, everybody shares in the failure. However, some of the players on the losing team may be satisfied with their individual performances, and this may soften the failure feeling. For example, if a player hit a home run or had four hits in four times at bat, for him the loss may not seem quite as severe. Pictures on the sports page of a newspaper frequently reflect the joy of successful accomplishment or the negative feeling of a failing attempt.

In individual and dual sports, these experiences are present without participating against an opponent. In golf, the player tries to beat par or perhaps his previous performance. His accomplishment is satisfying or dissatisfying by degrees. In bowling, the 300 game is the ultimate goal, although many bowlers are satisfied with a 200 game or just to improve their average. In track, a runner tries to break a record or improve his skill. For a young child, just being able to hit or catch the ball for the first time is success.

Success and failure elements exist whether in competition with others or as one tries to improve his skills. And it is the appropriate reaction to pleasant and unpleasant experiences in sports that is of inestimable value to an individual's development.

Physical Fitness

Where the physical begins and the intellectual ends is difficult, if not impossible, to determine. The question has long been debated and undoubtedly will be a source of discussion far into the future. There are also advocates of the term "total fitness" who suggest that fitness extends beyond muscle and that the individual must be viewed as a whole. However, physical fitness is a widely used term, and intramural participation makes a definite contribution.

Sports participation develops strength and endurance as well as the neuromuscular coordination that provides agility and confidence in the control of one's movements. Participation develops the ability to handle the body gracefully and efficiently. The qualities of strength, endurance, and agility are directly useful in meeting the stresses of everyday life. Indirectly, they comprise a great asset for any individual through the inner confidence and self-assurance they bring, and through the outward addition they make to his carriage and presence. The importance of bodily coordination and training in motor skills is receiving increased emphasis through the National Physical Fitness Programs of our country.

Constitutional soundness is an important feature of successful living. However, physical exercise, which is so necessary for securing this soundness, is not encouraged by our present way of life. Many of the student's occupations of today, both in regard to his studies and leisure time, are of the passive type. This is unfortunate because moderate exercise, in which the large fundamental muscles of the body are utilized, makes an important contribution to physical fitness. Exercise develops the muscles of the body and produces a healthy, balanced posture. The increased activity of the heart and lungs serves to eliminate waste products of the body and to hasten the assimilation of food energy into the body tissues.

Health examinations required for participation contribute to the development of a positive attitude of having periodic health examinations throughout life, an important objective of preventive medicine.

Mental and Emotional Health

Mental hygienists advocate the need for enjoyable, recreative activities, the kind which are sponsored in the intramural program. Dr. William Menninger, world famous psychiatrist, has stated, "To the individual, good mental health is directly related to his capacity and willingness to play." He further suggests that "competitive games provide an unusually satisfactory social outlet for the instinctive aggressive drive. It is a drive that constantly seeks expression in all of us. Where its direct expression is denied, symptoms may develop. There are perhaps specific values in varying degrees and types of competitive activity. The most aggressive outlet is seen in those sports in which there is bodily contact with an object, such as tennis, golf, badminton, bowling; and probably least, but still evident, in sports of primarily intellectual competition such as chess, checkers, bridge, poker, and so on. All these types of recreation meet the psychological need of many individuals whose jobs or daily work prevent sufficient expression of aggression." [1]

Participation in such activities gives objective interests and outlooks. It takes the individual's mind off himself and focuses it on outside, interesting objects, and thereby combats tendencies to become moody, too introspective, and too introverted. The individual also learns to adapt himself to group standards. There are too many people who do not know how to enjoy playing. From the standpoint of mental hygiene, intramural activities prove valuable in providing relaxation from work and study. Change of activity is important in relaxation, as is congenial companionship.

Emotionally, an individual participating in intramurals can attain personal satisfaction and meet personal needs. These include the need for accomplishment, need for self-expression and creativity, need for recognition, need for new experiences, and the need for belonging. A further emotional objective is development of self-reliance and self-esteem. Participants have an ideal opportuniy to develop their individuality and emotional maturity through intramurals.

Social Contacts

The opportunity to meet other individuals of similar age is one of the most valuable experiences a person gains during his school career. On the athletic field or sports court, these associations are carried on under conditions that simulate adult social and competitive life in many respects. Such an experience in group relations broadens the individual's

[1] William Menninger, *Living in a Troubled World* (Kansas City, Missouri: Hallmark Cards, Inc., 1967), pp. 32–38.

viewpoint; makes him a better judge of his associates; gives him greater self-assurance when in the company of others; teaches him the meaning of loyalty and cooperation; and teaches him lessons of acceptable sportsmanlike conduct. Participants receive actual experience in group living which is valuable for "getting along" in the numerous social involvements of everyday living. Friendships established in the classroom are often increased on the playing field and vice versa.

Use of Leisure Time

Through intramurals, an individual's leisure time is employed in a wholesome manner. Whether a person is playing or observing others performing, he is recreating. But the joy of participating in an actual sports experience is greater than the joy of watching one. Relaxation through physical recreation activities is an important part of his school career and postschool life.

The recreative concept of intramurals should be constantly emphasized. While certain rugged sports requiring tedious training are beneficial to the participants, constant attention should be given to sports that are enjoyed spontaneously without a great amount of preparation. Activity should never be organized to the point where the fun is organized out of them. Participation should be an enjoyable experience in addition to the quest for recognition.

The recreation or intramural concept tends to perpetuate itself through participation. A variety of activities is offered enabling the participant to develop a repertoire of leisure time pursuits which not only enrich his present life, but will add wholesome enjoyment to his life in the future. Intramural participation is one of the most fundamental methods by which students prepare for wise and joyful use of leisure time, and this is an important contribution in a world where there is enforced leisure because of the decreasing number of working hours.

Esprit de Corps

The feeling of group spirit and unity that a varsity team develops among students is a most praiseworthy feature of sports programs. This same spirit and loyalty is exemplified in miniature by the various participating units in the intramural program. The feeling engendered is that of belonging to a cause that is larger than one's self and of the willingness, if necessary, to sacrifice one's own interest for the welfare of the group. Pride and devotion is symbolic of the patriotism of a citizen to the state and nation and therefore is a worthwhile attitude to develop in the nation's youth.

This loyalty should not become a narrow partisanship which expresses an attitude of hostility or discourtesy toward opponents. Fortunately, such occasions are rare in intramurals; in fact, teams frequently gain mutual respect and good will as an outcome of meeting each other on the playing field. Rivalries in intramurals are natural and wholesome. There is no need for an artificial "build-up" because rivalries and the desire for competition develop spontaneously.

Permanent Participator—Spectator Interests

One of the drawbacks of highly specialized varsity athletic programs is that players do not have an opportunity to continue their interests in exercise and play immediately after graduation. They are usually trained in competitive sports that require numerous players, specialized facilities and equipment. These factors often preclude the possibility of engaging in these same team sports after their school career has ended.

Intramural participation does not promote a high type of specialization. The intramural athlete is apt to engage in a number of activities with the result that he gains knowledge in a variety of exercises and develops an average ability in most of them. To this extent the intramural program provides a broader base for greater carry-over interests in sports participation and spectation.

Rarely does an adult become interested in any form of sport unless the rudiments are learned in his childhood and youth. Herein lies the importance of programs with a wide variety of activities that may be continued after one's school days are over. When the spirit of play is once acquired, it continues to demand expression.

2

Intramurals:
Past, Present, and Future

To identify when the evolution of intramurals began is very difficult. There are theories about the previous existence of great civilizations such as Atlantis and Lemuria, submerged at the bottom of the Atlantic and Pacific Oceans. If these theories are true and the people were highly civilized as suspected, it is possible that they participated in physical exercise or athletic type activities. There are also many sporting events recorded in early Greek and Roman literature as well as in Scripture. It is highly possible that some of this early participation was intramural in nature.

When the word "intramural" was first used is not specifically known, but it may be related to the time when cities were surrounded by walls for protection from enemies. Although the early beginnings cannot be clearly established, there are some points of reference that identify the evolution of intramurals in America.

DEVELOPMENT OF INTRAMURALS IN AMERICA

The early growth of intramurals in America was haphazard. Until the 1920's, programs were hit or miss because the two more prominent departments of physical exercise, physical education and varsity athletics, were so involved with their own programs that the *athletic* needs of the masses of students were almost entirely neglected.

Early physical education departments fostered strictly formal gymnastic programs. As a result, the athletic programs developed independently under student and alumni control. Subsequently, the scope of these programs narrowed considerably to a point where they resulted in varsity training for the few. Winning became the paramount objective and all available revenues, facilities, and leadership were centered on these specialized teams. Therefore, intramurals grew up as a neglected orphan, uncared for by either the physical education or varsity athletic departments, and with limited support and design.

Student Organization

The sports club traditions of Great Britain and the Continent greatly influenced early American sports programs. Students formed sports clubs and participated in sports that were almost completely of English and European origin. Gradually rules of these games were adapted or changed to fit the American way of life and in some instances, new sports were invented.

The beginnings of athletics in colleges were intramural in nature and began because of student demand. The natural desire for sports and competition, a strong urge in normal youth, sought expression in impromptu, challenge games. Students, of their own accord, began loosely to organize intramural competition between classes. An example of this "organization" is cited below:

In the fall of 1857 at Princeton University, a few members of the freshman class met and organized, "The Nassau Baseball Club," to play baseball, although few members had seen the game and fewer had played it. But it became popular among members of the class, and a diamond was laid out in the "pasture" lot by the present casino . . . The object of the standing committee was to remove all bricks, stones and other obstructions on the ground which were liable to impede the operations of the energetic club.

After a few weeks' practicing, with an audacity unusual for freshmen, they challenged the sophomore class to a match game. The "Sophs" were as innocent of all knowledge regarding the game as new born babes but they were not to be downed by a lot of freshmen. One faction favored the contest, but another fearing it would go hard with them, declared it was beyond the dignity of their class to submit to such impertinence. However, after much consideration, the challenge was accepted, and the presidents of the classes were chosen as umpires. A referee was elected whose duty it was to decide between the umpires whenever they should disagree. Each side consisted of fifteen players, and the whole game was conducted with laudable and good feeling. After each side had played five innings the "Sophs" had beaten their antagonists by twenty-one rounds and were declared victorious. The announcement was received with deafening hurrahs. The freshmen throwing their caps into the air and showing other indications of a spirit unbroken by defeat replied by giving them three lusty cheers for their immortal class." [1]

Additional examples of class competition were recorded at Yale University and the University of Minnesota. In 1859 at Yale, boating clubs competed intramurally and subsequently served as the basis for interclass crews. At Minnesota in 1878, the freshman and sophomore classes played a football game which was won by the freshmen because "they had more men on their team than had the sophomores." The following year the sophomores and juniors challenged everybody else on campus, but the game failed to be played because of the "non-arrival of the ball."

Students later formed committees to arrange for competition among all four classes. This premeditated procedure lead to league championships, an advancement over the earlier custom wherein the challenge between two teams was the limit of competition. Classes elected managers to administer the details of organizing teams for the leagues. In some colleges, fraternities or associations established committees to conduct interfraternity athletics.

During this student organization stage, it soon became apparent that programs would need to be centralized under the direction of faculty supervision. Fraternity associations were not enthusiastic about relinquishing their own authority to faculty supervision and to newly organized intramural departments, but gradually they realized the value of merging their interests with the larger programs.

Departmental Control

Between 1904 and 1912, the number of student-controlled activities increased to the point that authorities recognized the necessity for stronger and more permanent, centralized authority. The various athletic associations, forerunners of present-day athletic departments, which permitted use of their facilities for intramurals, began to exert a form of control.

In 1904, the president of Cornell University emphasized combining in a practical way the indoor gymnasium work and outdoor athletics. It was proposed to allow students to specialize according to their individual interests in football, track, baseball, rowing, boxing, wrestling, and swimming. The coaching staff gave instructions within their specialities to students who were not out for intercollegiate teams. This was one of the first departments to give special emphasis to intramurals.

In 1913, Michigan and Ohio State Universities each inaugurated a Department of Intramural Athletics headed by one person who was expected to handle the demands for intramural competition in the various

[1] Frank Presbrey, *Athletics at Princeton* (New York: Frank Presbrey Co., 1901), p. 69.

leading sports. In 1917, the Committee on Intramural Sports of the Athletic Research Society, a group of scientific-minded physical educators, recommended a comprehensive classification of playing units in its annual report.

This move toward a unified system in place of students organizing leagues which had no relationship to each other, was very important to the athletic associations. It permitted them to exercise direct control over their own fields, equipment, and indoor facilities which, under the student control system, were loaned temporarily to the various organizations wishing to use them. This control meant that fields and courts were assigned impartially and without confusion; that games were better supervised; and furthermore, that responsibility for loss of or damage to equipment was easily traced. The athletic associations also found that the promotion of intramural activities, the "athletics for all" concept, stifled much criticism on the part of people who opposed varsity athletics because it favored only a few skilled performers.

In these early phases of intramural development, the athletic associations had the idea that the intramural program would provide a source of recruiting for future varsity material. However, time soon established the more comprehensive ideal of sports fun and benefit for all.

Additional Significant Developments

The success of recreation leaders in handling participants on a large scale, the increased interest of the public in all forms of athletics, the importance ascribed to athletics in the military training camps during the First World War, and the correspondingly great strides made in developing mass athletic programs—all contributed to the great boom in college intramurals which began in 1918.

In 1925 the first book on intramurals under the title of *Intramural Athletics* (the first edition of this textbook), was written by Dr. Elmer D. Mitchell, considered by many to be the "Father of Intramurals" in America. Because of his influence, the first intramural sports building was constructed at the University of Michigan in 1928.

Although intramural activities began to appear in high schools in 1925, these programs were not significantly under way until 1930. Prior to this time, the development of standards in interscholastic athletics engaged the major attention of physical education teachers and coaches in high schools; but after these standards were established, schoolmen turned their attention to the recreational needs of students. The intramural directors of the Western Intercollegiate Athletic Conference (The Big Ten) discussed high school intramural problems at their annual meeting in 1930.

Early Programs for Women

The informal characteristics of intramurals appealed to women physical education directors who were not impressed with the varsity competition concept. The nature of the intramural program readily adapted itself as a supplementary part of the more formal physical education program for women.

In 1917 at the University of Wisconsin, the National Athletic Conference of American College Women (currently the Athletic and Recreation Federation of College Women) was organized. This group maintained a firm stand against varsity athletics for women and promoted the intramural concept of "sports for all." In the same year, the American Physical Education Association (now the American Association for Health, Physical Education, and Recreation), established a Committee on Women's Athletics to standardize women's programs. This committee became an unofficial section of the American Physical Education Association in 1927, but it was not officially recognized as the National Section on Women's Athletics (currently the Division for Girls and Women's Sports) until 1932. In subsequent years this group continued to develop women's program policies including the advocation of a wide range of intramural activities.

Organized in 1923, the Women's Division of the National Amateur Athletic Federation became influential in women's physical education circles and attempted to avoid the intensified specialization and winning pressures of men's athletics. They affiliated with the American Physical Education Association in 1931 and merged with the National Section on Women's Athletics in 1939. The Division for Girls and Women's Sports is presently the guiding force in maintaining standards for quality women's sports programs.

FORMATION OF PROFESSIONAL INTRAMURAL GROUPS

As the intramural movement expanded, there was an increasing effort to set standards for improvement through the formation of various professional intramural organizations. The individual directors realized their problems could be solved by meeting as a group to share their experiences.

Since 1920, the intramural directors of the universities in the Western Intercollegiate Athletic Conference have held annual meetings to exchange successful ideas. In 1933, the College Physical Education Association provided a section meeting for the discussion of intramurals at its annual conference. In 1938, the Division of Men's Athletics in the

American Association for Health, Physical Education, and Recreation also established a section on intramural athletics, although reports on intramurals were given in the division prior to that time.

The National Intramural Association was formed in 1950 by Dr. William Wasson at Dillard University in New Orleans. This was the first national group devoted strictly to intramurals. The idea for the formation of the association grew from a Carnegie Grant-in-Aid Study of intramural programs in Negro colleges. Dr. Wasson observed intramural programs and facilities in 25 colleges, and during these visitations, intramural directors expressed the need for a medium of exchanging ideas.

Charter members of the N.I.A. are Albany State College, Arkansas State College, Bethuen-Cookman College, Dillard University, North Carolina College, Southern University, Texas State University, Tillotson College, Tuskegee Institute, Wiley College, and Xavier University of New Orleans. The objectives of the association are as follows:

1. To promote and encourage intramural and recreation programs.
2. To meet annually for professional growth.
3. To serve as a medium for the publication of research papers on intramurals.
4. To work in close cooperation with the American Association for Health, Physical Education, and Recreation; the National College Physical Education Association for Men; the National Recreation Association; the Educational Policy Committee of the respective institutions; and such other agencies that are consistent with the Association's ideals.
5. To act as a placement service agency.
6. To afford consultant services.

In 1955, the College Physical Education Association, the American Association for Health, Physical Education, and Recreation, and the National Association for Physical Education of College Women jointly sponsored an intramural conference in Washington, D.C., attended by 100 delegates from 79 institutions in the United States and Canada. Discussion centered on the role of intramurals in the education of college students, organization and administration, facilities, and types of programs.

Another significant step in the development of intramurals took place in 1966 when the National Intramural Sports Council was formed as a joint project of the Division of Men's Athletics and the Division for Girls' and Women's Sports of the American Association for Health, Physical Education, and Recreation. This council was established to provide leadership for initiating and improving the intramural programs at all educational levels.

In 1968, the American Association for Health, Physical Education, and Recreation sponsored a National Conference on College and University

Recreation to discuss the relationship of all phases of campus recreation including intramurals. Some of the problems and issues included organization and administration, financing, facilities, student participation and leadership, professional leadership and training, and identification of the responsibility for campus recreation.

SUMMARY OF HISTORICAL DATES IN THE DEVELOPMENT OF INTRAMURALS IN AMERICA

1857 At Princeton University, the freshman class organized the Nassau Baseball Club and challenged the sophomore class to a match game. This is an example of one of the first intramural type contests in the United States.

1859 Students at Yale University organized intramural boat clubs which subsequently formed the basis of interclass crews.

1861 The Pioneer Cricket Club sponsored cricket at the University of Michigan.

1878 At the University of Minnesota, the freshman and sophomore classes played a football game which was won by the freshmen because "they had more men on their team than had the sophomores." The following year the sophomores and juniors challenged everybody else on campus but the game failed to be played because of the "non-arrival of the ball."

1904 Cornell University combined in a practical way the indoor gymnasium work and outdoor athletics. It was proposed to allow students to specialize according to their individual tastes in football, "track athletics," baseball, rowing, boxing, wrestling, and swimming. The coaching staff gave instruction within their specialties to interested students who were not out for intercollegiate sport teams. This is believed to be one of the *first departments* to give special emphasis to intramural sports.

1913 The University of Michigan and Ohio State University inaugurated departments of intramural athletics under the direction of a faculty member.

1917 The Committte on Intramural Sports of the Athletic Research Society, an early group of scientific-minded physical educators, recommended a comprehensive classification of playing units in its annual report.

1917 The American Physical Education Association established a Committee on Women's Athletics to standardize women's athletic programs.

1917 The National Athletic Conference of American College Women (currently the Athletic and Recreation Federation of College Women) held its first meeting. They opposed varsity athletics for women and favored the promotion of intramurals.

1920	Intramural directors of the Western Intercollegiate Athletic Conference began holding annual meetings.

1923	The Women's Division of the National Amateur Athletic Federation was formed and recommended the selection and administration of activities which provided participation for all, rather than the few.

1925	The first book on intramurals, under the title of *Intramural Athletics*, was published by Elmer D. Mitchell, considered by many to be the "Father of Intramurals" in America.

1927	The Committee on Women's Athletics became an *unofficial* section of the American Physical Education Association.

1928	The first intramural sports building in the country was constructed at the University of Michigan.

1931	The Women's Division of the National Amateur Athletic Federation affiliated with the American Physical Education Association.

1932	The Committee on Women's Athletics was officially recognized as the National Section on Women's Athletics of the American Physical Education Association and further emphasized women's programs by developing standards which advocated a wide range of intramural activities.

1933	Under the Federal Emergency Relief Administration and later under the National Youth Administration, programs which offered financial aid to youth, many college students secured part-time assignments in intramural departments, the services for which were paid by the federal government.

1933	The College Physical Education Association provided a section for the discussion of intramural sports at its annual meeting.

1938	Under the Division of Men's Athletics, the American Association for Health, Physical Education, and Recreation established a section for intramural athletics, although reports on intramural programs were given in the division prior to that time.

1939	The Women's Division of the National Amateur Athletic Federation merged with the National Section on Women's Athletics.

1945	After World War II, as after World War I, returning veterans were interested in continuing the sports competition they enjoyed while in the military service and provided an incentive for the expansion of intramural programs.

1950	The National Intramural Association was founded by Dr. William Wasson at Dillard University in New Orleans.

1953	The name of the National Section on Women's Athletics (NSWA) was changed to the National Section for Girls and Women's Sports (NSGWS).

1955	The College Physical Education Association, the American Association for Health, Physical Education, and Recreation, and the National Association of Physical Education of College Women, jointly sponsored an intramural conference in Washington, D.C., attended by 100 delegates from 79 institutions in the United States and Canada.

1957 The National Section for Girls and Women's Sports became the Division for Girls and Women's Sports (DGWS).

1966 The National Intramural Sports Council was formed as a joint project of the Division of Men's Athletics and the Division for Girls and Women's Sports of the American Association for Health, Physical Education, and Recreation.

1968 A National Conference on College and University Recreation, sponsored by the American Association of Health, Physical Education, and Recreation, was held in Washington, D.C., to discuss campus-wide recreation, an important part of which was intramurals.

PRESENT STATUS AND FUTURE TRENDS

After the Second World War, as after the First World War, there was added momentum to the development of intramurals. Returning war veterans who had participated in mass athletics and physical training programs of the military services enrolled in colleges and universities and continued their interests in sports through participation in the intramural programs.

This momentum has continued to a point where intramurals are expanding at a faster rate than at any time in previous history. Participation statistics in some institutions have doubled and tripled in the last decade. In some instances, intramural participation is increasing faster than the rate of student enrollment.

Many schools previously without intramurals are introducing new programs. This is happening at all educational levels—elementary schools, junior high schools, senior high schools, junior colleges, colleges, and universities. The Armed Forces, Army, Navy, and Air Force, have placed increased emphasis on intramural programming. These units have long valued the sports experience as a basic ingredient for successfully training military personnel.

Never before has there been such wide acceptance of intramurals. Some schools include intramurals in the departmental title such as Department of Health, Physical Education, and Intramurals or Division of Intercollegiate and Intramural Athletics. In some institutions, separate intramural departments have been established. The youth of today are activists, and they are more interested in participating than in viewing sports. This pattern blends perfectly with the intramural participation concept.

Whereas the traditional intramural program fostered the organized competitive type of sport, the trend is to expand the equally important phase of informal physical recreation. Many programs have widened the scope of their activities to include outings such as camping, hiking, sailing, picknicking, and nature trips. The widespread movement of today emphasizes individual and dual sports, co-intramural activities, and sports clubs.

This tremendous expansion of intramural programs has created a demand for trained personnel and new indoor and outdoor facilities. To meet the personnel problem, the University of Illinois and the University of Minnesota have introduced Master's Degree Programs offering specialization in intramurals, and other schools are planning similar programs.

In 1957, Purdue University constructed a co-recreational gymnasium, the first structure devoted primarily to intramurals since the intramural sports building was built at the University of Michigan in 1928. In 1959, Michigan State University constructed two facilities, an intramural building for men and an additional one for women. The University of Illinois, University of Washington, and Oklahoma State University also have new structures designed to emphasize intramural programming. Other indoor and outdoor facilities have been and are being constructed to serve the expanded programs of intramurals, physical education, and varsity athletics.

The continuing increase in enrollments of the future will produce a corresponding demand for expanded intramural programs. With the leadership of groups such as the National Intramural Association and the National Intramural Sports Council the demand will be challenged, and the present momentum will move forward. A large measure of the "unlimited potential" of intramurals will be realized as staffs, facilities, and equipment are constantly expanded and improved. It is conceivable that in the distant future the importance of intramurals will increase to the extent that there will be "a sport for everyone, and everyone in a sport."

3

Administrative Organization and Personnel

If the intramural mission is to be fulfilled, the program must operate within some type of organizational pattern or administrative framework. The responsibility for the program must be assigned to someone whose primary interest is providing opportunities for participation in intramural activities. This person is administratively responsible to someone in a position of authority in the superstructure. His role is to supervise all of the internal affairs of the program and to relate with others in matters such as finance and facilities coordination. Administrative mechanisms must be devised before a program can materialize.

ORGANIZATIONAL PATTERNS

Intramural organizational patterns vary according to each local situation. Some programs may be supervised by a part-time person who has casual interests in these kinds of programs, while others may be administered by hundreds of students and several full-time staff members. Eight organizational patterns are presented in diagrammatic form in Figures 3–1 through 3–8. They represent a military program, industrial organization, junior or senior high school program, a high school program, a women's intramural program, a college intramural program, a large university program, and an organization for campus-wide recreation. The main features of these plans are applicable to local situations, although minor variations may be advisable.

25

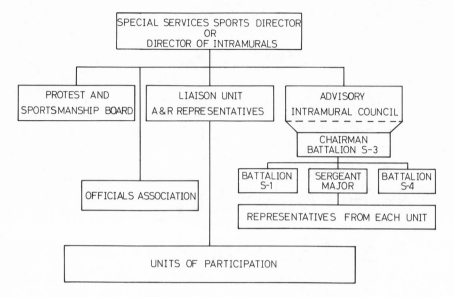

Fig. 3–1. Organizational Pattern for a Military Intramural Program.

Military Programs

Intramurals in military establishments are usually located in the special services division. (See Fig. 3–1). The special services sports officer or sports director has jurisdiction for these programs. The table of organization at a military installation lends itself most desirably to intramural programming. The program may be structured within certain echelons or at all levels of a military establishment, depending on how the program is defined. For example, competition may begin at platoon level with the winners advancing to company, from company to battalion, from battalion to brigade, from brigade to division, and from division to the corps championships. As is true in all intramural programming, civilian or military, strong command support at all echelons is the essential ingredient for successful programs.

Industrial Programs

Figure 3–2 illustrates the extension of the intramural programming concept to business and industry. The exact pattern of organization varies depending on the nature and function of a firm. In this illustration, employees and management share in planning and administering the various intramural and extramural activities through the advisory board, activities councils, and company clubs. Organized and informal participation take place within the company and between companies. For example, em-

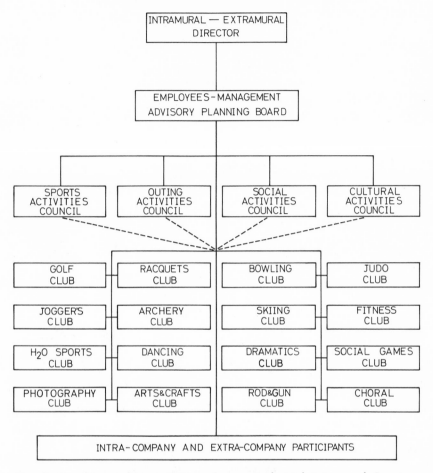

Fig. 3–2. Organizational Pattern for an Industrial Intramural Program.

ployees may represent departmental categories such as personnel, research, warehouse, sales, shipping, tool and die, and engineering in competitive sports activities or social and cultural events. One or more groups may participate extramurally in industrial leagues or tournaments composed of participants from several different firms.

Elementary, Junior High, and Senior High Programs

In elementary schools, junior high schools, and senior high schools, almost without exception, intramurals are administered by a physical education teacher or an athletic coach. (See Figs. 3–3 and 3–4.) In some instances, the assignment may be given to someone outside of the physical education area but to one who has a background in sports.

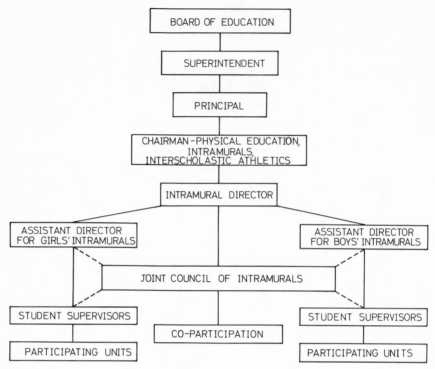

Fig. 3–3. Organizational Pattern for a Junior High School or Senior High School Intramural Program.

The person in charge of intramurals should receive compensation in the form of released time from classroom duties or compensatory remuneration comparable to the extra pay given to the various head coaches. Special attention should be given to equitable work loads. If a teacher is overloaded with physical education and coaching assignments and is also the intramural supervisor, the latter program will be the first to reflect this inequity. The intramural program is secondary in the estimation of most physical education personnel, and when pressed with other duties, intramurals will be neglected. Unless superintendents or principals have had experience in intramural programming, they will not understand the tremendous amount of organizational and supervisory detail necessary for operating an effective program. They should use great care in selecting someone who is vitally interested in intramurals, and then give this person more time than they feel would be adequate for intramural administrative work.

Some schools follow the community–school recreation plan wherein the program is administered by a municipal recreation director and all

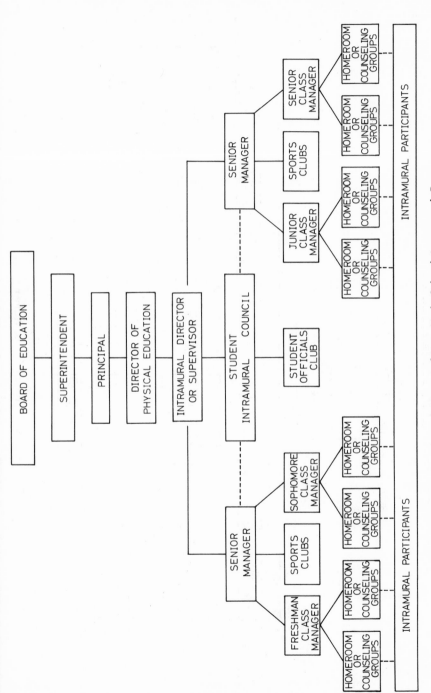

Fig. 3–4.   Organizational Pattern for a High School Intramural Program.

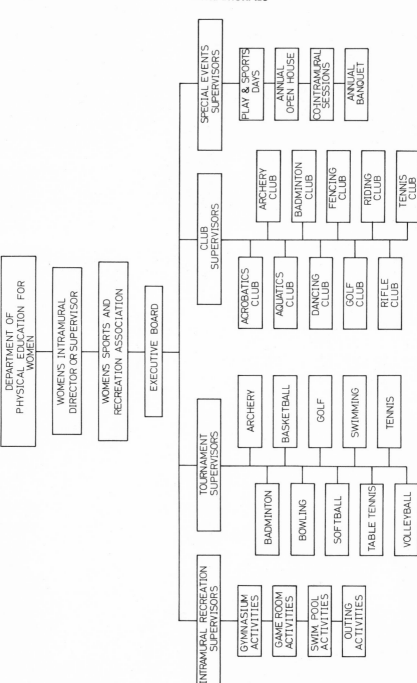

Fig. 3–5. Organizational Pattern for a Women's Intramural Program.

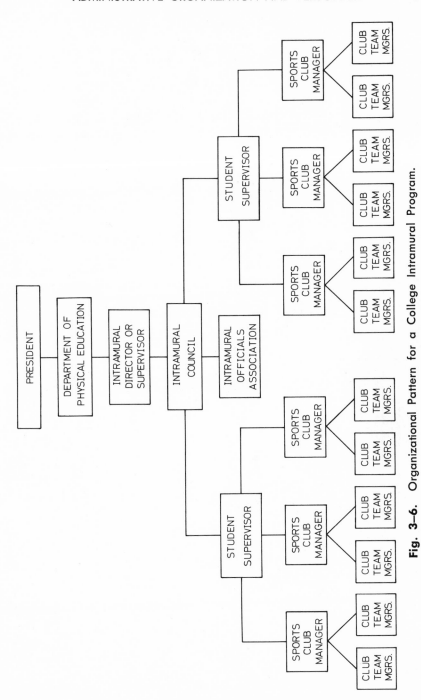

Fig. 3–6. Organizational Pattern for a College Intramural Program.

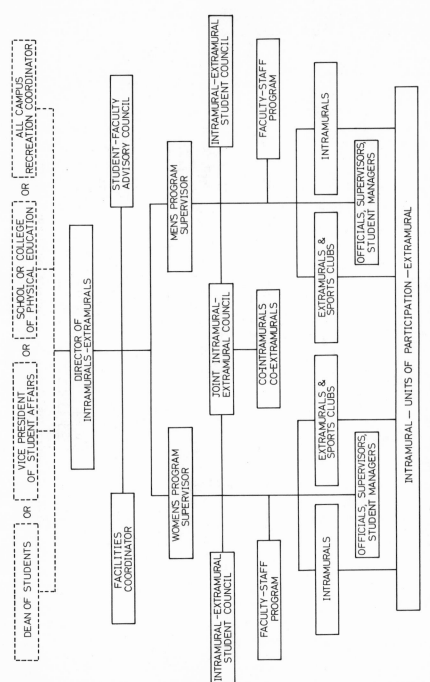

Fig. 3–7. Organizational Pattern for a University Intramural Program.

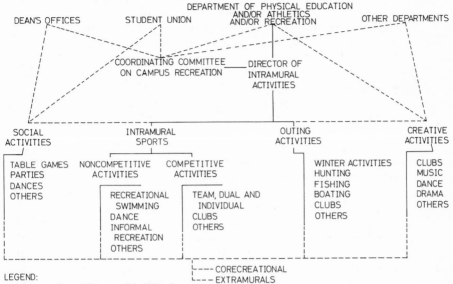

Fig. 3–8. Suggested Organization of Campus Recreation. From *Intramural Sports for College Men and Women,* American Association for Health, Physical Education, and Recreation, 1964. (Courtesy AAHPER.)

community, including school, facilities are used for all programs twelve months of the year. In smaller communities where less emphasis is placed on the community recreation program, an intramural director may administer intramurals from September through May and then turn his attention to the community recreation program for the summer months, again utilizing all facilities.

College and University Programs

In colleges and universities, intramurals are usually identified with one of the following organizational patterns:

1. Intramurals in some colleges and universities are aligned with the department of physical education. (See Fig. 3–6.) There may be one department for men's and women's programs, or if there are

separate departments of physical education for men and women, intramurals may also be separate. Sometimes intramurals are included in the departmental title along with other programs offered within the organizational structure such as Department of Health, Physical Education, Intramural and Intercollegiate Activities.

2. As a carry-over from earlier days when the varsity athletic department sponsored intramurals, some programs are part of a division or department of varsity athletics. The title of such a department might be "Intercollegiate and Intramural Athletics." At one time, this relationship had the advantage of financial support from athletic gate receipts, but recently, the high cost of sponsoring varsity programs has reduced this form of assistance. From a varsity standpoint, the existence of a comprehensive intramural program tends to offset criticisms that stadiums, fieldhouses, and athletic fields exist only for the benefit of a few highly trained athletes.

3. In some of the larger colleges and universities, intramurals are in a separate department of a school or college of physical education. There may be several departments including recreation leadership, physical education for men, physical education for women, health education, and a combined intramural–extramural department for men and women, or separate departments for each. (See Fig. 3–7.)

4. Some colleges and universities have organized all campus recreation under a recreation coordinator or committee. In this plan, intramurals operate as a separate unit which is responsible for physical recreation in much the same manner that the student union is responsible for social recreation. (See Fig. 3–8.)

5. Intramurals are also organized in a separate department and are identified with the office of dean of students, vice president of student affairs, or an executive dean. (See Fig. 3–7.) This plan is based on the recreation philosophy rather than physical education. The coordination of facilities is sometimes a problem because they must be scheduled for varsity athletics, physical education, and intramurals. This situation can be resolved by working through a facilities coordinator.

Organizational Associations

Intramural programs are often conducted under the auspices of various sports, athletic, and recreation association. This method is particularly popular among girls and women's programs. The words "girls" and "boys" are used in the names of elementary and secondary school associations, and "men" and "women" are a part of collegiate association titles. Examples of association names are the following:

Girls or Women's Athletic
Association
(GAA or WAA)

Boys or Men's Athletic
Association
(BAA or MAA)

Girls or Women's Recreation Association (GRA or WRA)	Boys or Men's Recreation Association (BRA or MRA)
Girls or Women's Sports Association (GSA or WSA)	Boys or Men's Sports Association (BSA or MSA)
Girls or Women's Sports and Recreation Association (GSRA or WSRA)	Boys or Men's Sports and Recreation Association (BSRA or MSRA)
Girls or Women's Athletic and Recreation Association (GARA or WARA)	Boys or Men's Athletic and Recreation Association (BARA or MARA)

These associations organize intramural and extramural activities through clubs, tournaments, special events, and informal participation. (See Fig. 3–5.)

Student Versus Faculty Administration

There is considerable disagreement among intramural personnel as to how much authority, if any, should be vested in students for administering and controlling programs. Some schools follow the democratic principle of delegating complete responsibility to students for administering intramurals. This question takes on even more importance at a period of time when students, particularly in colleges and universities, are demanding a greater voice in the administration of educational programs. There are many pros and cons, some of which will be presented to help identify both sides of the issue.

Arguments for Student Administration. Some administrators proclaim that one of the objectives of education is to provide leadership experiences and that this can be accomplished by teaching students how to organize and administer an intramural program. They suggest that the best way to teach responsibility is to give responsibility. Students want to be challenged, and they should be involved in the decision making processes of intramural programming. These advocates admit that mistakes will be made but suggest the adjustments necessary to correct them are part of the learning process.

Arguments for Faculty Administration. Opponents argue that history reveals early programs under control of students were administered on a haphazard, chaotic basis. With new students entering the program, others graduating, and some dropping out before graduation, there is no consistent pattern of program administration. Some insist that the basic purpose of intramurals is not to train student intramural workers, but rather to provide legitimate satisfying experiences for the participants. The opportunities to react to the kinds of mistakes made in administering the program are inherent in sports participation, and numerous participants should not have to suffer while a few profit from the experience of making administrative mistakes.

Students rarely possess the keen analysis and mature judgment often required in settling controversial issues which inevitably arise. Their decisions are not based on extensive experience and may interfere negatively with the quality participation of the masses. The academic pressures on students do not permit them to give appropriate attention to the many details of intramural administration.

Combined Student and Faculty Administration

When evaluating a program in terms of quality participation by the masses of students, there is little doubt that it is desirable to have a combination of a full- or part-time intramural director and student assistants to administer the program. Indeed it would be impossible to conduct a successful program without the aid of student officials, supervisors, lifeguards, etc., either paid or voluntary. Intramural councils composed of students and staff are invaluable in offering suggestions for program improvement. A director should be constantly aware of creating an atmosphere in which students know that new ideas or modifications of old ones are always welcome. It is undeniable that the best intramural programs will result from a proper balance of professional staff guidance supplemented by enthusiastic student assistance.

PROGRAM PERSONNEL

Although the organizational framework is a necessary ingredient of successful programming, an even more vital factor is the personnel involved in administering a program. The success of intramurals can never rise above the quality of its leadership. All programs succeed or fail in direct proportion to the appropriate decisions and actions of those who are responsible for administering them.

A summary of the kinds of personnel involved in intramural programming is presented to show not only the magnitude of a large operation, but to identify the areas of responsibility and the tremendous amount of detail involved in successful programming. Not all programs will have personnel for each of these positions. Indeed one full- or part-time intramural supervisor may play the role for many of these persons but on a much reduced scale.

Intramural Director or Supervisor

The intramural director or supervisor is responsible for the overall administration of the program. In large programs, he may be an executive in the sense that duties are delegated to subordinates. But in other situations, he may select, promote, and administer the activities with a limited amount of help. An intramural director must have many talents. He must have a very broad knowledge of sports and know how to structure them for competition. He must be an excellent organizer and be willing to give close attention to details. He must develop an awareness of what actions will produce what effects. Because he will be constantly approached by students with opposite points of view regarding won and lost situations, he must be an impartial judge. Above all, he must constantly strive to be of service to the program participants.

Assistant or Associate Directors

There may be one or more assistant directors in a program. As the name implies, this position relieves the director of numerous organizational details. In large programs with two or more assistant directors, they may be assigned areas of responsibility with one being responsible for supervising the paid and voluntary workers, including officials, and the other responsible for activity programming. Conferences between the director and assistant director(s) are most necessary to maintain an even flow of administration.

Secretarial and Clerical Assistants

An office secretary serves as the receptionist, answers the telephone, takes dictation, maintains office records and files, schedules the director's appointments, and in some instances becomes "the other intramural director." An experienced secretary is able to answer many questions about the program and can relieve the full-time professional staff of administrative details. Voluntary or paid students assist the secretary with the clerical affairs of the office and also provide a valuable messenger service.

Facilities Coordinator

Although the facilities coordinator may not be a part of the intramural administrative staff, he is very much involved in scheduling facilities for intramural, varsity, and physical education activities. If conflicts are to be avoided and intramurals are to be assured equitable use of facilities, this position is extremely necessary. A coordinator or director of facilities is also responsible for the maintenance of indoor and outdoor areas. Another of his responsibilities is to plan and develop new facilities.

Intramural Advisory Committee

Members of the advisory committee are students and faculty appointed by the administration or elected by the student body. They assist in establishing intramural policies and in evaluating the program. Although they are primarily advisory in nature, their support can be most helpful in influencing the administration on intramural matters.

Intramural Councils

Intramural councils are usually composed of representatives of the various participating units. They may take a very active role in administering the program or serve in an advisory, liaison capacity. Regardless of which role they assume, council representatives serve as an important link between the staff and participating teams. Information is transmitted from the intramural office to the teams through council members. In addition to making decisions about program operation, they serve as a sounding board for evaluating the program. Many changes are made in intramurals because of suggestions made by representatives of these councils.

Graduate Assistants

Graduate students are given assistantships, comparable to those offered for teaching and research, to administer certain phases of the intramural program. Because of their greater experience and mature judgment, they may be assigned more responsibility than undergraduates. Their position on the staff tends to lend stability and prestige to the program. Graduate assistants may be assigned the responsibility of conducting the faculty, co-intramural, and sports club programs. In addition to receiving excellent training in intramural education, they receive remuneration to help finance their graduate education.

Locker and Equipment Personnel

Locker and equipment personnel have frequent contacts with participants, and for this reason, they must be very personable and diplomatic. Often an individual judges the entire program on the basis of his association with persons working in the locker–equipment room. At this point of contact many individuals become satisfied or unsatisfied participants.

The major responsibility of these personnel is to issue, maintain, and inventory equipment and lockers.

Facilities Maintenance Personnel

Because of the heavy usage of intramural facilities, it is most desirable to have personnel assigned for the specific purpose of maintaining them. If maintenance crews are shared with varsity athletics or if they have other responsibilities, maintaining intramural areas may become secondary or tertiary in importance. The availability of these crews can make the difference between playing after a rain or postponing the schedule. Sometimes participants can assist with this task, but full-time personnel with appropriate equipment is most desirable.

Intramural Trainer

Provision must be made for first aid or training services in an intramural program. Some of the activities involve heavy body contact which produces injuries requiring immediate attention. A full-time or part-time trainer should be in attendance while those kinds of sports are being played. It is also advisable to have a first aid–training room available where students may receive care for injuries, wrap their ankles, and use whirlpools and other equipment.

Sports Club Supervisors

Better-than-average-ability students join together to form sports clubs in specialized activities such as judo, archery, karate, fencing, weight lifting, and soccer. Usually the best performer in the group serves as the instructor and supervisor. His services may be voluntary or on a paid basis. These clubs may conduct tournaments, give exhibitions, and compete with groups from other institutions. The sports club supervisor is responsible for the activities of each club.

Facilities Supervisors

Every indoor and outdoor area of participation should be supervised when an activity is taking place. These supervisors should be dependable, mature persons with an awareness for the safety and welfare of the participants. Their responsibilities may include directing teams and officials to the correct fields or courts, issuing scorecards and equipment, operating a central timing device, and referring injured players to the proper source of care. During competitive and informal participation, they may be responsible for checking the eligibility of users of the facilities.

Swimming Lifeguards

Lifeguards are a specialized type of facilities supervisor required for swimming pool areas. They have the very important responsibility of guarding the lives of persons swimming in pools. These persons must be trained in water safety, and they must be clearly indoctrinated with the importance of their responsibilities.

Publicity Reporters

Publicity reporters and photographers, paid or voluntary, are essential for collecting information to be reported to publicity media. If it is necessary to pay these individuals for their services, it is a most legitimate expenditure of funds. These persons observe the contests being played, take pictures, and write stories and releases for publication. They can develop a publicity file of photographs and statistical records to be used as source material for intramural handbooks, newsletters, publicity flyers, and other publications.

Officials' Supervisor and Officials

An officials' supervisor is responsible for organizing and training a core of officials such as referees, umpires, and timekeepers. Perhaps nothing contributes more to the quality of intramurals than good officiating. Numerous time consuming protests are avoided by good officiating. Clinics including practical and written examinations are given under the direction of the officials' supervisor. Officials are customarily paid by the hour or game, although in some programs volunteers officiate.

Officials may be varsity athletes, physical education majors, or anyone interested in sports' officiating. Varsity squad members and physical education majors who have completed sports' officiating courses are usually good officials because of their experience and prestige. The cause of good officiating can be furthered through the formation of an intramural officials' association or club.

Student Managers

There are two types of student managers in intramurals: unit or team managers and program managers. Unit or team managers form teams and enter them in intramural leagues and tournaments. Program managers are organized on a graded scale, seniors, juniors, sophomores, freshmen, and assist the professional staff with the administration of the program.

Senior Managers. Usually two senior managers are in charge of a core of student assistant managers. Managers relieve the intramural staff of numerous administrative details. A good managerial system produces thousands of man hours for the cost of a few manager's awards.

The primary responsibility of the senior manager is to assign work to the various junior, sophomore, and freshman managers. Assignments include assisting in making out schedules, notifying participants of scheduled playing times, recording scores and maintaining other office records, and aiding in the supervision of play areas. Senior managers, with the assistance of their subordinate managers, organize and promote some of the individual and dual type touraments. Final approval of tournament structures is given by the intramural staff. It is advisable for directors to assign duties of educational value rather than menial tasks such as cleaning basketballs or mending badminton nets.

In a managerial system, managers are promoted from year to year on the basis of their work performance. Two senior managers are selected from the junior managers by a committee consisting of the intramural director and outgoing managers.

The senior manager's position is comparable to the varsity manager with the exception that varsity managers perform their duties only while the varsity sport is in season, whereas intramural managers hold their responsibilities for the entire year. Managers are not paid, but in addition to valuable educational experience, they may receive awards, complimentary lockers, and equipment privileges. When senior managers are presented with a manager's letter and sweater, they also retain all rights and privileges of the official varsity letter club of the institution.

Junior Managers. Junior managers are selected by the intramural director and the senior managers from the sophomore managerial staff who have demonstrated proficiency in carrying out their assignments. The number of junior managers varies with the size of the program, but it is usually twice the number of senior managers and half the number of the sophomore managers. Junior and sophomore managers who do not qualify for promotions are permitted to stay on the staff as student officials or in some other student administrative capacity. Junior managers may receive minor intramural letters or monograms in addition to the usual departmental privileges.

Sophomore and Freshman Managers. Sophomore managers are picked by the selection committee from freshman managers who in turn are chosen from a group of students who "try out" for freshman managerial positions. The major requisite for any candidate is desire and enthusiasm. Freshman managers are oriented by the intramural director, but receive most of their on-the-job training from sophomore, junior, and senior managers. Intramural numerals are awarded to sophomore and freshman managers.

Not all managers are efficient, but when a good one is found, it is difficult to evaluate his services. It would require a considerable expenditure of money if he were employed on a paid basis. An effective managerial system is of vital importance to a successful, smooth operating department.

Programs not using a managerial system usually pay for the kinds of services described above. They may feel that paid help is more reliable and that greater demands can be placed on them. Because some programs are financed by student fees, some directors think it is logical to return these fees to the students in the form of employment to help finance their education. As is the case with all program decisions, each intramural director will choose whichever method he finds best suited to his framework of operation.

ADMINISTRATIVE CONSIDERATIONS

The basic purpose of an administration is to be of service to those whom it is supposed to serve. In some respects, intramural programming is comparable to merchandising a product in the business world. Every decision is made and every action is taken with the objective of placing the merchandise in the hands of the customer. Similarly, in intramurals every decision and every act should make the program so attractive and efficient that participants will be guaranteed a satisfying experience. The program should be desirable to a point that individuals *cannot afford not to participate.* Participation experiences should be satisfying to the extent that the "customers" will automatically become the program's best advertisers.

One of the greatest weaknesses of some administrators is their inability to count the costs of an administrative procedure in terms of time, effort, and money. Determinations must be made as to (1) what is going to be done, (2) how it will be done, (3) who is going to do it, (4) how much time and money will be required, and (5) who will follow-up to be sure it is done. A good administrator must mentally "walk through" the steps necessary to complete a project or proposal and then put the thoughts into action.

Administrative Aids

Considerable planning and follow-up are required to process the numerous administrative details involved in intramural programming. For this purpose, aids can be devised and utilized, examples of which are summarized below.

Programmed Responsibilities. A technique which is helpful in planning is the programmed responsibilities chart illustrated in Figure 3–9. Responsibilities are listed on the left-hand side of the chart, and the time they are scheduled to be performed is plotted for the various days of the week. A diagonal line designates the day, and the scheduled time is also recorded. If desired, A.M. times may be written above the line and P.M. times below the line. When they are completed or if they have not been finished at the appointed hour, a second diagonal line is placed in the box. If the item is not completed at the time specified, it is immediately reprogrammed to another period of time. This simple administrative technique eliminates two weaknesses of administrators: (1) the inability to remember what needs to be done, and (2) planning a time when the task will be performed.

Forward File. Another valuable administrative tool is the use of a "forward file." This consists of twelve file folders labeled with the months of the year. As ideas or suggestions are thought of for the future, they are

PROGRAMMED INTRAMURAL RESPONSIBILITIES

LEGEND

NAME____JONES____ WEEK OF_APRIL 21_TO _APRIL 27___

9:00 A.M. SCHEDULED | 9:00 A.M. COMPLETED

RESPONSIBILITIES	SUNDAY	MONDAY	TUESDAY	WED.-DAY	THURSDAY	FRIDAY	SATURDAY
I-M COUNCIL MEETING			4:00 P.M.				
SCHEDULE SOFTBALL TEAMS		9:00 A.M.					
TEACH CLASS		2:00 P.M.		2:00 P.M.		2:00 P.M.	
FACULTY GOLF LEAGUE					3:30 P.M.		
I-M OFFICIALS MEETING				4:00 P.M.			
REVIEW BUDGET PROPOSAL			2:30 P.M.				
STAFF MEETING					8:30 A.M.		
ORDER EQUIPMENT						3:00 P.M.	
STAFF RECREATION	2:00 P.M.						
LION'S CLUB LUNCHEON SPEECH				11:45 A.M.			
RESOLVE I-M PROTEST		4:30 P.M.					
ANSWER CORRESPONDENCE						9:00 A.M.	
EDIT HANDBOOK MANUSCRIPT			8:30 A.M.				
STUDENT AWARDS BANQUET						6:00 P.M.	
VARSITY BASEBALL GAME							2:00 P.M.

Fig. 3–9. Programmed Intramural Responsibilities Form.

placed in the appropriate month's file. For example, frequently an evaluation of an intramural event just completed is not remembered twelve months later when it is readministered. Notes in the forward file as to how phases of the program can be improved will provide excellent reminders when it is time to conduct the activity.

PROCEDURAL CHECK LIST FOR

ADMINISTERING AN INTRAMURAL ACTIVITY

1. ___Determine the activity and type of tournament structure.

2. ___Select starting and completion dates.

3. ___Review rules modification.

4. ___Purchase and display awards.

5. ___Prepare equipment and facilities.

6. ___Issue advance publicity.

7. ___Send out entry blanks.

8. ___Follow-up final notice via telephone.

9. ___Receive and classify entry blanks.

10. ___Check health status and eligibility.

11. ___Seed the entries.

12. ___Draw up the schedules.

13. ___Prepare daily master schedule.

14. ___Assign practice periods.

15. ___Distribute playing schedules.

16. ___Disseminate additional publicity to the news media.

17. ___Conduct rules interpretation meeting for student officials.

18. ___Prepare daily score cards and officials' rating cards.

19. ___Assign officials and supervisors.

20. ___Check accuracy of score cards after games have been completed.

21. ___Record scores, sportsmanship and officials' ratings.

22. ___Report game results to publicity media.

23. ___Structure and distribute playoff schedules.

24. ___Photograph winning teams.

25. ___Record participation statistics.

26. ___Tabulate all-year participation-performance points.

27. ___Present individual and team awards.

28. ___Record results in permanent records.

29. ___Send out final follow-up publicity.

30. ___File an evaluation of the activities' administration for subsequent reference.

Fig. 3–10. Procedural Check List for Administering an Intramural Activity.

Check Lists.   An excellent method of follow-up to be sure administrative assignments are completed is the use of a check list.   When administrative details are outlined in check list form and performed according to schedule, efficient program operation is assured.   The procedural check list for administering an intramural activity in Figure 3–10 is an example of how such a list is devised and also illustrates the many details necessary for programming one activity.   In an intramural program, it is not uncommon for several activities to be conducted at the same time, and the subsequent list of thirty items multiplied by several different activities, gives some indication of the multitude of details involved in administering intramurals.

If an intramural director understands the principles of administration and knows the basic ingredients of intramural programming as outlined in this text, he can administer a program for any age level, in any situation.

4

Ideas for Intramurals

An intramural program can never be any better than the ideas or thoughts that are applied to it. Intramural personnel must give constant attention to the relationship of ideas to program planning and problem solving. The purpose of any administration is to develop solutions for problems which in turn create new problems requiring new solutions. Thus, it is a never ending process.

Traditional, habitual thinking tends to prevent administrators from seeking new methods or to reject those which may be proposed. Frequently, individuals respond to progressive suggestions with these comments:

If it had any merit, the idea would have been used long ago.
It's never been done that way before.
What would happen if it didn't work?
Has someone else tried it?
It may work elsewhere, but not in our program.
Now doesn't seem to be the right time.

Supporting these comments may be a strong, self-styled feeling that their program is one of the best, and there really isn't any need for improvement. To this extent, intramural personnel may be the greatest inhibitors of program progress.

It has been suggested that there is an endless number of ideas existing in the universe just waiting for development in the minds of men. The degree to which this source is tapped varies greatly with the willingness to search for and accept new, unique ideas. Instead of immediately rejecting a new suggestion, the reaction should be an open-minded "why not" or "maybe it will work."

An excellent example of the force of a mental barrier is found in breaking the four-minute mile. For many years the theory was advanced that the mile could never be run in four minutes. Then Dr. Roger Bannister broke through the impossible time barrier by running the mile in 3 minutes, 59.4 seconds. Within three years, the four-minute mile was broken on 26 different occasions by 16 runners. In Dr. Bannister's opinion, the barrier for spectators and runners was psychological, not physical. The goals had not been set high enough.

POWER OF AN IDEA

If the element of time is eliminated, everything can be considered to be a thought or an idea. Every object or system has been created in someone's mind for a specific need or purpose. Subsequently, details of the design are developed through someone's thinking. Finally, the results of this thinking are realized in the form of a material object or a method of doing something. Actions are preceded by thoughts. Therefore, everything is an idea or thought which has originated in the mind, thus demonstrating the tremendous power of an idea.

An example of the power of a simple thought is found in dispensing over-the-counter soft drinks. A "man with an idea" approached soft drink distributors and suggested this method of increasing their profits. When customers asked for a soft drink, the soda fountain clerk was to respond with the simple query "large or small." Psychologically, people prefer better things in large quantities. The implementation of this idea only required the purchase of two different sized disposable cups. And the profits from soft drink dispensing increased many fold.

THE PROCESS OF PRODUCING IDEAS

Most people feel that creative thinking is reserved for the few and not available to the many. They generally believe that creativity is destined at birth, and nothing can be done to change it. However, Alex F. Osborn, a pioneer in the field of creative thinking, indicates in his book *Applied Imagination,* that scientific research has proven imagination or creativity can be deliberately developed through knowing and practicing the principles of ideation.

These principles may be applied collectively in group "brainstorming" or individually in the privacy of one's mind. Application requires a change of attitude for most people, a change that may positively alter the patterns of their living. Ideas must be germinated with an attitude that is free of criticism. By nature, people tend to criticize others or their suggestions. To avoid being the recipient of these critical thoughts, they are hesitant to offer suggestions unless there is reasonable assurance that their remarks will be favorably accepted. Consequently, the sphere of potential ideas is severely restricted.

Evaluation or judgment plays an important role in the ideative process, but it follows the noncritical, idea-producing period. Therefore, ideation requires a person to change roles, first turning on the free wheeling, uninhibited mind and then switching to the evaluative, discriminatory mind.

Aids for Individual Ideation

For the individual certain techniques aid the flow of creativity. These include the following:

1. Establishing a deadline by which ideas will be produced and setting a specific quota.
2. Carrying small note pads or slips of paper for making notes of ideas as they pass through the mind.
3. Making appointments with yourself to think creatively at a particular time and place.
4. Developing a check list of questions to be used for self-quizzing such as:
   a. Are there adaptations or modifications?
   b. What about other colors, shapes, materials?
   c. Are there other uses without changing it?
   d. Can it be made larger, smaller, wider, narrower?
   e. Could it be rearranged or reversed?
   f. Could something else be used in its place?
   g. Could it be combined with another method?

Group Ideation

In group sessions productivity is increased by the association of thoughts. A suggestion by one person stimulates the imaginations of others who have similar or related ideas lying dormantly under the surface of their consciousness. For successful group brainstorming, these guidelines should be followed:

1. *Organize the group.* Assemble a group of people for the purpose of producing solutions, in the form of ideas, to problems. From five to fifteen persons is a reasonable size for a group.
2. *Limit the scope of the problem.* Members of the group may offer suggestions as to how the problem could be more clearly stated. Appropriate definition of the problem is directly related to the success of the creative session.
3. *Create a noncritical atmosphere.* An informal, completely friendly environment must prevail. Negative thoughts or actions opposing someone's ridiculous idea must be eliminated.

4. *Record every idea.* With tape recorders or stenographers, record the ideas presented. It is helpful to keep the group periodically advised as to the number of ideas that have been generated.
5. *Solicit a large number of ideas—rapidly.* Good decisions are made from a choice of many alternatives. Setting goals of a certain number of ideas in so many minutes will increase idea production.
6. *Encourage "free thinking."* Wild, ridiculous, preposterous, impossible ideas are completely necessary for a successful session.
7. *Urge combination and improvement.* Participants should feel free to combine or improve previously stated ideas. This cross-fertilization will assure the quality as well as a quantity of ideas.
8. *Evaluate the ideas.* Mimeograph the ideas and distribute them to members of the brainstorming group. Reading the list after a day or two may release some additional ideas. Then ask the group or a few key members to judge the quality of the suggestions. Some ideas may be combined, duplicate ones eliminated, and the remainder may be ranked in order of significance.

Application of Ideas

Many of the ideas may be useless, but others will have immediate practical application. The percentage of usable ideas may be small, but if these guidelines are followed, the good ideas that will upgrade the program are the ones that undoubtedly would not have been uncovered without an ideation session. Also, after being exposed to this type of thinking, staff members and students will find themselves ideating on their own and offering new ideas.

Intramural personnel seek ideas for program improvement by attending professional conferences, visiting other programs, and reading professional literature. If they understand and apply the principles of ideation, they will discover that a source of ideas exists within themselves. However, effort is completely necessary. They must be willing to explore this source, accept new thoughts, and put them into action.

Although it is true that not all ideas will have application in all programs because of different personalities, facilities, and other local conditions, there is an idea waiting to be created that will apply to a particular situation. It must constantly be remembered that thoughts precede actions, and this process must prevail if intramural programs are to improve.

EXAMPLES OF IDEAS FOR INTRAMURALS

The remainder of this chapter contains examples of ideas that were produced in intramural workshop and clinic ideation sessions. Some may appear to be humorous, others routine, but all are presented to encourage the reader to "think up" new ones by applying ideation principles. Still further ideas for intramurals will be suggested in succeeding chapters.

Activities

1. Introduce "T" ball as an activity in the co-intramural program.
2. Play ice hockey with brooms and a volleyball or hockey sticks and a tennis ball and require the players to wear boots.
3. Schedule a donkey softball game in which the players ride donkeys around the base paths.
4. For boys and girls track, include a cycle relay using a bicycle instead of a baton. Title the event co-wreck.
5. Schedule "powder puff" touch football games for girls.
6. Schedule a tug of war between the faculty and the students using a long rope across a stream of water.
7. Play "instant" chess with a time limit of one minute for each move.
8. Schedule the basketball champions against the volleyball champions in a game in which one-half is basketball and the other half volleyball.
9. For swimming, include a sweatshirt relay in which one sweatshirt is used per team. The wet sweatshirt must be removed and passed on to the next team member.
10. Transport cross country participants to the country and require them to run back to school.

Awards

1. For a cross country "turkey trot" at Thanksgiving, award prizes as follows: first place—turkey, second place—goose, third place—duck, fourth place—chicken, fifth place—pigeon, sixth place—one dozen eggs.
2. Use a Polaroid camera to take team pictures, and present a print to each member of the winning team.
3. Sponsor a banquet or picnic at which intramural winners receive special recognition.
4. Award a scholarship to the outstanding intramural participant.
5. Present green stamps to every player who hits a home run.
6. Give members of both teams a "training table" meal before the championship game is played.
7. Present free movie passes to members of the winning teams.
8. Display the name of the winning team on the flag pole.
9. Provide the intramural champions with a special dinner to be served by the losers of the championship game.
10. Present a gift certificate to the winners instead of the usual trophies or medals.

Eligibility Rules

1. Organize a system to draft and trade intramural players in a manner similar to the pros.
2. Prohibit lettermen from participating in the intramural sport in which the letter was earned.
3. Allow track field-event letter winners to enter running events and vice versa.
4. Permit teams to have lettermen on the roster but with the provision that only one may be in the game at any time.
5. Install turnstiles at the entrance of facilities to count participants and to serve as a point where eligibility is checked.
6. Organize a league in which there are no eligibility rules.
7. Suspend ineligible players indefinitely until they agree to abide by the rules.
8. If teams do not have full complements, allow teams to use pickups, players watching the game, if it is agreeable with their opponents.
9. Do not permit players to switch from one team to another.
10. Establish cut-off dates after which team rosters are frozen.

Equipment

1. Invent a singing badminton bird so music lovers will enjoy playing badminton.
2. Equip the basketball teams with paper disposable shirts. Use letters A, B, C, etc., on one set and numbers on the other to identify players.
3. Imprint the word "Intramurals" on all equipment.
4. Use fluorescent colored balls that light up even under the lights.
5. Provide all-purpose uniforms and shoes for all of the teams.
6. Require touch football players to wear soft, rubberized headgears.
7. For tennis, require each player to furnish three balls. The loser receives the used ones, and the winner keeps the new balls for the next match.
8. Assemble a "picnic equipment kit" which may be checked out by participants over the weekend.
9. Charge a deposit for equipment, and do not return it if the equipment is damaged.
10. Provide junior size equipment for junior size participants.

Facilities

1. Construct fences around all softball fields to give players the thrill of "hitting one over the fence."
2. Install additional baskets on the walls of the gymnasiums for informal basketball shooting.

3. Install carpeting in all locker rooms.
4. Build a plastic dome over outdoor facilities.
5. Install electric scoreboards in gymnasiums and on fields.
6. Construct artificial ice rinks for skating activities.
7. Install lights for all softball and touch football fields.
8. Keep gymnasiums open 24 hours a day, seven days a week, and 365 days a year.
9. In ice hockey rinks, cushion the side boards with foam rubber.
10. In the gymnasium, install basketball rims that light up when a basket is scored.

Financing

1. If players go on the gymnasium floor with their "street shoes," take the shoes off and sell them back to the players.
2. Levy fines on participants who are guilty of profanity and other unsportsmanlike conduct.
3. Establish an endowment fund for intramurals and solicit contributions from business and industry.
4. Sell franchises to student teams.
5. Sell commercial advertising on the uniforms of intramural players.
6. Ask every student to contribute to a mile of pennies down the campus road.
7. Hold an annual raffle and raffle off the distinguished members of the faculty, such as the superintendent or president.
8. Fine the students who do not participate in the program.
9. Develop an intramural candy bar and sell it to the participants.
10. Sell intramural bumper stickers.

Game Rules

1. Play volleyball on the basis of a time limit rather than a specific number of total points.
2. Use the basketball screen instead of the body block in touch football.
3. For track and field, throw a six-pound medicine ball or a twelve-inch softball instead of the shot put, discus, or javelin.
4. In touch football, permit passes to be thrown in any direction and at any time.
5. In slo pitch softball, change pitchers every inning.
6. Play tennis matches on the basis of the best five out of nine games rather than the best two out of three sets.
7. Schedule touch football with 15 plays per quarter instead of the usual time limits.
8. Use free substitution rules in all intramural sports.
9. In cross country, ask players to guess how long it will take them to run the course and give prizes to those who are correct.

10. Keep a running team score in bowling, similar to basketball, so accumulative pins can be determined after each frame.

Military Programs

1. Establish sports schools in each of the commands to teach military personnel how to administer intramural programs.
2. Sponsor a softball game in which the commanding general and other staff officers participate.
3. Establish advisory intramural councils at all levels of the military command.
4. Include intramural participation as a criterion for officer and enlisted personnel promotions.
5. Post signs at the entrance of all athletic facilities that state "Rank stops here."
6. Schedule cross country meets with participants wearing complete combat gear.
7. Award three-day passes to the winners of the championship teams.
8. Distribute sports schedules at each place setting in the mess halls.
9. Award franchises to the companies permitting them to enter teams in the program; if a team forfeits, it loses the franchise.
10. On the day of a game, mark all streets "one way" to the ballpark.

Officiating

1. Use registered adult officials for the championship games.
2. Organize an intramural officials' association.
3. Require each team to provide one official for the game.
4. Require team managers to rate officials on performance and ask the officials to rate the teams on sportsmanship.
5. Play games without officials; let the players make the decisions.
6. Assign some women officials for men's games and vice versa.
7. Pay officials according to a two- or three-step pay scale to provide incentive for improvement.
8. Use a video tape recorder to film officials' performances and review their strong and weak points at a subsequent showing.
9. Install electronic automatic umpires for calling balls and strikes in softball and baseball.
10. Require intramural officials to sign a contract for the days on which they agree to work.

Publicity

1. Publish an intramural column in the student newspaper.
2. Distribute an intramural newsletter to all participants in the program.
3. Pay an intramural reporter on the basis of how much is published in the paper.

4. Sponsor an intramural queen contest.
5. Use a public address system at championship games to introduce the players of each team.
6. Employ student photographers for championship events to produce pictures for an "intramural highlights" bulletin board.
7. Mimeograph programs for championship games, listing players, numbers, won and lost records, season's scores, etc.
8. Sell or give away pencils with the name of the school and the word "intramurals" on them.
9. Post intramural notices on school buses to advertise the program in a manner similar to the advertising in commercial buses.
10. Identify a particular game as the "game of the week."

Scheduling

1. Schedule exhibition games in various sports prior to the regular league schedule to familiarize old and new players with rules modifications.
2. Schedule the cross country meet to end at half time of the football game with the 50-yard stripe serving as the finish line.
3. Schedule the intramural champion to play against the B-squad, preliminary to a varsity basketball game.
4. Design entry blanks in the shape of the ball of the sport for which entries are being submitted.
5. Insofar as possible, schedule teams to play the same day and time each week.
6. Call the team managers a day or two before the game to remind them of the time and place.
7. Solicit preferred playing times on entry blanks and also ask teams to identify times when it is impossible for them to play.
8. Publish the daily schedule in the newspaper and post it on bulletin boards.
9. Use different colored entry blanks, schedule sheets, and score cards for each of the various sports.
10. Schedule the finals of the intramural free throw contest for the half-time of a varsity basketball game.

Tournaments

1. Set up a tournament for the last place teams in each league.
2. Organize instant or quickie tournaments among students who are informally shooting baskets on the gymnasium floor.
3. For double elimination tournaments, use black lettering for the winner's and red lettering for the loser's names.
4. Establish a tournament or league for teams in which there are not participation points and no awards, just fun.

5. For individual or dual sports tournaments, ask all entrants to meet at a specified time, make the drawings, and play the first round matches.
6. Organize a special tournament for players that forfeit and use ineligible players.
7. Structure a triple or quadruple elimination tournament.
8. Conduct a contest in which the participants design "innovation" tournaments.
9. Set up a double or triple ladder challenge tournament to accommodate more players.
10. Use a different type of tournament structure for every sport in the program.

5

Finances, Facilities, and Equipment

Three of the most important ingredients of intramural programming are finances, facilities, and equipment. In addition to good leadership, these elements to a great extent determine the quality and quantity of a program. A formula which expresses this relationship is "dollars and cents = staff + facilities + equipment = qualitative and quantitative programs." For this reason an intramural program will be effective only if it is on a sound financial basis.

Every program must operate within the limitations of existing finances, facilities, and equipment, and in many situations, these are less than desirable. But even with these restrictions, through improvisation and innovation, meaningful experiences can be provided for the participants.

New well-planned facilities and quality equipment have a magnetic influence on participation. Their attractiveness tends to draw participants into the program. Therefore, intramural personnel should constantly seek financial support for better facilities and equipment.

FINANCES

If the values of intramural participation are valid, funding intramurals should not be regarded as a debit but a credit, not an expenditure, but an investment. On the basis of their educational contributions, intramurals ought to be financed with the same stability and consistency as any other phase of education. Although this is philosophically true, intramural funding in many programs does not approach this ideal.

An examination of budgets quickly ranks the importance of intramurals in the various institutions. Because there is no pressure for excellence in intramurals, administrators tend to divide revenues in favor of demands which are labeled "more essential" or "critical." This is one reason that some intramural programs are seeking affiliation with administrations other than physical education. Fortunately, a few programs are adequately financed, and they serve as a beacon for others who strive for comparable status.

Intramurals are definitely not expensive if one considers the large number of participants. In a properly planned and administered program, the cost for an individual may be as low as a few dollars per year and lower when considering the number of participations involved. This figure is even more significant when comparing it to the per pupil costs of other educational programs.

Sources of Income

There is no consistent pattern for funding intramurals. Reality forces support to come from whatever sources are available in a particular situation. Some of the financial practices are reviewed in the following paragraphs.

General Funds.   As indicated previously, the most ideal source of revenue for intramurals is the general operating fund of a particular institution. These funds usually emanate from taxes or similar broadly based revenues.

Student Activities Fees.   This method is becoming increasingly popular for funding student activities in educational institutions. Students pay an annual, semi-annual, or quarterly fee to help finance student activities, and a portion of this fee is budgeted for intramurals. In some institutions, the fee is not only used to maintain the program, but to amortize the construction of new indoor and outdoor facilities.

Physical Education Budgets.   In this plan, funds are allocated for intramural activities from the total physical education budget. Regardless of the amount of funds involved, a specific budget should be established for intramurals. With this method, equipment is shared for physical education classes and intramurals.

Varsity Gate Receipts.   When this system is followed, receipts should be placed in the general school fund and separate budgets should be approved for intramurals and varsity programs. Because of the increasing cost for administering varsity athletics, it may not be a desirable source of revenue. This type of income can be very unpredictable and unreliable because it is based on the won and lost records of athletic teams. If there is a shortage of funds, the intramural program suffers retrenchment.

Endowment Funds.   Some programs are supported by endowments that have been established to receive contributions from alumni or friends of the institution. Income generated from the interest on these funds is used to operate the program or for special projects such as sports clubs, intramural scholarships, and extramurals.

Entry and Forfeit Fees.   Additional funds may be raised by charging entry fees and forfeit fees. Entry fees are assessed at the time an individual or team registers for participation in a particular activity. The cost may range from $1.00 for individual and dual sports to $5.00 for team sports. In addition, an entry must be accompanied by a forfeit fee which is returned if the games are played or retained if a game is forfeited. These fees violate one of the basic principles of intramurals; namely, that activities should be "free and voluntary." They are a nuisance to the staff and the participants. When considering the administrative cost of collecting them, it is doubtful if there is any significant gain in revenue.

Dues.   In this method, dues are charged for membership in associations, councils, and sports clubs. Sometimes the cost of awards is defrayed through payment of dues by participating organizations.

Admissions Income.   Another source of funds is to charge admission for intramural events such as sports nights, sports carnivals, faculty–student competition, co-intramural sessions, sports club exhibitions, and championship games. Generally this means of raising funds is inadvisable because the intramural program should emphasize participation and not attendance at revenue-producing events.

Other Sources.   Additional funds may be raised for intramural expenses through special fund-raising projects. Sports clubs, associations, and athletic councils may assist with the organization and administration of these functions. The following list suggests types of activities that can be used for this purpose:

1. Sports film showings
2. Paper drives
3. Games concessions
4. Sports equipment sales
5. Car washes
6. Sports tag days
7. Varsity program sales
8. Light bulb sales
9. Magazine subscriptions
10. Soft drink and candy vending machine revenues

Some programs may be financed by a combination of the above methods. For example, facilities may be maintained from gate receipts with other phases of the program financed by student fees.

Budgetary Considerations

In intramural financial planning, there are three general categories of expenditures: (1) capital outlay for new or improved facilities, (2) maintenance costs of present facilities, and (3) programmatic operational costs. Most intramural personnel may not be directly involved in future facilities planning. Perhaps they will be consulted, but this planning is usually assigned to a specific person in the higher echelons of administration or to a special planning committee. Since facilities are shared with physical education and varsity athletics, maintenance may be the administrative responsibility of someone outside intramural jurisdiction. The intramural director's primary concern is planning a budget for the ongoing program.

For successful intramural programming, an annual budget, carefully identifying anticipated program expenditures, should be prepared. Too many programs do not follow the sound business practice of having a separate budget. It is never quite certain how much money is available for programming and, conceivably, money intended for intramurals may be used for other purposes via administrative manipulation.

Anticipating exact expenditures for an intramural program is not without difficulty because of the potential increases or decreases in participation. Accurate participation records aid in predicting budget requests. For example, the number of games played during the past year, plus the estimated increase for the following year, multiplied by the regular pay for the number of officials and supervisors required, yields a projected figure for this category. Examining records over a period of years provides a guide as to the amount of participation that may be anticipated.

The following outline lists the kinds of items that may be included in an intramural budget, the exact nature of each and amounts varying with the size and locale of the program. All figures must be adjusted to reflect program growth and increased costs of supplies, equipment, and services. Because it is impossible to predict the exact amount of participation that will take place, it is advisable to establish a budget item to cover these contingencies.

OUTLINE OF BUDGET ITEMS

I. PERSONNEL
    A. Full- and/or part-time staff
    B. Student miscellaneous employees
        1. Game officials
        2. Area supervisors
        3. Office clerks and messengers
        4. Swimming lifeguards
        5. Publicity reporters–photographers
II. EQUIPMENT
    A. Sports equipment

B. Office furniture
C. Office machines
III. SUPPLIES
  A. Office supplies
    1. Stencils, marking pens
    2. Stationery, envelopes
    3. Paper supplies
  B. Publicity
    1. Newsletters and posters
    2. Handbooks
    3. Orientation folders
    4. Photographic supplies
  C. Awards
    1. Individual and team trophies
    2. Medals, ribbons, certificates
    3. T-shirts, jackets, blankets
IV. EXPENSES
  A. Transportation
    1. Extramural participants travel
    2. National and regional meetings
  B. Professional literature and dues
  C. Insurance premiums
  D. Telephone and telegraph
  E. Special events
  F. Contingency fund

Comparisons are often made between budgets of different intramural programs in an attempt to determine the cost of intramural programming. Because of the lack of standard financial practices, these studies are usually invalid. What is defined as intramural in one institution may not be the same in another. For example, sports clubs, co-intramurals, and informal participation may be a part of one program, whereas another may include only the competitive concept of intramurals.

In comparing maintenance costs of facilities shared for physical education classes, varsity athletics, and intramurals, a percentage of these costs should be assigned to each program's budget, according to the amount of time each facility is used by the respective programs. This type of breakdown is seldom available. Unless it can be determined that identical budgetary items are being studied, such comparisons are impractical and illogical.

FACILITIES

When considering the "unlimited potential" of intramurals, the generalization may be made that all intramural facilities are inadequate. Obviously, some institutions have more ideal facilities than others. With the ever increasing enrollments, it is questionable if facilities will provide for the quantitative objective of "a sport for everyone and everyone in a sport," particularly when some schools have difficulty securing adequate classroom space.

There are certain tendencies that are encouraging for the growth of intramurals. Educators realize the value of these programs and are including improved facilities in new educational structures. As a matter of fact, they occupy a significant percentage of the total physical plant. This new construction in both indoor and outdoor facilities makes possible increased intramural activity. In some institutions, the old athletic facilities are remodeled for use by intramurals.

A very impressive trend is the construction of special facilities for intramurals. Some are already constructed and others are included in expansion plans. This type of intramural facility serves as a center for physical recreation, similar to the manner in which a student union is the center for social recreation. These facilities are either used exclusively for intramurals on a co-intramural basis, or they are used predominantly for intramurals but not to the exclusion of physical education classes and varsity practices. Some of them are named intramural buildings, recreational gymnasiums, or intramural–physical education gymnasiums.

One of the most important functions of the intramural program is to encourage individuals to make exercise a daily habit through participation in informal, self-directed, "walk-on or drop-in" activities. When facilities are scheduled, some activity areas should be retained throughout the day and evening for this purpose. Physical education classes and varsity practices often restrict these informal activities.

Students who do not have a continuous class schedule may desire to go to the gymnasium for a workout during their free periods, or exercise in the afternoon following their last class. To accommodate this type of activity, facilities must be available at the appropriate time. If a student has this desire but facilities are unavailable, he may seek other forms of recreation, perhaps too sedentary in nature.

Indoor Facilities

In planning new facilities, it should be remembered that substandard facilities usually result in a substandard program. For this reason, official court and field dimensions should be used whenever possible. The following list identifies the types of areas which should be considered in planning intramural indoor facilities.

1. *Main Gymnasium*
   - Regulation basketball courts with divider nets
   - Regulation volleyball, badminton, and indoor tennis courts

2. *Auxiliary Gymnasiums*
   — Regulation basketball, volleyball, badminton, tennis courts
   — Street shoe surface
   — Gymnastics area
   — Balcony track
3. *Swimming Pools*
   — Fifty meter pool
   — Diving pool
4. *Combative Room*
   — Wrestling, judo, karate
5. *General Exercise Room*
   — Weight lifting equipment, rowing machines, peg boards
6. *Handball–Paddleball Courts*
7. *Singles and Doubles Squash Courts*
8. *Golf Room*
   — Sand trap, putting area
   — Driving nets
9. *Rifle and Archery Range*
10. *Games Room*
    — Table tennis, shuffleboard
11. *Intramural Council Meeting Room*
12. *Dance Studio*
13. *Audio-Visual Room*
14. *Administrative Offices*
    — Director, secretaries, managers, sports clubs supervisors
15. *Lounge and Lobby Area*
    — Bulletin boards, trophy cases
16. *Training or First Aid Room*
17. *Men's and Women's Locker Rooms*
    — Full and half lockers, basket combinations
18. *Men's and Women's Shower and Drying Rooms*
19. *Faculty Locker Room*
20. *Steam and Dry Heat Rooms*
21. *Equipment Rooms*
22. *Storage Rooms*

Other Features. The installation of closed-circuit television aids in supervising areas from a central location. Also, portable video-tape recording equipment should be available for use in the various activity areas so participants can replay their performances and improve their skills. A public address system is essential for general announcements and locating persons in times of emergency. Additional baskets should be attached to the gymnasium walls to encourage informal basketball shooting. Consideration may also be given to the utilization of a synthetic surface rather than the traditional wood floor.

Most gymnasiums have a different colored line for each court, such as black for basketball, red for volleyball, white for tennis, and green for badminton. This maze of lines is often confusing for the players. A new lighting system eliminates the numerous lines by lighting specific court lines with the manipulation of a corresponding wall switch.

Ideas for Intramurals. Portable walls, hinged at the corner with a recessed adjustable roller on the opposite end, can be used for handball, paddleball, and squash courts in the gymnasium. In newly constructed facilities, they can be installed between permanent front and back walls. When not in position for handball, paddleball, or squash, the floor area can be utilized for badminton, volleyball, tennis, table tennis, fencing, karate, and judo.

Outdoor Facilities

Easy accessibility to intramural facilities is extremely important to encourage participation. Whenever possible, outdoor areas should be located adjacent to indoor facilities. Intramural outdoor facilities include the following: fields for touch football, soccer, field hockey, softball, baseball, cricket, and international handball; courts for tennis, volleyball, basketball, badminton, handball–paddleball, and horseshoes; and running tracks, golf courses, and skating rinks.

Many of these areas can be utilized for multiple purposes. For example, fields used for touch football in the fall can be converted for softball in the spring; tennis practice boards may be used for one wall handball–paddleball. Hard surfaced areas can be used for tennis, handball, paddleball, basketball, badminton, and volleyball in the summer, and for ice hockey and general skating during the winter.

Lighted fields for touch football, soccer, field hockey, softball, and baseball are ideal for intramural programming, and they provide a partial solution for the limited space problem. For example, from 4:30 P.M. to 10:30 P.M., 24 one-hour touch football games can be played on four lighted fields. Twenty-four fields are required to accommodate the same program where only one game can be scheduled during late afternoon daylight. Playing under the lights is popular among intramural participants, and if there is a choice between daylight or artificial light, they frequently request the latter. To encourage informal, drop-in participation on lighted fields, some systems include an automatic switching device which turns the lights on and off at specific times.

Cooperative Use of Facilities

In some programs, facilities are used for intramurals, physical education classes, and varsity athletic games and practices by both men and women. With this type of joint usage, it is advisable to appoint a facilities' coordinator to whom requests are made for scheduling various activity

64   INTRAMURALS

areas. Nothing is more discouraging to participants than to have them appear for an intramural game which must be canceled because of a varsity practice. Complete cooperation by all groups is essential to avoid conflicts.

One of the disadvantages of cooperative use of facilities is that intramurals, because of their traditional lack of importance, are often assigned the least desirable times. Policies should be established to identify which programs have priorities for use of the various facilities at specified periods of times.

EQUIPMENT

Purchasing quality equipment and making it readily available to the participants is an important ingredient for providing satisfying program experiences. Intramural personnel should not be satisfied with the use of second hand, inferior equipment. A program's status can only rise to the level of standards established by intramural personnel. If they are satisfied with mediocre equipment, undoubtedly the rest of the program will reflect mediocrity. The high standards of varsity athletics should be followed in purchasing quality equipment for intramurals.

Ideally, all equipment necessary for conducting activities should be made available to the participants. Individuals will be more likely to participate if it is not necessary for them to buy expensive equipment. Realistically, however, most programs do not have sufficient funds to purchase all of the essential equipment. In some programs, equipment is shared by physical education and intramurals; others utilize equipment previously used by the varsity teams. The following policies are recommended when it is not possible to provide all of the equipment.

General Policies

For team games, it is customary to furnish game equipment: balls, bats, bases, and nets. Personal equipment such as tennis shoes is seldom furnished. Some participants provide their own bats, gloves, racquets, shoes, and jerseys. When possible, equipment should be available on a checkout basis for teams and individuals who cannot supply their own and who would not be able to participate unless equipment were available to them.

Equipment should be furnished to individuals playing a specific hazardous position in a sport. For example, a baseball catcher should be supplied complete catcher's gear because this position requires protective equipment, unnecessary for the other members of the team. Similarly in hockey, goalie equipment should be provided.

Informal, self-directed activities are greatly enhanced if participants can check out equipment. Also, some groups organize challenge games or picnics and it is not logical for them to buy materials that would be used only once or twice. The intramural image is greatly improved by helping these groups with their equipment needs.

The formation of sports clubs may be encouraged in activities such as judo, weight lifting, archery, fencing, cricket, and karate, if equipment for these activities is made available to the participating individuals or teams.

Ideas for Intramurals. Printing the name of the institution and the word "INTRAMURALS" on sporting equipment adds prestige and also helps to identify equipment belonging to the program. Sporting goods companies usually provide this service at no additional cost.

Purchase of Equipment

An up-to-date inventory is necessary to identify which items of equipment need to be replenished. The perpetual or periodic inventory (see Figs. 5–1 and 5–2) should include information about the type, quantity, and condition of the items in stock, as well as which materials should be repaired, destroyed, and reordered. It is also advisable to establish minimum numerical levels for the items in stock. When these levels are reached, the equipment manager submits an order for additional equipment.

In purchasing sporting equipment, consideration should be given to the quality and design of the material, safety, cost, and the source of supply. Purchasers should not buy on price alone. Most equipment experts agree that it is more economical to spend more money for quality merchandise than to purchase inexpensive materials. For example, poor grade softball bats necessitate numerous reorders due to breakage, are less safe for the participant, and result in "unsatisfied contestants and customers." Participants are usually good judges of superior and inferior equipment. Many problems are eliminated if orders are placed with reputable sporting goods dealers.

Some institutions require that bids be submitted for equipment purchases. This procedure saves money when buying from the lowest bidder but caution should be exercised to eliminate the possibility of receiving low quality merchandise. Specifications of each item must be clearly outlined with particular emphasis on the degree of quality desired. It is wise for the purchaser to compare prices carefully and if possible, to secure samples of the items to be purchased. For limited budgets, the practice of buying "close-outs" or reconditioned equipment is a practical means of getting fairly good material at low cost.

FORM NO. ____

PERIODIC INVENTORY OF EQUIPMENT AND SUPPLIES

PAGE NO. ____

____ ACTIVITY

____ PROGRAM

____ ORANIZATION

____ DATE OF INVENTORY

ITEM DESCRIPTION	UNIT: EACH PAIR DOZEN GROSS	USAGE RATE: PER YR. PER ACTIVITY	LOCATION	PREVIOUS INVENTORY	PURCHASED SINCE LAST INVENTORY	TOTAL TO BE ACCOUNTED FOR	USABLE		NEEDS REPAIR	NOT ACCOUNTED FOR	ESTIMATED NEEDS		
							NEW	USED			QUANTITY REQUIRED	UNIT COST	TOTAL COST
SOFTBALL, RUBBER, 12"	each			50	10	60	10	49	0	1	20	$.50	$10.00
VOLLEYBALL STDS., ALUM.	pair			4	2	6	2	3	1	0	0	0	0

____ SIGNATURE

____ DATE

Fig. 5–1. Periodic Equipment Inventory. From *Equipment and Supplies for Athletics, Physical Education, and Recreation,* Athletic Institute, 1960. (Courtesy Athletic Institute.)

PERPETUAL INVENTORY FORM

FORM NO. ___
CODE NO. ___

ORGANIZATION

ITEM DESCRIPTION _____ Tennis shoes, low cut, white _____

VENDORS 1. _____ 4. _____

2. _____ 5. _____

3. _____ 6. _____

CRITICAL BALANCE (4) [40]   USAGE RATE (5) [   ]

DATE	REFERENCE (1)	REQUISITIONED		QUAN RECD	DISBURSED		BALANCE	UNIT COST	TOTAL COST
		HOW (2)	QUAN.		HOW (3)	QUAN.			
1-1 —							40		
1-5 —	VENDOR (1)	P.O. 1963	25 pr.					$3.00	$75.00
1-20 —				25 pr.			65		
1-25 —					I	20	45		

(1) Vendor Code	(2) Code	(3) Code	(4) Critical Balance (order when
_____	PO—Purchase Order	C — Consumed	balance reaches quantity
_____	PC—Petty Cash	I — Issued for Use	shown)
_____	D — Donation	T — Transferred	(5) Usage Rate (quantity used
_____	T — Transferred	D — Discarded	per year or activity)
_____	O — Other	L — Lost or Broken	
		LO— Loaned Out	

Fig. 5–2. Perpetual Equipment Inventory. Adapted from *Equipment and Supplies for Athletics, Physical Education, and Recreation,* Athletic Institute, 1960. (Courtesy Athletic Institute.)

Sporting goods companies emphasize the value of prevenient ordering. Early orders result in early deliveries which alow ample time to make necessary adjustments or evaluations. Blanket requisitions, covering a specified amount of money for a limited period of time, provide a method of making minor or urgent purchases and in overcoming order and voucher delays.

Care of Equipment

Because the cost of equipment represents a sizable percentage of the budget, definite policies should be established to protect this investment. In small programs, the maintenance and issuance of equipment may be assigned to a faculty member who receives extra compensation for his services. Larger programs employ full- or part-time equipment managers who have the responsibility for cleaning, repairing, and issuing equipment. Student equipment managers may assist with these responsibilities.

The equipment room should be sufficiently large to accommodate all intramural equipment. The room should be systematically arranged to reduce the number of man hours necessary to issue and care for equipment. If it is properly desigend, it can serve as an issue point for men's and women's equipment. The room should have adequate bins and racks for storage of equipment in a cool, clean, dry environment. Good air circulation is extremely important for storing off-season sporting goods. Equipment stored without proper ventilation often mildews or rusts.

All equipment should be labeled for check-out purposes with an identifying number or letter which also indicates the year in which the equipment was purchased. For example, the numbers A4, B4, C4, and D4 indicate that this particular piece of equipment was purchased in the year 1974. These symbols may be inscribed with a marking pen or electric burning needle.

Equipment Issue Procedures

Participants desiring to use equipment should fill out a requisition slip which includes the following information:

1. Borrower's printed name, address, telephone, and locker number.
2. Quantity and name of each item desired.
3. Identification number of each item.
4. Date and time of issue.
5. Date and time of return.
6. A statement indicating that the borrower agrees to pay for any unreturned or carelessly damaged equipment.

Some check-out systems require a deposit until the equipment is returned. This deposit may be in the form of money, identification card, fee statement, or any other item that is of value to the individual.

The length of time items may be retained depends on the amount of equipment available. Some regulations require equipment to be returned immediately following the activity; others, within a day or two. Unless this regulation is enforced, participants might keep it for the entire season, thus preventing maximum use of equipment.

Equipment may also be distributed by facilities supervisors at the fields or courts to be used for a specific set of games. In this system, equipment is reissued to individual team managers, who must return it after the games have been completed. This supervisor also checks out game equipment to the referees and umpires who are accountable for each item used in their respective games.

CONCEPTS FOR FACILITIES AND EQUIPMENT
IN THE FUTURE

Present day technological advancement and concepts will have a tremendous impact on the kinds of facilities and equipment that will be used in future intramural programs. The following paragraphs suggest some of these concepts, many of which have been advanced and tested by the Educational Facilities Laboratories.

1. Geodesic or dome-shaped gymnasiums have been constructed and may be an even more important part of future facilities construction. It is also possible that smaller units will be portable, even to the extent of rolling on wheels to a new location.
2. Outdoor fields and swimming pools will be completely enclosed in domes, thereby making the facility available on a year-round basis. It is also conceivable that rather than any physical structure, walls of forced air will keep the cold air out and the warm air in or vice versa, depending on environmental conditions.
3. Instead of lighting fields with many different lights on several different poles, the lighting system of the future may be one lamp strategically placed to light the entire area. This type of lamp may not only produce light, but heat as well. In other words, it will imitate the sun.
4. Outdoor fields, tracks, and playgrounds will be completely surfaced with synthetic materials such as astroturf and tartan. As competition increases between manufacturers and the volume expands, costs of these materials will reach a lower level, making them obtainable on a wide scale.
5. For those who do not have synthetic surfaces, moistureless synthetic dirt is being developed which does not turn to mud, but has all of the other properties of nature's dirt.
6. Unrefrigerated plastic ice will enable ice hockey, figure skating, and other ice activities to take place in the warm climates as well as in the cold.
7. Locker rooms will have an "athletic club" atmosphere. In place of the usual musty, odoriferous, uninviting atmosphere, these areas will contain carpeted floors, steam and dry heat rooms, sun and heat lamps, whirlpool baths, scented climate-controlled air, and a masseur.

8. Electronic automated umpires are being developed to identify the strike zone and "call" balls and strikes for softball and baseball games. An umpire will still be needed for the bases and to determine fair and foul balls. It is predicted that these automated umpires will be coin-operated, which will permit teams to insert a coin and have the services of an errorless balls and strikes umpire.

9. In the future it may not be necessary to arrange for track and swimming judges and timers for intramural meets. Computerized totalization boards have been devised for swimming and track, which not only select the final places, but time each lane to a small fraction of a second.

10. Throw-away paper clothing will be used by participants. Swim suits, shirts, and paper towels will be discarded after one use, thereby eliminating laundry charges.

11. The new synthetic surfaces will eliminate the need for cleats on shoes. Psychologically, players may wish to retain them, but eventually they will be proven unnecessary.

12. Golf balls with built-in transistors will speed up the game of golf because the player will be directed to the lost ball by a tiny wrist radar set.

13. The traditional coin flip at the beginning of football games will give way to a transistorized coin flipper which requires the captain to choose a red or green light instead of "heads or tails." An alternating current produces a red or green light when a push button breaks the circuit. The same proportion of red lights and green lights appears as the number of times a flipped coin falls heads or tails.

14. No longer will it be necessary to take the chains out on the field to measure for a first down. A football liner-upper has been developed to locate on the sideline the corresponding position of the ball on the field of play. This device, a system of properly angled mirrors, is infinitely more accurate than the deceptive eye of a human football official in spotting the ball after an incompleted pass and determining when the line to gain has been reached.

Intramural personnel must be ready to accept future changes when they arrive, if intramural programs are to keep pace with a society that is ever changing.

6

Units of Participation

Units of participation are part of the organizational framework of an intramural program. They are natural or artificial groupings of individuals that serve as the basis for programming activities. Properly chosen, they create and maintain participant interest in these activities. The competitive, highly organized and the informal, self-directed phases of intramurals take place within these units. Other names frequently used are loyalty units and units of competition.

The success of intramurals is directly related to the appropriate selection and development of these participating units. An attempt should be made to discover the most logical, natural existing associations in which group spirit and program enthusiasm can be generated. If such relationships are not apparent, it is necessary to create them artificially.

SELECTING UNITS OF PARTICIPATION

In selecting or establishing units for participation, consideration should be given to these factors:

1. Type of institution
2. Geographical location
3. Size of enrollment
4. Group relationships
5. Living accommodations
6. Age and interests
7. Institutional traditions
8. Program facilities

For effective units, it is important to utilize established traditions, or in the case of a new program, to initiate practices that will become traditions. Units based on a common residence or meeting place, such as dormitories, barracks, fraternities, and home rooms, are usually successful because there is opportunity to make announcements, discuss activities, display

71

awards, and generally stimulate group spirit. Conversely, participants living separately or commuting do not have strong loyalty ties and require more encouragement to take part in intramural activities.

The attitudes and interests of participants are important factors to consider when selecting units. For example, elementary and junior high school youths do not demand high specialization in play because they are naturally interested in belonging to and playing in a group. The "gang" spirit is so strong that teams are easily formed by the supervisor, whereas older participants need greater associations to motivate them. Players of this younger age spend much time together and *espirit de corps* is quickly aroused with minimum effort.

Because of the many variables in different programs, not all units will be successful in all situations. The chart in Figure 6–1 suggests the kinds of units which may be applicable in elementary schools, junior high schools, senior high schools, junior colleges, colleges, universities, industrial programs, and military organizations. Each of these units is described in the following paragraphs.

Athletic Club Units

Participants form athletic clubs and participate intramurally over an extended period of time rather than for just a sport's season. They may stay together for a year or several years, depending on the strength of their leadership. The cohesiveness of this group permits them to be a part of the point system competition. Their sporting relationships often extend to social and cultural activities.

These clubs may be organized by an enthusiastic intramuralist, or a team entered in one sport may decide to expand and continue their activities throughout the year. Some athletic clubs are formed by the intramural staff. Individuals are arbitrarily assigned to one of several clubs and participate with that unit throughout their collegiate career. Nicknames from the sports' world, professional or collegiate teams, or names of no significance may be chosen. The initials A.C., representing Athletic Club, accompany the name, such as Tiger A.C. or Untouchables A.C.

Boarding Club Units

Boarding clubs may serve as a unit of participation wherever eating cooperatives exist. The tie that holds team members together is mainly the friendship from frequent association at meal times. This common meeting place has an advantage over groups that are similarly based on social acquaintance but do not get together except for practices or games. Interest in these units is enhanced when the club honors its players at a post season banquet.

UNITS OF PARTICIPATION	ELEMENTARY SCHOOLS	HIGH JUNIOR SCHOOLS	HIGH SENIOR SCHOOLS	JUNIOR COLLEGES	COLLEGES	UNIVERSITIES	INDUSTRIAL ORGANIZATIONS	MILITARY ORGANIZATIONS
ATHLETIC CLUBS	U	U	U	U	U	U	U	U
BOARDING CLUBS				U	U	U		
BOY AND GIRL SCOUTS	U	U						
COINTRAMURALS	U	U	U	U	U	U	U	U
DEPARTMENTS-DIVISIONS			U	U	U	U	U	U
DORMITORIES				U	U	U		U
FACULTY-STAFF	U	U	U	U	U	U	U	U
FOREIGN STUDENTS					U	U		
FRATERNITIES-SORORITIES				U	U	U		
GEOGRAPHICAL-RESIDENTIAL	U	U	U	U	U	U	U	U
GRADES-CLASSES	U	U	U	U	U	U		
GRADUATE STUDENTS					U	U		
HOMEROOMS-ADVISORY	U	U	U					
MILITARY UNITS			U		U	U		U
PHYSICAL EDUCATION SECTIONS	U	U	U	U				
RELIGIOUS GROUPS				U	U	U		
SPECIAL INTEREST GROUPS		U	U	U	U	U	U	U
SPORTS CLUBS		U	U	U	U	U	U	U
UNAFFILIATED UNITS	U	U	U	U	U	U	U	U
UNSTRUCTURED PARTICIPATION	U	U	U	U	U	U	U	U

Fig. 6–1. Units of Participation Chart.

Scout Units

Institutions that have boy and girl scout troops can combine group competition in intramurals with scouting activities. Camp fire girls and Indian guides also offer this possibility. These units require close cooperation between those in charge of scouting and the intramural supervisor. The intramural program should not be stressed to the point that it overshadows interest in scouting activities. This type of unit leads to much individual interest and practice because considerable proficiency is required to pass scouting tests in athletics, physical development, and health.

Co-Intramural Units

One of the most progressive developments in intramurals is the emphasis on co-intramural or co-recreational activities. Numerous activities can be conducted on a co-participation basis to give students meaningful experiences in a wholesome atmosphere. Participation may take place on an informal, noncompetitive basis, or some scheduled competition may be involved using modified rules to equalize opportunities for successful competition.

Some schools organize co-intramural competition on a play day basis. Each student maintains his identity with one of two color groups throughout his school career. School colors are used to identify the two competing sides. Field day events are set up with modified rules for boys and girls. On pre-arranged dates, perhaps once during fall, winter, and spring, classes are dismissed for participation in the play day, and the color winner is determined on the basis of field meet points. The reader is directed to additional information on co-intramurals in Chapter 14.

Departmental or Divisional Units

When intramural programs operate in large organizations, departments or divisions may be used to organize participation. In an industrial organization, competition may involve the production, sales, personnel, and engineering departments. In colleges and universities, competition may be scheduled between teams representing various departments or divisions. Some departments may be sufficiently large so that an intradepartmental league may be established, with the winner competing in a tournament involving comparable winners from other departments. At large universities, interschool or intercollege units may be formed.

In high schools, these groups may be organized on the basis of curriculum interests: college preparatory, industrial, commercial, agricultural, and specialized trade. Vocational schools may establish units in the pre-vocational departments of mechanics, electricians, carpenters, etc.

Dormitory Units

Dormitories have some of the advantages of fraternal groups, i.e., loyalty and social tradition already exist, members can communicate easily, team trophies may be centrally displayed, and the permanency necessary for the use of successful point systems is present. Some residential colleges and living–learning centers offer the same advantages.

Participation may be organized on the basis of one team representing each dormitory, or more frequently, teams representing various divisions in the dormitory structure such as houses, wards, blocks, floors, wings, and precincts. If there is more than one dormitory, champions can be named within each complex and the winners of two or more dorms may play for the all-dormitory championship.

Faculty–Staff Units

Faculty and other staff members participate in self-directed, informal activities as well as in individual, dual, and team competition. Establishing faculty–staff sports clubs encourages this type of participation. In institutions where the number of faculty is small, they may play challege games with student teams or with other adult teams chosen from representative groups in the community. Where a competitive program is organized, teams may represent different departments, or they may be organized across departmental lines. Faculty–staff family sessions, during which facilities are reserved for family participation, are popular features of intramural programs.

Foreign Students' Units

In institutions where the number of foreign students is significantly large, separate units of participation may be established for them. Although they may be sensitive to their inability to play American sports successfully, efforts should be made to provide them with this type of experience. Utilizing methods of equalizing competition may provide the necessary encouragement. Activities that are common in their homelands should also be a part of the program. These include soccer, volleyball, cricket, international handball, and rugby.

Fraternities' and Sororities' Units

In institutions of higher education in which they exist, fraternities and sororities are very successful units for intramural participation. They are usually well organized, and loyalty is present to a very high degree. It is relatively simple to transfer this spontaneous loyalty to intramural activities.

The permanency of these groups makes them well adapted for maintaining a competitive program through the entire school year. Some intramural systems conduct separate leagues for national and local fraternities–sororities, but the more common practice opposes any differentiation. However, some directors segregate participation for professional fraternities–sororities, whose representatives are primarily graduate students, from academic or social fraternities–sororities.

Separate active and pledge or class A and B leagues are formed for the popular intramural activities. These leagues provide opportunities for those who do not have the necessary skills to play on the first team but are eager to be a part of the program.

Geographical or Residential Units

Participants may be grouped according to the geographical or residential areas in which they live. These units can be determined by plotting enrollments on a map and making equitable divisions of the community. In forming these divisions, it is desirable to follow natural boundaries if they permit fair competition. If a school includes several wards of a city, it is feasible to use the official boundaries of these wards. Where sharp social distinctions exist between sections of a community, care must be exercised in developing these units, or feelings of antagonism could be intensified.

Another geographical unit is the campus zone. The campus is divided into several areas from which intramural teams are organized. Population rather than area size should determine the pattern of the zone. Other units in this category are bus routes, clubs representing counties or regions, and units composed of the alumni from a previous school.

Grade or Class Units

In small programs, classes or grades such as sixth, seventh, eighth, ninth, and tenth, make up units of competition. Class spirit and traditions already exist and can be channeled into program activities. One objection to participation between grades is that pupils in the higher grades have an advantage in physical development, but this disadvantage may be offset by using classification and handicap methods. Units may also be arranged to provide competition within each class and then the winners play off for the all-institutional championship. Although this system is more frequently found in the elementary, junior, and senior high schools, some colleges and universities organize class teams for certain sports and supplement these with other units of participation.

Graduate Student Units

In large institutions, units of participation are established for persons studying for advanced degrees. These individuals are interested in taking part in individual and dual sports as well as some team sports, although the latter should be of a less vigorous nature. Because they are usually involved in a concentrated course of study, the less demanding schedule of intramural activities is appealing to them.

Home Room or Advisory Units

Students are usually assigned to one counselor or teacher for advising them in their educational pursuits. In some schools, the home room serves this function, and units of intramural participation are organized on this basis. Students report to these rooms at the beginning of the morning and afternoon sessions and during periods when they do not have classes. This method facilitates informing participants about intramural activities because it is given to the players with other general school announcements. These units are sometimes called "session rooms, house, or study rooms." Friendly rivalries between home rooms are easily fostered because of the common place of assembly. One team may represent each home room or if the group size permits, players can be classified according to ability so that two or more teams may be entered from each home room.

Military Units

Military organizations provide ideal units for intramural participation within or among all echelons, depending on how the program is defined. The entire training mission operates within an organizational framework that provides natural rivalries and logical arrangements for intramural programming. Most military authorities regard the competitiveness of sports participation as a valuable asset in training military personnel and for maintaining morale. Categories of participating units are listed below.

In educational institutions with military programs, intramurals may be organized using the same types of units. Activities may be scheduled specifically for military personnel, or military students may wish to enter teams in competition with other members of the student body.

AIR FORCE	ARMY	NAVY
Squadron	Squad	Division
Group	Platoon	Department
Wing	Company	Element
Division	Battalion	Unit
Major Air Command	Brigade	Group
	Division	Force
	Corps	Fleet
	Field Army	
	Major Command	

Physical Education Section Units

Physical education section students are divided into teams for intramural participation. The squad leaders of the respective classes serve as team managers or captains. Competition should take place outside of the physical education class period because this time should be utilized to teach physical skills which can subsequently be voluntarily exercised in intramural activities. However, a few schools with limited facilities, a predominantly rural enrollment, or a full academic class schedule, sometimes use one of the physical education class periods each week for intramural competition.

These units are satisfactory for the lower grades because almost all students are required to take physical education. In some schools, physical education classes are elective for the upper grades and not all students would be included in this type of unit arrangement.

Religious Units

Some educational systems include religious denominational organizations that serve as units for intramurals. Their activities are coordinated through a student religious council or association which can be helpful in organizing intramural activities. Some interesting intramural rivalries can be developed because of the strong feeling that sometimes accompanies a person's religious beliefs.

Special Interest Units

Special interest groups frequently enter participants in intramural activities to supplement the primary activities for which they are organized. Some of these interests include politics, honor societies, philosophy, science, band, choir, debate, drama, literary, and social service groups. Members of these organizations are usually so devoted to their own specialized objectives that their interest in intramurals is secondary. Nevertheless, all organizations should be encouraged to take part in intramurals, because this may be one of the few opportunities they have to participate in physical recreation.

Sports Club Units

In some programs, intramural participation centers around sports clubs. These clubs are organized and supported by participants who are interested in promoting a particular activity. Knowledge of the activity is shared by the participants with the most skilled performers serving as leaders of the group. These clubs conduct intramural tournaments and in some instances, extramural competition when they compete with teams from other institutions.

Sociability is stressed along with interest in a particular sport. Outing clubs include hiking and picnicking as a part of their activities, an example of combining sporting and social interests. Skiing, figure skating, cricket, judo, karate, fencing, water polo, soccer, rugby, archery, canoeing, sailing, riding, rifle shooting, and weight lifting are examples of sports that lend themselves to the formation of sports clubs.

Unaffiliated Units

In most programs, there are some individuals who do not have any affiliation with a particular group or organization. Because they do not seem to fit into the existing units of competition, they are sometimes referred to as independents or limbos. There are several methods of arranging teams in these categories, some of which are identified below.

1. Independent participants contact others in the same category and of their own free choice, make up a team.
2. Participants sign up individually for placement on one of the teams. It is a meaningful experience for players to associate on pick-up teams with others whom they have never met previously. Once organized, these groups can be encouraged to form athletic clubs and participate with the same players throughout the entire year.
3. The intramural director can assemble all of the individuals who wish to take part in competition and at that time, organize several teams. Division of the players may be made alphabetically, numerically, by arbitrarily assigning them to teams, or by choosing up sides. Attention should be given to distributing players' talents as evenly as possible. When choosing up sides, it is advisable to make the selections when the players are not present, so poorer performers are not subjected to the humiliation of being chosen last. Captains, after choosing teams, may draw to see which team they will manage.
4. Teams may be formed on the basis of various classifications. For example, age, height, and weight may be used to categorize the participants. They are often grouped in physical education classes, using a battery of youth fitness tests, and these same classifications may be used for making up teams in intramurals.

Open tournaments are sometimes scheduled in which participants and teams do not represent any particular unit of participation. In other words, the units of participation are set aside for this type of tournament which names an all-school or all-unit champion. In a sense, all teams are unaffiliated for this competition.

Teams choose names representing colors—blues, golds, grays, maroons, animals—bears, lions, tigers, wolves, badgers, or professional teams—Yankees, Cubs, Indians, Braves, Twins. The names follow a particular pattern, or if no theme is involved, the teams may try to think up the most ridiculous name that comes to their imagination.

Ideas for Intramurals. A unique method of determining intramural teams
is the draft system used in professional sports. With this system, the
poorest teams are allowed first draft choices. Although this method involves detailed planning and organization, it creates considerable enthusiasm among the teams. In addition, teams trade, buy, and sell
players throughout the season. The medium of exchange may be paper
money, a certain number of points, such as 100,000, or real money with a
limit of $1.00 on each transaction. When legal money changes hands, it
can be utilized for purchasing awards.

Unstructured Participation

Another element of participation is the informal, self-directed, walk-on,
drop-in, unstructured exercise, referred to as intramural recreation in some
programs. It is not a competitive unit as such, but this type of participation may be a part of all of the above units. Although not scheduled in a
manner similar to team competition, it should be included in the schedule
arrangements for facilities, equipment, and supervision.

7

Program of Activities

Selecting appropriate activities is another phase of the intramural programming pattern. It may be suggested that with proper planning and administration, any activity can be programmed for intramurals. However, there are hundreds of possible activities available, and each director must make wise determinations as to which ones will provide the most successful program for his particular situation. Selection should be made on the basis of individual interests, number and age of the participants, climatic conditions, and the available facilities, equipment, and supervisory staff.

Intramural activities vary geographically. Sports such as basketball, touch football, tennis, volleyball, softball, and track are popular in most programs, while other sports have greater acceptance in different areas. Lacrosse, soccer, squash racquets, rifle shooting, and fencing are conducted more extensively in the East than in the Midwest and West. Hockey, skiing, figure skating, speed skating, and other snow and ice activities are usually confined to the northern sections of the country.

The program should include team, individual, and dual sports, some of which should be vigorous and others less strenuous. Some should be highly competitive and several should be informally recreative. Many should encourage participation on a co-intramural basis. It should be remembered that a program does not need large numbers of activities to be successful. A better program will result from a few well chosen and properly administered activities than a hodgepodge of less meaningful, poorly organized activities.

In general, intramural players prefer activities which provide active enjoyment without depleting their reserve energy. Most intramural athletes do not wish to carry on extensive training programs and therefore, prefer sports that do not require long preliminary practices. Certain vigorous sports, wrestling for example, should not be sponsored unless participants agree to submit themselves to a conditioning schedule.

The following comprehensive list includes numerous activities which are used in intramural programs representing all age levels.

INTRAMURAL ACTIVITIES

(A)
aerial darts
archery

(B)
badminton
baseball
basketball
(a) dribbling relays
(b) end zone
(c) lay-up shooting
(d) one basket
(e) one-on-one
(f) three man
(g) twenty-one
bicycling
boating
boccie ball
boxing
bowling
(a) duck pins
(b) nine pins
(c) progressive
(d) swing-du-lum
(e) table
(f) triangle
broom ball

(C)
camping
canoeing
car economy run
chariot races
chins and dips
code ball
crew
cricket
cross country
croquet
curling

(D)
dance
(a) folk and square
(b) modern
(c) social
darts
decathlon
distance walking races
dodge ball

(F)
fencing
field meets
figure skating
fitness meet
fly and bait casting
football
(a) agility tests
(b) flag
(c) forward pass
(d) knee tackle
(e) net
(f) pass or punt
(g) powder puff
(h) punting relays
(i) tackle
(j) touch
(k) rope tackle
free throw contest
frisbee

(G)
golf
(a) archery
(b) blind bogey
(c) chip-in
(d) clock
(e) drive for distance
(f) hole-in-one
(g) one club

(h) putting
(i) tin can
gymnastics

(H)
hand balancing
handball
(a) one wall
(b) three wall
(c) four wall
(d) rotation
hexathlon
hockey
(a) broom stick
(b) field
(c) ice
horseback riding
horseshoes

(I)
ice carnival
ice skating

(J)
jogging
judo

(K)
karate
kickball
korfball

(L)
lacrosse
life saving

(M)
marbles

(O)
obstacle course

(P)
paddleball
pentathlon
polo
(a) broomstick
(b) water
pool
(a) billiards
(b) snooker
push ball

(R)
relay races
rifle shooting
rodeo
roller skating
rope climbing
rugby

(S)
sailing
shuffleboard
Sigma Delta Psi

skeet shooting
skiing
skin diving
snow shoeing
soccer
softball
(a) four-man
(b) multiple team
(c) one pitch
(d) one swing
(e) rollum
(f) six base
(g) slo pitch
(h) T ball
(i) twelve player
space ball
speedball
speed skating
splashketball
squash racquets
standing long jump
steeplechase run
swimming

(T)
tennis
(a) aerial
(b) deck
(c) paddle
(d) racquet
(e) table
tetherball
tobogganing
track and field
trampoline
triathlon
tug-of-war

(V)
volleyball

(W)
water skiing
weight lifting
wrestling

Seasonal Activities

Sports activities are generally seasonal in nature and in most programs, can be logically scheduled during the fall, winter, spring, and summer. However, local conditions such as limited facilities and scheduling conflicts sometimes require greater flexibility than the traditional seasonal pattern. Where weather is not a factor, touch football may be scheduled during the fall and winter seasons. Some institutions on the trimester system must schedule softball programs in the fall rather than in the spring. Whether seasonally selected or otherwise, it is advisable to arrange an equal number of activities for fall, winter, and spring because unbalanced scheduling may result in over-activitied participants. A sample breakdown of intramural activities is presented to illustrate the balanced pattern.

FALL

Women	*Men*
field hockey	touch football
bowling	bowling
soccer	cross country
badminton	table tennis
table tennis	paddleball
gymnastics	volleyball
co-intramurals	co-intramurals
sports clubs	sports clubs

WINTER

Women	Men
volleyball	basketball
modern dance	ice hockey
basketball	handball
figure skating	free throw contest
free exercise	wrestling
synchronized swimming	swimming
co-intramurals	co-intramurals
sports clubs	sports clubs

SPRING

Women	Men
softball—slo pitch	softball—slo pitch
lacrosse	softball—fast pitch
golf	baseball
track and field	tennis
tennis	golf
archery	track and field
co-intramurals	co-intramurals
sports clubs	sports clubs

SUMMARIES OF SELECTED ACTIVITIES

Some of the principal activities from the previous comprehensive list are presented herein to highlight certain features important to intramural programming.

Archery

This activity is suitable for boys and girls, men and women. The muscular strength required can be reasonably controlled by use of a variety of bows. Archery participation usually involves competitive target shooting, clout shooting, archery golf, and flight shooting.

1. In target shooting, an archer shoots a certain number of arrows from several distances which is called a round. After completing an end, the shooting of six arrows, the score is determined on the basis of the position of the arrows in the target.
2. For clout shooting, arrows are shot into the air so that they drop "mortar" style on the face of a target on the ground.
3. Archery golf is played like golf, except that the bow and arrow replaces the club and the ball.
4. In flight shooting, participants attempt to shoot the greatest distance.

In addition to the above activities, bow and arrow hunting is popular, as is field archery in which the conditions of hunting are simulated. Participation interest can be enhanced by forming an archery club.

Disadvantages of archery include the expensive equipment and possible danger resulting from carelessness. Target areas should be carefully selected and supervised.

Badminton

Badminton is an excellent co-intramural activity. It can be played indoors and outdoors and as a singles or doubles game. Team competition involving four players, two singles and two doubles, can be arranged for intramurals. (Refer to the discussion of team competition in the handball section, page 95.) Two of the disadvantages are the expense of the equipment and the limited number of players that can be accommodated.

Baseball

Baseball ("hard ball" or league) is a popular activity among youth, but the major difficulty in promoting it on a large scale is the amount of space required. Usually, intramural games are scheduled at times when varsity and freshman teams are not using the diamonds. Lack of sufficient space for baseball has caused many schools to limit the number of entries and to introduce softball for the majority of the students.

For intramural purposes, a game shortened to five or seven innings or played according to an hour and a half time limit is preferable to the regulation nine-inning game. For safety reasons, complete catcher's equipment and batting helmets should be provided.

Basketball

Basketball is an ideal intramural activity and practically everywhere is the most popular event in the program. For intramurals, it does not require extended preliminary practice and almost every participant has played the game sufficiently to enjoy it. The number of players required for a team is small, and they can be readily assembled. Leagues can be promoted successfully in practically any unit of participation, the amount of available playing time and space usually being the only limitations to the activity.

Games can be played in quarters of six to ten minutes or halves of twelve to twenty minutes. Rules may require clock stopping or the game can be played on a straight running time basis. When the latter method is used, championship games may be played according to regulation basketball rules. Where facilities include adjacent basketball courts, a central timing device can be used to time several concurrent games on the straight running time system.

Ideas for Intramurals. (1) A rules modification which can be success-fully applied to intramural basketball involves taking the ball out of bounds, rather than shooting free throws, for all fouls except those which occur during an unsuccessful try for goal. In the last few minutes of the game, regular free throw procedures prevail. This modified rule speeds up the game by eliminating excessive time at the free throw line and re-duces the foul calling pressure on officials. (2) The "ice hockey" free substitution rule may be utilized by permitting basketball players to enter the game at any time provided the incoming and outgoing players cross the boundary line at the same time and place.

Bowling

Bowling in the intramural program depends entirely on the availability of bowling lanes. Some institutions have bowling facilities in the gym-nasium or the student union building. When these are not available, it is necessary to use commercial establishments.

Competition may be organized with singles and doubles tournaments, or leagues may be established for three-, four-, or five-man teams. If facilities are adequate, entries can be divided into leagues to be followed by an elimination tournament of the league winners. If facilities are lim-ited, it is advisable to conduct the sport on a qualification basis, picking a certain number of high score teams to compete in a final elimination series.

Interest in bowling is maintained by posting high averages, high single game and high three game totals for teams and individuals. For league bowling, the seven point system can be used to determine winners. Two points are allowed for each of the three games bowled, and a seventh point is awarded to the team with the higher three game total.

Another method of interesting new bowlers and poor bowlers in team competition is to conduct the league on a handicap or "overaverage" basis. The purpose of this procedure is to equalize the competition by giving a certain number of pins to the team with lesser ability as determined by bowling averages. For exact handicap procedures, refer to bowling hand-icap methods in Chapter 9.

Boxing

Boxing is not a popular intramural sport in school intramurals, but it is successful in military programs. It requires careful training, and should only be promoted when proper conditioning can be required and super-vised. Participants should be carefully matched according to weight and ability.

Three rounds of two minutes each, with one minute intermission pe-riods, are advisable for tournament bouts. Weight classifications are as follows:

Bantam weight, 119 lbs.
Featherweight, 125 lbs.
Lightweight, 132 lbs.
Light-welterweight, 139 lbs.
Welterweight, 147 lbs.

Light-middleweight, 156 lbs.
Middleweight, 165 lbs.
Light-heavyweight, 178 lbs.
Heavyweight, over 178 lbs.

Experienced referees and judges should be carefully selected, because the determination of a winner in a close bout requires keen judgment of boxing maneuvers. As a safety precaution for practice and competitive bouts, large gloves should be used. For intramural matches, 14-ounce gloves should be worn by the participants. Younger age groups are advised to use 16-ounce gloves. In some programs, the written consent of the parents is required before a minor is permitted to engage in any scheduled boxing match.

Cross Country

Although cross country is free from the element of physical contact, it is a very strenuous activity. A minimum number of practice periods should be a prerequisite for entering a meet. A course of one or two miles is sufficiently long for intramural purposes. Some cross country races scheduled at Thanksgiving time are titled "turkey trots" or "gobbler chases," and the first place winner is awarded a turkey.

All contestants should wear numbers so the judges can differentiate the order of finish as players enter the chute. This also aids the checkers on the course who are responsible for patroling the runners and reporting "short cuts."

The cross country meet can be scheduled as an open meet or a team event. If the latter method is adopted, five men may be picked to represent a team. Any number of participants can run but only the first five to finish are counted in the team scoring. The respective places of finish in the race are recorded and added together. Totals are then compared and the lowest score represents the winner. For example, if the five best runners of a team finish 1, 3, 4, 7, and 8, the total for this team would be 23, and it would be the victor over teams possessing a higher total.

Ideas for Intramurals. (1) The jogger's mile, when added to cross country racing, offers opportunities for all runners to be winners. Before the race starts, each runner is asked to estimate how long it will take him to finish the race. Those whose estimates match the finishing times are winners in this event. (Refer to the jogger's mile chart in Figure 7–1). (2) Another variation for cross country is to run for a specified length of time, for example, six minutes. A pistol is shot at the end of this time, and everyone remains in his position until the order of finish is tabulated. The runner covering the greatest distance in this period of time is the winner. (3) When large numbers of cross country runners enter a meet, recording participant numbers in proper order as they enter the chute is sometimes cumbersome. An idea which expedites this process and reduces potential errors is to attach numbers to the runners' shirts with an adhesive, or pin tear-away numbers with perforations inside the pinned edges. As runners cross the finish line, numbers are easily detached from the shirt and placed in the correct order of finish.

JOGGER'S MILE CHART

T = TIME
P = PLACE

T	P	T	P	T	P	T	P	T	P	T	P	T	P	T	P
7:30		8:00		8:30		9:00		9:30		10:00		10:30		11:00	
7:31		8:01		8:31		9:01		9:31		10:01		10:31		11:01	
7:32		8:02		8:32		9:02		9:32		10:02		10:32		11:02	
7:33		8:03		8:33		9:03		9:33		10:03		10:33		11:03	
7:34		8:04		8:34		9:04		9:34		10:04		10:34		11:04	
7:35		8:05		8:35		9:05		9:35		10:05		10:35		11:05	
7:36		8:06		8:36		9:06		9:36		10:06		10:36		11:06	
7:37		8:07		8:37		9:07		9:37		10:07		10:37		11:07	
7:38		8:08		8:38		9:08		9:38		10:08		10:38		11:08	
7:39		8:09		8:39		9:09		9:39		10:09		10:39		11:09	
7:40		8:10		8:40		9:10		9:40		10:10		10:40		11:10	
7:41		8:11		8:41		9:11		9:41		10:11		10:41		11:11	
7:42		8:12		8:42		9:12		9:42		10:12		10:42		11:12	
7:43		8:13		8:43		9:13		9:43		10:13		10:43		11:13	
7:44		8:14		8:44		9:14		9:44		10:14		10:44		11:14	
7:45		8:15		8:45		9:15		9:45		10:15		10:45		11:15	
7:46		8:16		8:46		9:16		9:46		10:16		10:46		11:16	
7:47		8:17		8:47		9:17		9:47		10:17		10:47		11:17	
7:48		8:18		8:48		9:18		9:48		10:18		10:48		11:18	
7:49		8:19		8:49		9:19		9:49		10:19		10:49		11:19	
7:50		8:20		8:50		9:20		9:50		10:20		10:50		11:20	
7:51		8:21		8:51		9:21		9:51		10:21		10:51		11:21	
7:52		8:22		8:52		9:22		9:52		10:22		10:52		11:22	
7:53		8:23		8:53		9:23		9:53		10:23		10:53		11:23	
7:54		8:24		8:54		9:24		9:54		10:24		10:54		11:24	
7:55		8:25		8:55		9:25		9:55		10:25		10:55		11:25	
7:56		8:26		8:56		9:26		9:56		10:26		10:56		11:26	
7:57		8:27		8:57		9:27		9:57		10:27		10:57		11:27	
7:58		8:28		8:58		9:28		9:58		10:28		10:58		11:28	
7:59		8:29		8:59		9:29		9:59		10:29		10:59		11:29	

Fig. 7–1. Jogger's Mile Chart.

Dance

The rhythmic activity of social, modern, and folk and square dancing has great appeal for intramural participants of all ages. Dancing is an informal type of activity, although it can be organized on a club basis. It may only be competitive to the extent that individuals try out for the various roles in the club. Activities of clubs may be purely recreational, or artistic in that dance routines are created for public presentations.

Fencing

Fencing involves contests between two opponents, who attempt to touch each other legally with the tip of a sword. All maneuvers take place on a strip 40 feet long by 6 feet wide. Removable rubber mats can be placed on the gymnasium floor for practices and meets.

Divisions include foil, épée, and sabre. Electrical equipment can be used to help eliminate the judgment factor of determining a "touch." Beginning, intermediate, and advanced groups should be organized to encourage equalized competition. Ladder tournaments are effective for developing tournament contesting, judging, and directing.

Field Hockey

Field hockey is a fast moving game played by two teams of eleven members each on a football-type field. It is played almost exclusively in women's and girls' intramural programs in America, although it is a popular men's activity in other parts of the world. The nature of the game is similar to ice hockey in that an attempt is made to hit the ball with a curved stick into the opponent's goal.

The game consists of two thirty-minute halves which may be reduced for intramural purposes. Equipment includes the hockey stick, which is flat on one side and rounded on the other, shin pads, goalie pads, and goalie shoes with pads over the instep.

A field hockey club may be organized in which the membership plays intraclub games. Additionally, the best players can compete extramurally against teams representing outside groups.

Field Meets

Field meets may be organized using some of the basic skills of sports such as baseball and football. A point system is established to determine the top performers in the meet. Baseball and football meet events are as follows:

BASEBALL

1. Base running
2. Bunting and running
3. Fungo hitting
4. Baseball pitching
5. Target throwing
6. Throwing for distance
7. Catcher's throw to second base

FOOTBALL

1. Passing for distance
2. Passing for accuracy
3. Punting for distance
4. Drop kicking for field goals
5. Place kicking for field goals
6. Place kicking for distance

Football

Touch Football. Touch football is an extremely popular intramural activity. It capitalizes on the nationwide interest in tackle football and requires a limited amount of skill, training, and equipment. Strict field supervision and good officiating are necessary to keep game injuries at a minimum. Although it is played primarily by men participants, some programs include leagues for girls.

The rules of touch football have been freely modified to meet the needs of local playing conditions. Examples of these modifications are listed below:

1. The number of players on a team varies from six to eleven.
2. The method of touch-tackling may be one or two hands on a specific area of the body such as a one-handed touch between the shoulders and the knees.
3. Field sizes include the regulation tackle football field and smaller areas 300 ft. x 150 ft. or 240 ft. x 120 ft.
4. First downs are determined by advancing the ball to the next twenty-yard zone.
5. Games are played with stopped clock time or straight running time.
6. Restrictions are placed on the blocker to the extent that he cannot leave his feet on the block.
7. On a kick the ball is run out of the end zone, and if the runner is unsuccessful, it is placed on the twenty-yard line.
8. If the extra point is kicked, one point is scored and if it is advanced from the three-yard line by running or passing, two points are scored.
9. For another extra point method, the ball is placed on the ten-yard line. If the runner advances to or beyond the five-yard line, one point is scored, and if he crosses the goal line, two points are scored.
10. To eliminate ties, the team with the greater number of first downs is the winner. If the score and the number of first downs are tied, the ball is positioned on the fifty-yard line, and each team runs four alternating plays, a total of eight plays. At the end of the alternating series, the team that has the ball on the opponent's side of the fifty-yard line breaks the tie, and unless other scores have been made, the score of the penetration series is 1 to 0. These scores may be represented as follows: 6–4d–1 to 6–4d–0. The tournament draw sheet in Figure 10–3 illustrates this system of scoring.

A committee of the National College Physical Education Association for Men surveyed and standardized touch and flag football rules modifications. These rules have been published by the Athletic Institute under the title "National Touch and Flag Football Rules Handbook."

Flag Football. A variation of touch football is the game of flag football. The rules are comparable to touch football with the major differences being the method of "tackling" the player. In flag football, the runner is stopped by pulling a small cloth strip or flag from the runner's belt. This procedure eliminates the judgment as to whether the ball carrier has been touched.

Flags may be made from heavy cloth strips or they may be purchased from sporting goods firms. The commercial product includes a belt with two or three flags attached to the back and sides. It is advisable to use different colored flags for opposing teams.

There is a disagreement among intramural personnel as to the roughness of flag football compared to touch football. Some claim that the pushing roughness involved when the player tags a runner with one or two hands is eliminated by simply pulling a flag from the belt. Others claim that players hold or practically tackle the runner in an attempt to get the flag. The degree of roughness undoubtedly depends on the temperament of the players and the adequacy of officiating and supervision. Flag football is played extensively in military intramural programs.

Tackle Football. While tackle football is a very popular varsity sport, it is played limitedly in intramurals. The game requires intricate plays and teamwork which cannot be acquired without a considerable amount of practice. The cost of equipping large numbers of players is prohibitive for most programs.

Tackle football is played in some programs with a limited number of teams. In teacher education institutions, these are coached by physical education majors. Younger aged players sometimes wear only headgears and shoulder pads, the roughness not differing too much from the type of contact that occurs in a neighborhood play fight.

Ideas for Intramurals. Knee tackle football reduces player momentum, minimizes falling distance, and eliminates the necessity for expensive equipment. It can be played indoors on a wrestling mat or out of doors in a restricted area. All maneuvers of the game are performed on the hands and knees. A closed fist replaces the foot for kicking kick-offs, field goals, and extra points. A new series of downs is earned when a team crosses the midpoint of the field.

Free Throw Contest

Shooting free throws requires limited physical movement, but it creates considerable interest, as indicated by the thousands who participate in these contests. The activity can be introduced by requesting varsity basketball players to shoot free throws for the event. Their scores are publicly announced, and intramural participants attempt to beat the varsity players.

If the basis of the tournament is one hundred attempts, winners usually average between 70 and 85 successful throws. With a large number of entries, the task of supervising a maximum number of throws by every candidate is enormous; therefore, a qualification system should be adopted. Supervision is facilitated if participants from opposite teams record each other's scores. Figure 7–2 illustrates a type of score sheet which can be used for a free throw contest.

One method of conducting the qualification series is as follows: all candidates shoot 25 free throws and those scoring 15 or more qualify to shoot 25 more times, making a total of 50 attempts. The ten candidates with the highest scores are permitted 50 additional attempts; the winner is the one making the most free throws out of 100.

Another way to complete the contest in one day is to require each contestant to shoot two rounds of 25 throws. A team enters any number of players with the ten best rounds applying to the total team score. Both rounds or just one round of any player can be counted toward the team total. The highest possible team score is 250. For additional individual competition, players successfully completing 40 out of 50 throws may be awarded another 50 attempts, or a total of 100 throws. The highest total out of 100 identifies the individual free throw contest winner.

Golf

The popularity of golf is such that little stimulation is required to interest participants in an intramural tournament. Unfortunately, many institutions do not have sufficient golfing facilities to meet the demand, and it is necessary to use public courses. When intramural tournaments are conducted on public or private courses, green's fees of the participants may be paid out of intramural funds. Intramural golf competition can be organized in several ways, some of which are discussed below.

Medal or Stroke Play. Medal or stroke play is the number of times a player strokes or swings at the ball to complete a round. The total number of strokes is posted for each player and the one with the lowest number is the winner. In a sense, medal play is an attempt to beat the established par of a golf course. Medal scores may also be used to determine various tournament flights or classes.

For intramural stroke play or team competition, groups may enter any number of players. Each player's score is recorded at the end of 18 holes, and the total of the four lowest scores makes up the team total, the lowest aggregate score being declared the team winner.

Match Play. Match play involves competition between two players, each attempting to win a greater number of holes by taking the least

FREE THROW CONTEST

PRINT NAME_____   TEAM OR ORGANIZATION_____

SHOOT TWO ROUNDS OF 25 FREE THROWS: After 10 practice throws are completed, the contestant should advise the checker he is ready to start. The count begins when the first free throw is made. The contestant may take a break at the end of his first round. No practice is allowed between rounds and the first throw attempted after the break counts. Only these two rounds count toward team scores.

SAMPLE ROUND

1	2	3	4	5	6	7	8	9	10	11	12	13	14	15	16	17	18	19	20	21	22	23	24	25	TOTAL
1	X	X	2	3	4	X	5	X	X	6	7	8	9	X	10	X	X	11	X	12	13	X	14	X	14

X equals a Miss--Numbers indicate the running score.

FIRST ROUND

1	2	3	4	5	6	7	8	9	10	11	12	13	14	15	16	17	18	19	20	21	22	23	24	25	TOTAL

SECOND ROUND

1	2	3	4	5	6	7	8	9	10	11	12	13	14	15	16	17	18	19	20	21	22	23	24	25	TOTAL

CHECKER'S SIGNATURE_____   SUB TOTAL_____
CHECKER'S TEAM_____
NOTE: Checker may not be a teammate of contestant!

INDIVIDUAL CHAMPIONSHIP

Any contestant making 40 or more free throws in the first two rounds is entitled to 50 additional throws for the Individual Championship. These throws are attempted immediately and recorded below in rounds three and four. No practice throws are allowed.

THIRD ROUND

1	2	3	4	5	6	7	8	9	10	11	12	13	14	15	16	17	18	19	20	21	22	23	24	25	TOTAL

FOURTH ROUND

1	2	3	4	5	6	7	8	9	10	11	12	13	14	15	16	17	18	19	20	21	22	23	24	25	TOTAL

CHECKER'S SIGNATURE_____   SUB TOTAL_____
CHECKER'S TEAM_____   GRAND TOTAL_____

Fig. 7-2. Basketball Free Throw Contest Score Sheet.

number of strokes per hole. If the score is posted as 1 up, it means that one player won one hole more than his opponent. If the score is 2 and 1, it means a player has won two holes more than his opponent, with only one hole left to play. If a tie results at the end of 18 holes, additional holes are played until the tie is broken. Match play winners are usually decided on the basis of a single elimination tournament.

Nassau Scoring Method. In this scoring method, the number one players of each team play against each other, number two players are paired together, number three's together, etc. In the Nassau system, three points are awarded for each match on the basis of the number of holes won. One point is awarded to the winner of the first nine holes, one point to the winner of the second nine holes, and one point to the player who wins the greatest number of holes for a complete round of 18. Thus, it is possible for A to defeat B by 3–0, 2½–½, or 2–1. The score of 3–0 indicates A won the first nine holes, the second nine holes, and the total out of 18 holes. In case of ties at the end of the round, winners can be determined by playing extra holes. A variation of this system for intramurals is to award points to the player with the low medal or stroke score at the end of each nine holes and at the end of 18 holes.

Blind Bogey. The blind bogey golf tournament is appropriate for intramurals because anyone can win regardless of ability. It may be conducted as a separate event, or concurrently with a medal play tournament.

Participants record their estimated handicaps with the starter before teeing off. If the individual's actual score minus the guessed handicap equals the blind par, he is one of the tournament winners. Blind par is established by drawing a number between 70 and 80 after all of the golfers have left the first tee. In estimating handicaps, players should think of what number subtracted from what they expect to shoot will equal the number which will be drawn as the blind par. For example, an actual score of 110 minus a guessed handicap of 36 equals the blind drawn par of 74. For increasing the number of prizes, more than one blind par may be drawn.

Flag Match. The flag match may be conducted as a novelty intramural golf activity. By adding an individual's handicap to the par of the course, the total number of strokes for a round is established. Each entrant then plays a regular round and places a flag wherever his ball stops on the last of the allotted strokes for the round. Usually the flags are placed close to the 18th green.

For example, player A adds his handicap of 15 strokes to the par of 72, to give him 87 strokes for the round. After the 87th swing, he places his flag where the ball rolls to a stop. Player B adds his handicap of 20 to the par of 72 which gives him 92 strokes. B makes the 18th hole in 87 strokes. He still has five strokes to play which may take him beyond the 19th hole where his flag would be placed. The player whose flag is the greatest distance beyond the 18th hole is the winner.

A variation of the flag match is *par golf*. Each contestant is permitted a number of strokes equivalent to the par of the course, for example, 72. Flags are placed in the relative positions after players have taken their allotted number of strokes and the individual whose flags is farthest advanced is the winner.

Other competitions which can be used to add interest to intramural golf are the following:

1. Fewest number of putts
2. Low net score for handicaps of 10 and under
3. Low net score for handicaps of 11 and over
4. Low net scores for those with odd numbered handicaps
5. Low net scores for those with even numbered handicaps
6. Longest putt on a specific hole
7. Longest drive on the first hole
8. Low gross scores for selected holes

Ideas for Intramurals. Shotgun golf is unique for simultaneously starting several foursomes of golfers. Players are positioned at each tee and wait for the noise of a shotgun blast before teeing off. They play a complete round, ending at the hole prior to where they began.

Gymnastics

An intramural gymnastics meet can be successful if it is coordinated with a physical education teaching unit on gymnastics skills. Intramural gymnastics events include floor exercise, long horse, side horse, high bar, parallel bars, and rings. Participants are judged on the basis of their individual performances and winners are named for each event. A team winner is decided by combining the best individual scores in each event. Additional information about conducting meets is presented in Chapter 9.

Handball

One-wall, three-wall, or four-wall handball games are popular with intramural participants. Singles, doubles, and challenge tournaments or team competition may be included in the schedule.

Each team consists of two singles players and two doubles players. Rules specify four different players or two players may play both singles and doubles. Winning each match counts one point. For example, the number one singles players play three matches (not the best two out of three) totaling three points. Matches involving the number two singles players and the doubles players are each worth three points. The total number of possible team points is nine, thus resulting in potential scores of 9–0, 8–1, 7–2, 6–3, and 5–4. An alternative is to use five-man teams with two doubles players (counting two points for the match) and three singles players (each match counting one point). These team plans of competition are adaptable for other individual and dual sports.

Horseshoes

Horseshoes or "barnyard golf" is a desirable intramural activity because courts require relatively little space and can usually be placed in areas that are otherwise unused. The game also attracts participants who are physically incapable of strenuous participation.

As in handball, tournaments may be arranged for singles players, doubles players, or teams. A team may consist of six players who are paired for three doubles matches. The winning team is determined on the basis of two victories out of the three matches, or by following the team scoring procedure described above in handball. The cancellation method of scoring can be used in which the player closer to the stake cancels opponent's points, or all points can be counted if the shoes are within six inches of the stake.

Ice Hockey

Intramural ice hockey games are played where the climate is conducive to producing natural ice and at institutions that have artificial indoor or outdoor rinks. On occasion, warm weather melts natural ice and interferes with the completion of the hockey schedule. Because of the strenuous nature of the game, each period may be reduced to ten or twelve minutes, straight running time. Many intramural players play without pads, and for this reason rules should be modified to eliminate body checking and boarding. Goalies should be supplied with a complete set of equipment including face masks.

Where ice time is limited and to assure adequate rest between periods, the following scheduling method, dove tailing periods of two separate games is advisable. Teams A and B play their first period and then rest while teams C and D play their first period. Subsequently, A and B play their second period while C and D rest, and so on throughout the game. To encourage participants of all levels of ability, it is helpful to schedule both major leagues for the skilled players and minor leagues for the less skilled players.

Jogging

Jogging, a popular method of physical conditioning, has several advantages as an intramural activity. It is primarily an informal, noncompetitive activity, but interest and competition may be developed by setting common goals or objectives. Some of the advantages are the following:

1. Jogging is easy to perform, requiring absolutely no skill.
2. It is suitable for men and women, boys and girls, without any limitation on age.

3. No specific equipment or special facilities are needed.
4. It can be scheduled at the convenience of the participant and may be performed individually or collectively.
5. It develops the lungs, muscles, and heart; slims and trims the appearance; and tones or firms the body.

Jogger's mile clubs may be established to encourage participation. A jogger's mile chart can be developed which lists members' names and shows the corresponding number of miles they have run. This chart may be calibrated in squares with each square representing one mile. It may be designed to reflect the distance between two cities within a state or two points from coast to coast which are traversed over an extended period of time. This type of chart may be termed "jogger's journey" or "jogger's jaunt."

Ideas for Intramurals. To encourage running or jogging, distances equaling a mile in and around facilities should be posted. For example, X number of laps around the track equals a mile; X number of laps around the gymnasium equals a mile; X number of laps around a city block equals a mile; X number of trips between two buildings equals a mile; and X number of trips between the locker room and a specific facility equals a mile.

Judo

Judo is an oriental type of wrestling which has become extremely popular as a year-round intramural activity. The major emphasis is on the sporting or contesting aspect rather than self-defense, although the latter is a concomitant of participation. The objective is to outmaneuver the opponent by using leverage techniques.

A contestant may win by five different methods:

1. Throwing
2. Holding or immobilizing the opponent for 30 seconds on his side or back
3. A strangling submission hold
4. An arm lock submission hold
5. A judge's decision

One point determines a match and is awarded for throwing, holding, or one of the submission holds. A contestant may earn a half-point for a 25-second hold down or for a poor throw. A match may be three or five minutes in length, and if no match point is awarded, judges determine a winner on the basis of judo technique.

Competition is organized in the form of a double elimination tournament or the bad point system. In the latter method, each participant begins with five points to his credit. If he loses a match on a one point

basis, he also loses three of his five points. If he loses the match by a
decision, two points are subtracted, and if he wins by a decision, one
point is deducted from his five point total. Half points count the same
as a decision. It is possible for a participant to win five matches by decision and be out of the tournament because his five points have been
spent.

As participants perfect judo techniques, they are promoted through
four belt categories: white, green, brown, and black. These are further
subdivided into 16 classes or degrees: 10 black, 3 brown, 1 green, and 2
white.

Competitors are categorized in six weight classes:

139 lbs. and under	176 lbs. and under	Heavyweight
155 lbs. and under	205 lbs. and under	Open class

Karate

Karate is an oriental art of self-defense based on striking an opponent
with the arms and legs. However, as in judo, the emphasis is placed on
the sporting aspects in which the blows do not actually make contact.
There are five colored belt classifications: white, green, purple, brown,
and black, all of which denote a person's relative proficiency in the activity. These belts are further subdivided into 20 kyus or classes: black, 1
through 10; brown, 1, 2, and 3; purple, 4 and 5; green, 6; and white, 7,
8, 9, and 10.

Competition consists of katas or lessons and free style fighting. There
are five katas which a participant must be able to perform against an
imaginary assailant. The referee and judges select one of these for pairs
of participants and the one who is judged to be better remains in competition while the other is eliminated. For advanced competition, more
complex katas are performed, and these are judged on the basis of a
point system.

In free style fighting, a referee judges the timing, control, and speed
with which defense and attack movements are executed. Points and half
points are awarded by the referee.

Lacrosse

Lacrosse is a football-type field activity in which the objective is to
advance a smaller rubber ball into the opponent's goal. The ball may be
batted, carried, or thrown with the stick or "crosse." The game involves
the strategy of basketball in that players are paired off to obstruct each
other's movements, and it includes the type of body checking found in

ice hockey. The side stepping and dodging of a football open field runner is also part of the game.

It is played in an area slightly larger than a football field, and the playing time consists of four 15-minute quarters. Ten player. represent each team. It is played predominantly in the eastern portion of the United States, although it is becoming increasingly popular in other sections of the country.

Paddleball

Paddleball is played in a handball court and the rules are similar to those of handball except that paddles are used. The game was developed in 1930 by Earl Riskey at the University of Michigan. The game was originally conceived while watching tennis players practice in handball courts. Equipment consists of a rubber ball and paddles which are attached to the wrists with a leather thong.

Paddleball requires less skill than handball or squash. Most participants discover they can be reasonably successful the first time the game is played and this adds to its popularity. Paddleball can be played according to one-wall, three-wall, or four-wall rules. Where handball courts are unavailable, a gymnasium wall can be substituted for one-wall paddleball.

Push Ball

Push ball, played on a football-type field, is a highly competitive, exhausting game. Each team consists of ten to 50 players who attempt to propel a ball, six feet in diameter, across the opponent's goal line by rolling, passing, carrying, or pushing it. Any means of interference may be used to impede an opponent's progress except striking and throwing the body across the back of an opponent's legs.

The game is played in four 10-minute quarters. A goal scores five points and a team is allowed to try for an additional point after making a goal. For this purpose, the ball is placed on the opponent's five-yard line and a team is allowed one minute to penetrate the goal line. This activity is extremely popular in military programs.

Rifle Shooting

Rifle shooting is a desirable intramural activity but it can only be promoted if a rifle range is available. Institutions with ROTC units usually conduct riflery in cooperation with the military authorities. Supervision and instruction is provided by military personnel. For younger aged participants, air rifles can be used in competition.

Rifle shooting is an important phase of military training and comprehensive schemes of competition can be developed for military intramural programs. Matches can be conducted on a shoulder to shoulder basis or by transmitting the results between opponents via telephone, telegraph, or postal services.

Sigma Delta Psi

Many colleges and universities have established chapters of Sigma Delta Psi, the national honorary athletic fraternity. Trials for passing membership requirements are usually conducted by intramural personnel. These requirements may be modified for younger age participants.

Information about the fraternity and its requirements should be distributed during the fall season to give candidates an opportunity to practice and pass the tests throughout the year. To promote interest, yearly records of individual performances should be posted. Sigma Delta Psi activities may be organized on a team basis or similar to a field day or track meet in which points of five, four, three, two, and one are awarded to the place winners of each event.

Another method of team scoring involves the application of individual performances to national scoring tables. Scores of the best ten entrants are compiled, and the high total determines the winner. Appendix C includes Signa Delta Psi requirements, scoring tables, and a sample membership certificate.

Skiing

Skiing is an exciting intramural activity, but the expense of owning or renting equipment may limit participation. However, it requires considerable skill and most persons having the ability possess their own equipment. Skiing involves the following types of competition:

1. Downhill skiing is the fastest form of competition in which the skier attempts to negotiate a downhill trail in the least amount of time.
2. Slalom is a form of controlled downhill skiing wherein the skier passes through or goes around pairs of flags called gates. These maneuvers require quick reactions and complete coordination of the body and skis. The winner is determined on the basis of time.
3. Cross country competition requires the skier to traverse over hilly and flat terrain. The race may be several miles in length, as many as five or ten.
4. Ski jumping involves skiing down an inclined plane to a take off area and leaping into the air. The jumper earns points on the basis of form and distance.

Soccer

The popularity of soccer varies with the locality and is particularly related to participant nationalities. Where a large portion of the participants are of European or Canadian descent, or are from other foreign lands, soccer is usually an ideal intramural activity. In many foreign countries, soccer is the national pastime similar to baseball in the United States.

Coordinating intramural soccer with a unit in the physical education instructional program aids in generating interest. From an intramural standpoint, one of the disadvantages in soccer is the infrequent scoring. This produces tie games, often scoreless games, and the schedules are held up by the necessity of rescheduling them.

One method which can be used to overcome this discrepancy is to score one point for a corner kick and two points for a goal. Another scheme is to score one point for fouls which result in free kicks. This tends to limit body contact, the cause of most fouls in soccer.

Softball

Softball ranks with basketball as a leading intramural activity, both in the number of programs sponsoring these activities and the number of participants. In many respects, the game does not demand the exacting skills of baseball; therefore, it is a desirable sport for all age levels. Softball requires less space; approximately two fields occupy the same amount of space as one baseball field. Several variations of the original game of softball have been developed and are commonly used in intramural programs.

Fast Pitch. Fast pitch softball is played according to the regular rules and is favored by many of the highly skilled players. However, a good pitcher can dominate the game which sometimes leads to a game of catch between the pitcher and the catcher. This has a tendency to produce inactivity among the other players and is the main reason why slo pitch softball has become popular in intramurals.

Slo Pitch. Where slo pitch softball has been introduced in intramural programs, it has almost completely replaced fast pitch softball, particularly after a few years of experimentation. Slo pitch softball emphasizes hitting, fielding, and running with pitching being a less dominant factor in the game. The most distinguishable feature between slo pitch and fast pitch is the fact that the pitcher must throw a slow nonspinning ball which has a perceptible arc of not less than one foot nor more than ten feet. Some of the other components of slo pitch softball are as follows:

1. There are ten players on a team instead of nine.
2. An illegal pitch is counted as a ball, and runners do not advance.
3. Bunting or chopping at the ball is not legal; the ball is dead and the batter is out.
4. On a missed third strike, the ball is dead and runners cannot advance; the batter is out.
5. Base stealing is not allowed.
6. A runner can lead off from a base only after the ball crosses home plate.

There are some other variations found in slo pitch softball such as the use of a 12-, 14-, or 16-inch softball. Sizes of fields vary with 45-, 50-, or 60-foot base paths. If games result in large scores, a time limit or a ten-run per inning rule may be enforced. When games are played according to a time limit, teams may forfeit their turn at bat to conserve time. Still another modification is using two strikes and three balls rather than the customary three strikes and four balls.

One-Two-Three Pitch. Allowing only one, two, or three pitches per batter in a softball game speeds up play considerably. In restricted pitch softball, there are two pitchers, a fielding pitcher and a pitcher furnished by the batting team who throws the ball so it is easily hit by teammates. The batter is out if he hits a foul ball, swings and misses, or fails to swing at his allotted pitches. The batting team's pitcher must take his turn at bat and is replaced by someone else on the mound.

> **Ideas for Intramurals.** Four-man softball provides rapid action on either a fast or slo pitch basis. The players for each team are the catcher, pitcher, infielder, and outfielder. An imaginary line is drawn from home plate through the pitcher's mound, second base, and center field. When a right handed batter is at bat, the ball must be hit to the left side of this imaginary line and conversely for left handed batters, which causes the fielders to move to the opposite side of the field. If the ball is hit to the wrong side of the field, the batter is out. In four-man softball, the pitcher's rubber is substituted for first base. If a legally hit ball is fielded and thrown to the pitcher with his foot on the pitcher's plate before the runner gets to first base, he is out. No stealing is permitted.

Speedball

Speedball was developed by Elmer D. Mitchell, the "Father of Intramurals" in America, at the University of Michigan in 1921. The simple rules are easily mastered, and it is therefore easily adapted for intramural competition. It involves some of the skills of soccer, basketball, and football, those already known to most participants. Consequently, the game is enjoyed by new players in their initial attempt.

The use of hands is permitted, and the combination of ground and overhead play is appealing to the players. This variety permits more scoring possibilities so that tie games are a rarity. It is played with a soccer ball or a slightly larger official speedball on a football field or comparable area.

Squash Racquets

Squash racquets is a game played in an enclosed four-wall court. It is an extremely fast game, requiring more skill than handball and paddleball. Because of the unavailability of courts, the game is usually limited to larger institutions. Generally, there are fewer squash courts than handball courts. It is an excellent activity for faculty–staff personnel. Competition can be arranged in singles, doubles, or team events, although doubles matches require a larger court than singles matches.

Swimming

Where indoor or outdoor pools are available, swimming is a satisfying, competitive or informal intramural activity. A variety of dual, triangular, quadrangular, open, and novelty meets can be arranged. To prevent a few outstanding performers from dominating a swimming meet, the number of events in which an individual may enter should be limited to three. Awarding points for at least ten or twelve places in each event, if place times are available, also encourages less skilled participants. Records should be maintained from year to year to add interest to this sport. (Refer to Chapter 9 for additional information about conducting swimming meets.)

A popular novelty meet is the sweat suit race in which swimmers wear sweat shirts and pants. It may be used to equalize competition between men and women contestants. The men's speed is reduced when wearing water soaked sweat suits. Splash parties are also an important part of the co-intramural program.

Individuals can be encouraged to work out informally by posting a swimmer's mile board in the pool or locker room on which pool laps are recorded. The board should be designed to indicate the number of laps necessary to swim a mile. Over an extended period of time participants swim as far as twenty-five miles, and those reaching this goal may be presented with an award.

"T" Ball

"T" ball or post ball is a very useful activity to teach elementary age participants the games of baseball and softball. It eliminates the disadvantage of numerous walks and actionless play caused by the pitcher's inability to control the ball. In addition more time is spent in the fielding, hitting, running, and throwing phases of the game. The ball is placed on an adjustable, pliable rubber tee which is anchored to a portable, hard rubber home plate. Batters hit the ball from the tee after the pitcher goes through the motions of pitching the ball. Other modifications adapted to the ability of the players are as follows:

1. A game consists of five innings or a time limit of one hour.
2. A batter is allowed three swings and if the third one is a foul ball, the batter is out.
3. Base runners cannot lead off, nor can they steal bases.
4. Base runners may advance only on a hit ball.
5. After one team warning, a batter is out if he throws his bat.
6. Other options include:
   a. Hitters run on any hit ball, fair or foul.
   b. The inning ends when there are three outs or any other specified number such as six.
   c. If a team scores ten runs in their half of the inning, the sides change even if there are no outs.
   d. The inning ends when all players have batted, not when there are three outs.
   e. An inning terminates after seven players have batted regardless of the number of outs.

To assure everyone's participation in the game, all team members bat in order, even if there are as many as 18 players, but only ten team members play in the field. Fielders may be substituted at any time during the game.

As the ability of the players improves, a six-inning game can be played using "T" ball for three innings and pitching for the final three innings. Another variation that can be introduced after players have improved their skills is to provide an adult, everlasting pitcher who pitches for both teams. Each team has the advantage of batting against the same pitcher, and play is speeded up because of controlled pitching. The adult pitcher can guide player's learning experiences by throwing faster balls to the better players and slower ones to the players of lesser ability.

Table Tennis

Table tennis requires very little space and can be played in the gymnasium, a lounge, hallway, balcony, or a room in which furniture may be shifted to accommodate playing tables. Portable, folding table-tennis tables may be rolled into position and quickly prepared for play. If official tables are not available, others may be improvised.

Individual and dual competition may be scheduled as well as team matches. Because of the brevity of the game and its less strenuous nature, quickie or instant tournaments may be organized in which all matches are played in one evening. The activity also lends itself to challenge-type tournaments which can be posted in the living quarters of participants or in a table-games room.

Tennis

Tennis may be a year-round activity if both indoor and outdoor courts are available. It is an ideal co-intramural activity. As in other individual and dual type activities, tournaments may be arranged for singles, doubles, and team competition. Instead of having six ranked players compete in singles and doubles for each team, two or four players may represent a team in playing number one and number two singles and doubles as described in the team procedures for handball.

Scoring may also be modified for intramural purposes. According to regular tennis rules, a set consists of winning six games with a two game advantage and a match consists of the best two out of three sets. For intramurals, a match may consist of a specific number of games such as five, seven, or nine rather than playing sets. Another modification adapts the table tennis concept of changing serves after each five points and playing a match which consists of 21 or any other specified number of points.

Track

Indoor and outdoor track and field activities offer a wide range of opportunities for intramural participants. The events should be modified to correspond to the ability of the participants. Long distance races should be eliminated for young intramural participants. As in swimming, no individual should be permitted to enter more than a limited number of events, and conditioning sessions should be encouraged or even required.

Novelty races and events are effective if they are repeated annually and are well publicized. Relay races, pentathlons, tugs-of-war, and chariot races are examples of events which may be included in an intramural meet or conducted on separate occasions. (Refer to the detailed discussion of conducting track and field meets in Chapter 9.)

Ideas for Intramurals. For 440- and 880-yard relays in which the races are run in lanes all the way around the track, require runners in every other lane to run in opposite directions. With this arrangement, half of the participants will run counter to some opponents and parallel with the others. As they approach the finish line, they will be challenged to defeat runners coming from the opposite side and others running with them.

Volleyball

Volleyball is a game that intramural participants of all ages and abilities can enjoy. It is played with teams consisting of the regulation number of six players, or modified numbers of seven, eight, and nine players. For co-intramurals, four women and four men may represent one team. The game may be played on the basis of fifteen points or a time limit.

To adapt the game for intramural purposes, beginning players may be permitted to assist the server in hitting the ball over the net and to have additional taps of the ball on each side of the net. Another modification provides for the scoring of a point by either team on every serve instead of the regular scoring procedure of only the serving team scoring. The regulation method sometimes produces lengthy games and affects the scheduling pattern. The modified scoring plan tends to standardize the length of games, and consequently, starting times for subsequent matches can be properly programmed.

Foreign students attending American educational institutions show unusual interest and adaptability to the game. The skills of striking the ball are learned much more readily than the catching and throwing skills required in most other American games.

Water Polo

Water polo is a contact game that requires a tremendous amount of endurance. Unless it is played in a shallow pool permitting the players, seven per team, to touch the bottom, it is suitable only for highly skilled swimmers. The object of the game is to throw or place the ball in the opponent's goal.

The defensive team attempts to prevent the opposition from advancing the ball by using tactics that include immersing and holding under water the player with the ball. The length of playing time is 28 minutes divided into two 14-minute halves. This amount of time may be reduced for intramural water polo. In addition to being a strenuous, competitive intramural activity, it is suitable for the formation of a sports club.

Weight Lifting

Competitive weight lifting may be a part of the program, but weight training plays a more significant role in intramurals. Through the latter, individuals lift weights to improve their muscular strength and physical appearance. Weight lifting facilities should be available to encourage this informal type of participation. Circuit training devices permitting ten or fifteen individuals to work out at one time offer the possibility of unsupervised participation. There is no danger of injury and the equipment cannot be removed from the area.

In competitive weight lifting, three lifts, the military press, clean and jerk, and snatch, are contested. A contestant is given three trials for each of the three lifts, and he is credited with the heaviest weight for each lift. These three weights are added together for a total score, and the participant with the highest score in each weight class is the winner. The body weight classes are 123½ lbs., 132¼ lbs., 148¾ lbs., 165¼ lbs., 181¾ lbs., 198¼ lbs., and heavyweight (up to 242½ lbs.).

Wrestling

Wrestling is an appropriate intramural activity because it is an outgrowth of the kind of "backyard scuffling" that takes place between young boys as they attempt to demonstrate their superiority. It is a strenuous activity and participants should be encouraged to take part in preliminary conditioning periods. Competition is usually scheduled on a single elimination tournament basis, and it is desirable to include a consolation tournament for all first match losers to provide a minimum of two matches for every participant.

Weight classes at the collegiate age are 118, 126, 134, 142, 150, 158, 167, 177, 190 pounds, and unlimited. For the younger high school age group, the classes are 95, 103, 120, 127, 133, 138, 145, 154, 165, 175 pounds, and unlimited. All heavyweights must weigh a minimum of 175 pounds for high school competition. One or two pounds overweight may be permitted at weigh-in time.

It is advisable to limit preliminary matches to four or five minutes and final matches to six or seven minutes. "Advantage" time can be adjusted proportionately. In case of a draw the referee's decision may determine the winner.

8

Scheduling:
When and How

After selecting units for participation and program activities, a subsequent important programming step is scheduling. Determinations must be made as to when the program functions, specifically the times contests will be played, and when facilities will be available for informal participation. The person in charge of intramurals should carefully evaluate the local scene to select time periods that best fit the total pattern. These periods must be coordinated with other groups using the facilities and with other potentially conflicting events in the institution. The task of time selection should be approached with the idea that there is a time and a place for all intramural programs.

Activities must be scheduled when individuals are available to participate, or the program cannot exist. Normally, participants take part in scheduled, competitive contests once or twice each week and perhaps more frequently in the self-directed activities. Because of varying academic schedules and other conflicting interests, several alternatives must be available, some beginning in the morning and intermittently extending throughout the day and evening.

An intramural director must develop an awareness for time problems and scheduling conflicts. To assist program coordination, future events should be plotted on weekly, monthly, and yearly calendars. (See Fig. 8–1.) It is also advisable to locate large schedule boards at heavy participant traffic points to identify daily and preferably weekly facilities' schedules. These should include intramural activities, varsity practices and games, and physical education classes to assist participants in planning their "work-out" periods.

INTRAMURAL DIRECTOR'S MONTHLY CALENDAR

MONTH JANUARY — YEAR 19—

2	3 CLASSES BEGIN	4 INTRAMURAL SPORTS COUNCIL	5 INTRAMURAL OFFICIALS ASSOCIATION	6 INTRAMURAL SUPERVISORS MEETING	7 COINTRAMURALS	8 INTRAMURAL RECREATION
9 FACULTY-FAMILY RECREATION	10 INTRAMURAL SPORTS CLUBS COUNCIL	11 BASKETBALL ROUND ROBIN BEGINS	12 BOWLING LEAGUES BEGIN	13 HOCKEY TOUNAMENT BEGINS	14 COINTRAMURALS	15 INTRAMURAL RECREATION
16 FACULTY-FAMILY RECREATION	17 WHITE WATER CANOE SPORTS CLUB	18 FACULTY BOWLING BEGINS	19 JUDO AND KARATE SPORTS CLUBS	20 FACULTY SPORTS CLUB	21 COINTRAMURALS	22 INTRAMURAL RECREATION
23 FACULTY-FAMILY RECREATION	24 FENCING AND ARCHERY SPORTS CLUBS	25 INTRAMURAL ADVISORY COUNCIL	26 FREE THROW CONTEST BEGINS	27 TABLE TENNIS TOURNAMENT BEGINS	28 COINTRAMURALS	29 INTRAMURAL OPEN HOUSE
30 FACULTY-FAMILY RECREATION	31 SCUBA SPORTS CLUB	1 INTRAMURAL OFFICIALS ASSOCIATION	2 FACULTY VOLLEYBALL BEGINS	3 TRAMPOLINE SPORTS CLUB	4 COINTRAMURALS	5 INTRAMURAL RECREATION

Fig. 8–1. Intramural Director's Monthly Calendar.

TIME PERIODS

Various time patterns currently used for intramurals are presented as points of reference to be considered by those who wish to choose and evaluate program time periods.

Early Mornings

Although a seemingly undesirable time for intramurals, some programs are scheduled during the early morning hours between 7:00 and 8:00 or 7:00 and 9:00. Students frequently arrive early for school and it is possible to schedule 7:30 activities prior to 8:30 classes. Also, some industrial firms schedule bowling leagues and other activities during the wee hours of the morning for employees who work the late shift.

Middays

Noon-hour intramural programs are successful in elementary, junior, and senior high schools. Administrators appreciate the supervision of students who do not go home for lunch. This plan permits students who must work after school to participate in the program. The midday program is particularly well adapted to rural communities where the majority of students ride home on buses after the last afternoon class.

Activities should not be too strenuous, particularly if the program is scheduled after lunch. Sufficient time should be allowed for students to eat their lunches leisurely. There is a tendency for students to rush through eating in anticipation of starting play as soon as meals have been completed.

In some programs, noon-hour activities are conducted at the beginning of the lunch period. Games are followed by showers and lunch. Open or free periods are sometimes scheduled before or after lunch which provides extended time for intramural participation. In schools with split shifts or split lunch periods, it is necessary to conduct programs for both groups of participants.

Co-intramural activities are effective for midday programs. The less strenuous activities required for co-participation are most appropriate for noon-hour programming.

Late Afternoons

Perhaps the most satisfactory time for intramurals is the late afternoon period. Participants are present, eliminating the necessity of going home and returning to activity areas later in the evening. In schools, faculty supervision is more easily secured for afternoon hours, and parents are usually pleased to have their children play under supervision in a safe environment.

After a full day of comparatively sedentary work, participants enjoy the opportunity to "let off steam." This exercise and play is truly recreative after heavy concentration on the work of the day. One disadvantage is that some individuals may have tasks to perform at home or elsewhere. Other scheduling arrangements should be made to accommodate these individuals. Some school administrators delay school bus departures until after intramural activities have been completed.

Evenings

Evenings and late afternoons are undoubtedly the most frequently scheduled times for intramurals. Some programs are so extensive that activities are scheduled in the afternoon and continue through the late evening. Where facilities are shared with physical education classes and varsity athletics, there is usually less conflict in use of facilities during evening hours. Although participants must return to the activity area for evening participation, an attractive program will produce the enthusiasm necessary to overcome this disadvantage. Many participants prefer to play outdoor activities under the lights rather than during natural day light.

Weekends

Weekend intramurals are scheduled for Friday evenings, Saturdays, and Sundays. In some programs these times are used for playing postponed games. Certain weekend time periods are more desirable than others, depending on the age and interests of the participants. For example, in collegiate programs, Fridays and Saturdays are not good times because students go home for the weekend and leave immediately after the last class has ended. Also, Friday and Saturday nights are traditional dance and party nights. In these situations, Sunday afternoons and evenings seem to be preferred because students return to the campus and there are fewer conflicting social affairs. Weekends are desirable for scheduling co-intramural activities. Participants may wish to take part in these activities before attending other social affairs of the evening.

For younger aged participants in elementary, junior, and senior high schools, Saturday mornings and afternoons can be effective times for scheduling intramurals. Participants may have paper routes, delivery jobs, or other part-time employment during late afternoons that prohibit participation in intramurals. These individuals are usually willing to participate in a Saturday intramural program.

Activity or Club Periods

Special activity or club periods are sometimes a part of the regular school schedule and may serve as a suitable time for intramurals. These periods are scheduled daily or at various times throughout the week. Cocurricular or extracurricular activities take place during these intervals such as varsity practices, band and choir practices, drama rehearsals, as well as intramurals. Activity clubs may be organized to involve all students in some type of extracurricular participation. Club activities center around music, dramatics, arts and crafts, mechanics, aeronautics, home economics, business economics, and sports. Intramural tournaments can be conducted as part of the activity club program, or several clubs may function to promote interest in different kinds of sporting activities.

Vacation Days

Vacation days related to Christmas, Easter, Thanksgiving, Lincoln's Birthday, Washington's Birthday, Columbus Day, etc., provide additional opportunities for scheduling intramural activities. It is a particularly convenient time for extramural tournaments involving teams from several different institutions.

Gymnasium Classes

Although some schools use gymnasium class periods for intramural participation, physical education authorities advocate that class time should be primarily for instruction. If no other time is available for intramurals, it is acceptable. This can be accomplished in several ways: (1) using squads for units of participation during the regular class period; (2) assigning one complete physical education class period each week for intramurals; or (3) arranging an additional period as an extension of the physical education requirement to be used exclusively for intramural participation.

Special Intramural Days

Administrators are often willing to set aside classes to permit the entire student body to participate in a field meet, track meet, play day, or sports day. Afternoon classes are suspended and the entire school assembles for sports activities. The holiday from classes adds enthusiasm and interest to such programs. Half days may be set aside during fall, winter, and spring with outdoor activities promoted in fall and spring and indoor–outdoor activities emphasized in winter.

The previous presentation identifies several possibilities for times which may be selected for intramurals, the choice of which must be coordinated with many factors in a specific locality. The creative, enthusiastic director will be able to find an appropriate time to conduct the intramural program.

SCHEDULING PROCEDURES

A well-planned and appropriately administered activities schedule often means the difference between a highly successful intramural program and one that appears to be so on paper. Perhaps nothing is more detrimental to intramural programming than poor scheduling. It is demoralizing if participants report for a contest and their opponents or the officials fail to appear. If this condition exists even occasionally, interest deteriorates and pride in the program is destroyed.

Scheduling factors including processing entries, devising forms, notifying participants, and handling postponents and forfeits are reviewed in the following sections. (The mechanics of structuring competitive tournaments are presented in Chapter 9.)

Scheduling Considerations

Careful attention must be given to the following items when developing schedules:

1. Available equipment and facilities
2. Time allotted for the activity
3. Number of teams or individuals entered
4. Number of games required to complete the schedule
5. Conflicts with other activities
6. Allowance for postponements due to inclement weather
7. Seeding exceptional performers
8. Assignment of practice times

Schedules should be arranged as far in advance of actual playing dates as possible. In some instances, scheduling may be restricted because entries are not available until a few days before the event begins. This is particularly true of activities which start the first or second week of a new school year.

Scheduling a team to play the same night each week is another important consideration. This permits participants to arrange other activities accordingly. If two or more sports are sponsored at the same time and members of the same unit play on both teams, they must be scheduled to play on different nights. Whenever feasible, preferred playing times should be honored in drawing up schedules. Eventually, some teams will

.

be required to play at different times in order to meet winners of other divisions in the playoffs.

It is desirable to set specific times and dates for tournament matches or league games. For some elimination and challenge-type tournaments, participants are required to set their own times with the provision that games must be played on or before a certain date or with instructions to play one game per week. This flexibility may be necessary for certain kinds of competition, but it is difficult to attain success without constant supervision and reminders from the intramural staff. Opponents wait for each other to call, and soon the tournament is behind schedule or is on schedule, accompanied by several forfeits. Slow tournaments and forfeits result in unsatisfied participants. This type of scheduling is most effectice when competitors are enthusiastic and do not require constant prompting.

Some program directors make up a partial schedule covering first round games and after they have been played, complete the schedule, eliminating forfeiting teams and drop outs. Partial seeding is permitted by scheduling undefeated teams for the final rounds of league play.

Entry Blanks

The first step in making up schedules for competition is the solicitation of entries. There are several types of entry forms, but generally they may be classified as follows: (1) team entries, (2) individual and dual entries, and (3) meet entries. Team entry blanks (see Fig. 8–2) as used for basketball, bowling, touch football, softball, and volleyball, or for individual and dual sports that are promoted on a team basis. Individual and dual sports entry blanks (see Fig. 8–3) are used for badminton, table tennis, handball, tennis, paddleball, etc., when organized on a nonteam basis. Meet entry blanks (see Fig. 8–4) are used for swimming, wrestling, gymnastics, and track when students enter several different events.

Entry blanks should request information necessary to complete an effective schedule. The following list indicates the kinds of items that should be included on entry blanks:

1. Name of the activity
2. Name of the entrant
3. Manager's or captain's name, address, and telephone number
4. Specified hours participants prefer and/or cannot participate
5. Date of entry
6. Alphabetical listing of the team roster
7. For meets, identification of players in appropriate events
8. Signed statement of eligibility
9. Initials of staff reviewer
10. A space to indicate the entry has been scheduled

DATE_____

CHECKED BY___
SCHEDULED___

Team   Sports   Entry   Blank

SPORT_____

TEAM_____   MANAGER _____
        (PRINT)   (PRINT)

ADDRESS_____ TEL. NO. _____

CIRCLE HOURS YOUR TEAM CANNOT PARTICIPATE. DRAW A LINE UNDER PREFER-
RED PLAYING TIMES.

MONDAY	4:00-5:00	5:00-6:00	6:00-7:00	7:00-8:00	8:00-9:00	9:00-10:00
TUESDAY	4:00-5:00	5:00-6:00	6:00-7:00	7:00-8:00	8:00-9:00	9:00-10:00
WEDNESDAY	4:00-5:00	5:00-6:00	6:00-7:00	7:00-8:00	8:00-9:00	9:00-10:00
THURSDAY	4:00-5:00	5:00-6:00	6:00-7:00	7:00-8:00	8:00-9:00	9:00-10:00
FRIDAY	4:00-5:00	5:00-6:00	6:00-7:00	7:00-8:00	8:00-9:00	9:00-10:00

- PRINT TEAM ROSTER -

1._____ 11._____
2._____ 12._____
3._____ 13._____
4._____ 14._____
5._____ 15._____
6._____ 16._____
7._____ 17._____
8._____ 18._____
9._____ 19._____
10._____ 20._____

-ELIGIBILITY-

THIS CERTIFIES THAT I UNDERSTAND THE INTRAMURAL ELIGIBILITY RULES
AND HAVE COMPLETELY CHECKED THE ELIGIBILITY OF ALL THE PLAYERS ON
MY TEAM. IF THERE IS ANY DISCREPANCY, I WILL ASSUME FULL RESPONSIBIL-
ITY. FAILURE TO COMPLY WITH THESE RULES WILL RESULT IN DISIPLINARY
ACTION OUTLINED IN THE INTRAMURAL SPORTS HANDBOOK.

_____
MANAGER'S SIGNATURE

Fig. 8–2. Team Sports Entry Blank.

Tournament or game rules are sometimes printed on entry blanks. However, a less complicated and neater entry form can be provided if rules
are published on supplemental sheets.

To avoid possible misscheduling, one entry blank should be filled out
for each team if organizations enter more than one team. When entries

```
┌─────────────────────────────────────────────────────────┐
  DATE_____                        CHECKED BY___
                                            SCHEDULED ____
                     ENTRY BLANK FOR
                  INDIVIDUAL AND DUAL SPORTS

  PRINT NAME_____

  ADDRESS_____

  TEL._____    _____
                              (AFFILIATION)


                     CIRCLE ONE

  HANDBALL      GOLF          BADMINTON      TABLE TENNIS
  PADDLEBALL    SQUASH        HORSESHOES     TENNIS

  SINGLES___              DOUBLES___            GOLF AVE.___



          MY DOUBLES PARTNER WILL BE:

  _____
└─────────────────────────────────────────────────────────┘
```

Fig. 8–3. Entry Blank for Individual and Dual Sports.

are received, they should be carefully checked for errors and properly classified. If entries are returned to the office in person instead of by mail, the intramural staff can eliminate inconsistencies by immediately checking the entry and eligibility status of the players. Inquiries can also be answered in a friendly, cooperative manner, thereby establishing important participant-staff relationships.

After checking the entries against the list of teams that usually participate, it is advisable to notify the nonentered teams by telephone or a card to determine if they wish to enter the tournament. However, this procedure may encourage groups to be delinquent in submitting entries because they will rely on the office contact to remind them about entering a team.

Two different practices are followed with regard to setting entry deadlines. Some intramural directors feel that deadlines should be established for all entries, and others utilize an open end deadline. In the latter, entries are due by a certain date, but additional ones may be accepted if the schedule can be adjusted to accommodate them. Entrants may change their mind and withdraw from the schedule, or drop out after

SWIMMING

ENTRY BLANK

ORGANIZATION OR TEAM _____ DATE _____ 19_____

100 YARD MEDLEY RELAY _____   _____
                       _____   _____

100 YARD FREE STYLE

_____   _____   _____

50 YARD BACKSTROKE

_____   _____   _____

50 YARD BREAST STROKE

_____   _____   _____

50 YARD BUTTERFLY

_____   _____   _____

50 YARD FREE STYLE

_____   _____   _____

DIVING

_____   _____   _____

100 YARD INDIVIDUAL MEDLEY

_____   _____   _____

200 YARD FREE STYLE RELAY _____   _____
                          _____   _____

Teams are limited to one team in each relay. Individuals may enter a maximum of three events (any combination). Points are scored as follows: For All-Meet: Individual events – 7,5,4,3,2,1; Relays – 14,10,8,6,4,2. For Division Championships: Individual events – 8,6,5.5,5,4.5,4,3,2.5,2,1.5,1,.5; Relays – 16,14,11,10,9,8,6,5,4,3,2,1.

Fig. 8–4. Swimming Meet Entry Blank.

the first game. Late entries can be used to fill these gaps in the schedule.

In certain programs, the intramural director automatically enters one team from each unit for every sport. If the unit decides not to participate or if the unit wishes to have more than one team, the intramural staff is notified.

Scheduling Forms

Intramural scheduling may involve one or more combinations of the following: original work schedules, office master or daily schedules, mimeographed or dittoed schedules, card schedules, newspaper schedules, or daily schedules posted in the playing area. Original work schedules are prepared from entry blanks, and the master or daily schedule is compiled from work schedules. The master schedule includes the sport, time, date, court or field, opponent, officials, and a telephone notification check column or space to list the name of the person notified.

Figure 8–5 illustrates two types of intramural daily schedules. The advantage of Type I is that duplication of games on a court or field is easily discernible. A disadvantage is that a separate sheet must be used for each sport, whereas several activities can be included on Type II.

Schedules can be mimeographed or dittoed for distribution to team managers. These schedules should include name of the sport, opponents, dates, times, courts or fields, blanks for scores, parentheses for final league position, and minimal directions. Duplicated schedule sheets list several divisions and provide players with the opportuinty to follow the progress of other teams. Figure 8–6 shows a schedule arrangement for a touch football league. Card schedules, suitable for mailing or other means of dissemination, offer comparable information but only for one game or match. Schedules are distributed to team managers through the mail, intramural council meetings, post office boxes, or intramural information boxes reserved for each manager.

Daily schedules of intramural events may be published in student or community newspapers. This schedule is derived from the master schedule, and someone must be assigned the responsibility of relaying correct information to the newspaper. Also, daily schedules should be posted in the lobby of the gymnasium building or on a portable blackboard or bulletin board in the playing area. A small but important detail that adds interest to the program is listing the league position of each team in parentheses behind their names, for example, Alley Cats (4) versus Pin Splitters (2).

In addition to notifying teams via schedules, it may be advisable to remind managers two days in advance of the game by calling them on the telephone or sending cards. When teams are called, a check mark

INTRAMURAL DAILY SCHEDULE
TYPE I

SPORT___Softball_____   DATE___Tues., May 3___

TIME	FIELD VI	FIELD VII	FIELD VIII
4:30	ARROW INN	THE OTHERS	SOB'S
	CHATEAU CLUB	DROP OUTS	MINI-MAX
6:00	KOSMIC KIDS	TIGER A.C.	STRANGE CASES
	BALL BUSTERS	AMIGO CLUB	FUNGOES
7:30	WOODEN BATTERS	MIGHTY MITES	STANDARD DEVIATES
	GROUND BALLS	NO ACCOUNTS	COMBO'S
9:00	NEWMAN CLUB		
	SAD SACKS		
UMPIRES	ANDERSON & TUTT	STEVENSON & BLASS	ZISKE & SYKES

INTRAMURAL SCHEDULE FOR TODAY
TYPE II

DATE___Wed., Jan. 20_____

SPORT	TIME	COURT	TEAM	NOTIFIED	VS	TEAM	NOTIFIED
BASKETBALL	7:00	1	GUNNERS	MAAS	VS	SWISHERS	HALSTENSON
''	''	2	SKINS	GRIAK	VS	SHIRTS	DONNELLY
''	8:00	3	MISSION POSSIBLES	TROCHLIL	VS	BUCKET HOUNDS	SCHMIDT
''	8:00	4	TRIANGLE	PYLE	VS	EX-ISLES	CARLSON
VOLLEYBALL	4:15	6	SPIKERS A.C.	SELDON	VS	SOME TEAM	BENSON
''	''	8	BORN LOSERS	RIONS	VS	SCRAMBLERS	MILLER
''	7:30	6	THE SET-UPS	LINEWEAVER	VS	PUFFIN 6	ROSKENS
''	''	8	VALLEY FIVE	FALLON	VS	MERCURY'S	DAVIS
''	8:30	6	2-4-D'S	STRAND	VS	WHIZ KIDS	BURKE

Fig. 8–5. Types of Intramural Daily Schedules.

should be placed behind the team name on the master schedule, or the name of the person taking the call should be recorded in case the team claims it was not notified.

A procedure which places complete responsibility on the manager is to send out just one schedule indicating it is the only notification he will receive. For the most effective programming, several combinations of scheduling and notification should be used such as daily newspaper schedules, mimeographed schedules, and telephone or card reminders. There

```
----------------------------------------------------------------
|              TOUCH  FOOTBALL  SCHEDULE                        |
|                                                              |
|  DIVISION I                          DATE    FIELD  TIME      |
|                                                              |
|  EVANS SCHOLARS (3)  12 vs 20  SAFTIES    (1)  10-7    1    6:00 |
|  WASH. AVE. BUMS (0)  6 vs 8   END ZONERS (2)  10-7    3    6:00 |
|                                                              |
|  EVANS SCHOLARS   7d vs 2d  WASH. AVE. BUMS  10-14   2   7:00 |
|  SAFTIES          7 vs 6    END ZONERS       10-14   2   8:00 |
|                                                              |
|  EVANS SCHOLARS   14 vs 21  END ZONERS       10-21   4   7:00 |
|  SAFTIES          18 vs 12  WASH. AVE. BUMS  10-21   4   9:00 |
|                                                              |
|  DIVISION II                                                 |
|                                                              |
|  MILLARDERS   ( ) __vs__  BOMBERS      ( ) 10-8   1   7:00   |
|  WRONSKIANS   ( ) __vs__  TIGER A.C. II ( ) 10-8  1   8:00   |
|                                                              |
|  MILLARDERS   __vs__  WRONSKIANS     10-15   2   5:00        |
|  BOMBERS      __vs__  TIGER A.C. II   10-15   2   6:00       |
|                                                              |
|  MILLARDERS   __vs__  TIGER A.C. II   10-22   3   8:00       |
|  BOMBERS      __vs__  WRONSKIANS      10-22   3   9:00       |
|                                                              |
|                     DIRECTIONS                               |
|                                                              |
|   At the completion of the divisional round robin, undefeated |
|   teams compete in continuous play-back Class A Play-offs. Teams |
|   with one loss enter the Class B Play-offs. Teams with two losses |
|   play in the Class C Play-offs. Winless teams compete in the |
|   Class D Play-offs.                                         |
----------------------------------------------------------------
```

Fig. 8–6. Schedule for a Touch Football League.

can be no acceptable excuse for forfeiting if schedules are carefully drawn and teams are properly notified.

Two types of time-saving schedule forms are shown in Figure 8–7 for six-team leagues. Type I may be used as a worksheet from which the schedule is typed or mimeographed, or it may be posted on the bulletin board and serve as the final copy. The team names listed at the top of the form are positioned wherever the corresponding numbers appear for each round. Simply list the sites, dates, and times for the games and the schedule is complete for a six-team round robin. As matches are completed, scores may be recorded in the appropriate spaces. This same form may be used for five teams by substituting the word "bye" for number six. (Refer to Figures 15–10, a through f, for additional round robin schedule forms.)

Type II is not as functional for scheduling, because it is necessary to post the dates, times, and sites on another sheet. The rounds are not clearly identified, thus increasing the possibility of double scheduling. However, it has the advantage of providing space for four six-team divisions, whereas Type I requires an entire sheet for one six-team division.

Ideas for Intramurals. (1) When entries are submitted for challenge-type tournaments and single and double elimination activities, photograph the participants with a Polaroid camera or similar device. Pictures of opponents for each match may then be posted on a large tournament board or draw sheet. Winner's names and pictures are advanced as the tournament progresses. (2) Display large schedule boards on the wall of the intramural office and when submitting entries, request team managers to select the day, time, and field or court for their first game. After all entries are received, the remainder of the schedule is completed and distributed to team managers. First come, first served choices under crowded scheduling conditions encourage early submission of entries. (3) Utilize telephone tape devices for recording daily intramural schedules. By dialing a number, participants may obtain instant schedule information.

Postponements and Rescheduling

Postponed games or matches are inevitable in intramural programming, particularly for reasons of inclement weather. One rainy day can postpone an entire schedule and result in twice as much staff work for rescheduling. Two or more days may be lost depending on the amount of rainfall and the drainage of the playing fields.

If the weather is such that postponement is determined several hours before game time, the I-M office can perform a valuable service by notifying all of the team managers who in turn can contact their players. It is advisable to establish a cancellation deadline, and if games are not called by this time, the decision to cancel them will be made at the field of play. This eliminates the possibility of making cancellations too early. After teams are at the field and weather conditions become worse, the decision to continue or terminate activities rests with the intramural supervisor or officials.

When weather causes several daily softball schedules to be postponed, it is possible to double up the schedule by playing abbreviated doubleheaders. For example, a five-inning double header may be scheduled or, if absolutely necessary, a three-inning triple header could make up two or three weeks of the postponed schedule. Similar modified playing arrangements can be made for touch football and other sports.

An intramural director receives various requests for postponements, some of them unusual and unjustified. Illness of team members is legitimate, but conflicting social events or other excuses should be viewed with caution. If intramural schedules are continually changed to meet all postponement situations, it is next to impossible to complete the schedules.

```
┌─────────────────────────────────────────────────────────────┐
                          TYPE I

  SPORT____SOFTBALL_____ DIVISION_____I_____ DATE __5/21__

      TEAMS       WON  LOST  PLACE   POINTS  MANAGER'S NAME  TEL.NO.
  1._BEARS____    ___  ___  _____  _____  _____  _____
  2._BEAVERS__    ___  ___  _____  _____  _____  _____
  3._BUNNIES__    ___  ___  _____  _____  _____  _____
  4._BOBCATS__    ___  ___  _____  _____  _____  _____
  5._BULLDOGS_    ___  ___  _____  _____  _____  _____
  6._BRONCOS__    ___  ___  _____  _____  _____  _____
```

ROUND 1 TEAM*	SCORE		TEAM	SITE	DATE	TIME
1 BEARS	vs	2	BEAVERS			
4	vs	3	BUNNIES			
5	vs	6				
ROUND 2						
6	vs	4				
2 BEAVERS	vs	5				
3 BUNNIES	vs	1	BEARS			
ROUND 3						
5	vs	3	BUNNIES			
4	vs	1	BEARS			
2 BEAVERS	vs	6				
ROUND 4						
3 BUNNIES	vs	2	BEAVERS			
1 BEARS	vs	6				
4	vs	5				
ROUND 5						
5	vs	1	BEARS			
6	vs	3	BUNNIES			
2 BEAVERS	vs	4				

* RECORD TEAM NAMES IN SPACES THAT CORRESPOND WITH TEAM NUMBERS ABOVE.
NOTE: FOR 5 TEAMS SUBSTITUTE THE WORD "BYE" FOR NUMBER 6.

Fig. 8–7. Types of Six-Team Round Robin Schedule Forms.

Such teams should be encouraged to make a choice as to which activities are more important.

There are occasions when both teams mutually desire to postpone their contest. In this situation, each team should officially notify the intramural office of its intention, or one of the teams may falsify the request to their advantage. A mutual request may be granted when it is possible to reschedule the game without disrupting the completion of the tournament. It is important, however, that requests be made as early as possible so the intramural staff can substitute another game in the schedule.

Following a postponement, arrangements must be made to reschedule the game(s). Different methods are required with elimination-type tour-

```
TYPE II

SPORT___SOFTBALL____  LEAGUE ___INTRAMURAL____        DATE _5/21___
```

DIVISION I								
NO. TEAMS		SCHEDULE		SCORES	WON	LOST	PLACE	POINTS
1. BEARS	1x4	1x5	1x6	___ ___	___	___	___	___
2. BEAVERS	2x1	2x3	2x6	___ ___	___	___	___	___
3. BUNNIES	3x1	3x5	3x6	___ ___	___	___	___	___
4. BOBCATS	4x2	4x3	4x6	___ ___	___	___	___	___
5. BULLDOGS	5x2	5x4	5x6	___ ___	___	___	___	___
6. BRONCOS					___	___	___	___
DIVISION II								
1. CO.A	1x4	1x5	1x6	___ ___	___	___	___	___
2. CO.B	2x1	2x3	2x6	___ ___	___	___	___	___
3. CO.C	3x1	3x5	3x6	___ ___	___	___	___	___
4. CO.D	4x2	4x3	4x6	___ ___	___	___	___	___
5. CO.E	5x2	5x4	5x6	___ ___	___	___	___	___
6. CO.F					___	___	___	___
DIVISION III								
1. ARROW INN	1x4	1x5	1x6	___ ___	___	___	___	___
2. SAD SACKS	2x1	2x3	2x6	___ ___	___	___	___	___
3. COMBOS	3x1	3x5	3x6	___ ___	___	___	___	___
4. SCHOLARS	4x2	4x3	4x6	___ ___	___	___	___	___
5. TIGERS	5x2	5x4	5x6	___ ___	___	___	___	___
6. AMIGOS					___	___	___	___
DIVISION IV								
1. WARD A	1x4	1x5	1x6	___ ___	___	___	___	___
2. WARD B	2x1	2x3	2x6	___ ___	___	___	___	___
3. WARD C	3x1	3x5	3x6	___ ___	___	___	___	___
4. WARD D	4x2	4x3	4x6	___ ___	___	___	___	___
5. WARD E	5x2	5x4	5x6	___ ___	___	___	___	___
6. WARD F					___	___	___	___

Fig. 8–7. (Continued.)

naments and league games. In an elimination series, games are simply postponed for a day or two because future games are contingent upon the winning of previous games. For league games where round robin schedules are made out for the entire season, games are already scheduled for succeeding days. Therefore, the schedule must proceed as previously arranged, and the postponed games remain undecided until the league is completed or there is an open date in the schedule.

To save staff time in rescheduling postponed games, it is advisable for the two managers to arrange a mutually agreeable date. Both managers should subsequently contact the intramural office to confirm the new schedule. This eliminates numerous "middle" calls by the staff.

Every attempt should be made to avoid postponements, but when they are necessary, rescheduling procedures should be carefully implemented. If postponement policies are not consistently enforced, participants may be encouraged to seek game changes for the slightest reason, and the importance of intramurals reaches a lower level.

Forfeits

One measure of the effectiveness of intramural programming is the number of forfeits that occur among scheduled games and matches. In some programs, it may not be unusual for 25 percent of the contests to be forfeited and a few leagues or tournaments in which only half of the games are played. Preferably, this percentage should be below five percent, and every effort should be made to eliminate them completely. The absence of forfeits usually indicates efficiently administered programs and satisfied participants.

Forfeits discourage the necessary *espirit de corps* which is essential for good programming. Participants look forward to playing intramural games and are greatly disappointed when their opponents fail to appear. Repeated disappointments result in decreased participation. If individuals are permitted to participate in a haphazard manner, they can never be taught responsibility.

Frequently, negative techniques are used to prevent or eliminate forfeits. A forfeit fee is required when submitting entries for a tournament. This procedure provides an "out" or alternative to participating; namely, paying instead of playing. Another negative feature is requiring teams to forfeit if they do not have a full team or are not ready to play at the scheduled game time. Certainly tardiness cannot be condoned, and managers must be encouraged to have their teams ready to play at the appointed time. However, keeping in mind the basic intramural principle of participation, it seems logical to follow procedures which encourage participation in these situations.

For example, a team should be permitted to begin a game with less than the required number of players. If a team arrives late, the other team should be given advantage points such as one goal in hockey for every five minutes or portion thereof the opposing team is late, two points per minute in basketball, one run in baseball and softball for every five minutes or portion thereof, in addition to having their choice of field or at bat. When both teams are tardy, they should play a shortened game. Other examples of negative emphasis are subtraction of participation points for forfeits and charging a forfeit to a team if it does not list first and last names on scorecards.

TO: Intramural Team Captains

FROM: Intramural Director

SUBJECT: Forfeited Games

    Your touch football   team,   Tiger A. C.   ,
forfeited its last game. Please keep in mind that forfeits are
unfair to your opponents, demoralize your own team, and have a
detrimental effect on the entire intramural program. Elimination
of forfeits will result in a better program for everyone.

    We solicit your complete cooperation and request that
you check (X) your intentions below:

       _____Drop our team from the schedule. When
           entering teams in the future, we shall
           pledge our complete cooperation.

       _____Please continue to schedule our team.
           We will definitely be present for all
           future contests.

               Signed_____
                       Team Captain

RETURN THIS LETTER IN THE ENCLOSED SELF-ADDRESSED, STAMPED ENVELOPE.

Fig. 8–8. Sample Intramural Forfeit Letter.

Although it is practically impossible to reach this goal, no intramural director should be satisfied until all forfeits are eliminated. A positive approach to the problem must be followed in an effort to attain this objective. First, the director must evaluate all procedures to be certain there is no administrative reason for forfeits. Schedules must be carefully arranged with proper notification being given to the contestants. Rules and regulations must include the possibility of postponing games in case of an emergency.

Second, after eliminating customary reasons for forfeiting, the director must conduct a positive campaign to eliminate forfeits. This may be done through intramural council meetings, mimeographed materials, and other publicity media. Participants must be made aware that forfeits are not only demoralizing to their team, but have a detrimental effect on the entire program.

It should be emphasized that, in essence, an entry blank is a contract. When the entry is submitted, the team requests participation and agrees to be present for all scheduled contests. The director fulfills his part of the contract by providing opposition, equipment, facilities, supervisors, and officials. If teams fail to live up to their part of the agreement, it is impossible for the director to fulfill the opposition clause of the contract, and a great deal of time and effort is wasted. It should be made very clear that the participants are the only ones who can eliminate forfeits, and the effort will result in a better intramural program for their benefit.

When a forfeit occurs, the team should be contacted immediately to determine the cause. This aids in preventing future forfeits and also provides an additional opportunity to carry the campaign to the participants. They appreciate the personal attention of the intramural staff and are pleased to know that attempts are being made to upgrade the program. If staff limitations do not permit personal contact, a letter similar to the one in Figure 8–8 may be used. Every intramural director confronted with this problem should apply realistic, positive actions to prevent and eliminate forfeits.

9

Structuring Tournaments

Tournaments are participation schemes or plans designed to identify one or more winners. There are many different types, and when used in various combinations, the number of choices exceeds several hundred. Selecting the appropriate tournament method is an extremely important factor in successful intramural programming. Sometimes the simplest form of activity becomes fascinating by adding an element of competition.

Tournaments must be structured or selected to accomplish the intended purpose. Some questions to be considered before designing tournament patterns are the following:

1. Will a valid champion be determined?
2. Is evenly matched competition desirable?
3. Will participants play an equal number of games?
4. Is keen rivalry assured for all participants including those who lose several games?
5. Does the plan accommodate the maximum number of teams or players?
6. Will the activity be conducted on a team, individual, or dual basis?
7. What are the ages, interests, and abilities of the participants?
8. Will interest be maintained throughout the tournament?
9. How much time will be required to complete the tournament?
10. Are adequate facilities and equipment available for the tournament selected?
11. How many winners are desirable?
12. What accuracy is desired for ranking the participants?
13. Is sufficient personnel available to officiate and supervise the tournament?
14. What classification and equalization methods can be incorporated with the scheme of competition?

Every tournament director must be familiar with the advantages and disadvantages of each competitive plan to match the correct one with whatever objectives he wishes to accomplish. This chapter comprehensively reviews methods of structuring tournament competition, divided into categories of meets, round robins, elimination tournaments, challenge tournaments, informal-type tournaments, and classification and equalization methods.

MEETS

Meets are participation arrangements in which contestants compete in a number of separate events during an afternoon or evening session or over a two- or three-day period. A complete schedule is prepared in advance and each event takes place at a designated time. Some examples of meets are track, swimming, gymnastics, field days, speed skating, and sports festivals.

Track and Field Meets

Track and field meets are held during the outdoor and indoor seasons with events adapted for each situation. Sample schedules for both kinds of meets are included in the following sections.

Outdoor Meets. A carefully arranged plan of operation accompanied by a detailed schedule of events is completely necessary for conducting an efficient track meet. Qualified supervisory personnel must be assembled to assist with the administration of the meet. Equipment should be properly located and track markings such as starting and finishing points and hurdle positions should be plainly marked.

Officials for an intramural track meet may include the following:

One referee–starter	Three timers
One clerk of course	Two finish judges per place
One scorer	One judge for each field event
One announcer	

For large meets, it is advisable to provide assistants to help the clerk of course, starter, scorer, and announcer. In addition to the head judge, there should be at least two judges at the finish line for each place picked in the event.

The success of a meet is directly proportional to the selection of qualified personnel. The referee–starter especially must be experienced, and the clerk of course and announcer are key persons for administering events according to the time schedule. The head varsity or assistant track coach may serve as the starter, and members of the varsity team can be solicited for other responsibilities.

A large number of entries requires trial heats in the dashes and hurdles, and the time schedule must be appropriately adjusted to accommodate preliminaries and finals. The field events schedule must be integrated with running events because participants may wish to enter several activities. The high jump and pole vault require a considerable amount of time and should be started as early as possible. Below is a schedule of events for an outdoor track meet.

OUTDOOR TRACK MEET

FIELD EVENTS

1. Pole vault .... 1:15 P.M.
2. High jump .... 1:15 P.M.
3. Shot put .... 1:30 P.M.
4. Long jump .... 1:30 P.M.
5. Discus .... immediately following shot put

TRACK EVENTS

1. 120-yard high hurdles, trial heats .... 2:00 P.M.
2. 100-yard dash trial heats .... 2:20 P.M.
3. One-mile run .... 2:35 P.M.
4. 440-yard dash .... 2:45 P.M.
5. 100-yard dash .... 2:55 P.M.
6. 120-yard high hurdles, finals .... 3:10 P.M.
7. 220-yard dash, trial heats .... 3:25 P.M.
8. 180-yard low hurdles, trial heats .... 3:40 P.M.
9. 880-yard run .... 4:00 P.M.
10. 220-yard dash, finals .... 4:10 P.M.
11. 180-yard low hurdles, finals .... 4:25 P.M.
12. Half-mile relay .... 4:45 P.M.

When there are numerous intramural track entries, the meet may be scheduled over a period of two or three afternoons. Preliminaries can be arranged for the first two days with the finals on the last day or preliminaries and finals of several events may be scheduled for each day. For example, on Monday schedule the long jump, shot put, 220-yard dash, 120-yard high hurdles, and the mile; Tuesday, high jump, discus, 180-yard low hurdles, and 880-yard run; Wednesday, pole vault, 100-yard dash, 440-yard dash, and half-mile relay. A two- or three-day scheduling pattern is also much less strenuous for the competitors.

For younger groups, the previous track schedule can be followed, but events should be modified to meet the physical limitations of the participants. Some events may be eliminated entirely resulting in a shorter program. Participants are usually restricted in the number of events they may enter.

Managers should submit team entries prior to a track meet to aid them in organizing their participants. However, it is not always advisable to arrange heats from these entries because there may be numerous "scratches" requiring the rearrangement of heats. An excellent method of eliminating forfeits or "scratches" is to require each individual to fill out an event slip, similar to the one in Figure 9–1, just prior to performing the activity. Small pencils and entry slips may be provided at strategic places in the track area.

```
┌───────────────────────────────────────────────┐
│                                                 │
│           I-M  TRACK  ENTRY  SLIP               │
│                                                 │
│   PRINT  NAME_____           │
│   TEAM_____            │
│                                                 │
│                 (CIRCLE ONE)                    │
│   100 YD. DASH           120 LOW HURDLES        │
│   220 YD. DASH           440 YD. DASH           │
│   880 YD. RUN            MILE RUN               │
│                                                 │
│              HALF  MILE  RELAY                  │
│   1. _____           │
│   2. _____           │
│   3. _____           │
│   4. _____           │
├───────────────────────────────────────────────┤
│   HEAT_____ LANE _____           │
│                                                 │
│   TIME_____  PLACE _____ POINTS__          │
└───────────────────────────────────────────────┘
```

Fig. 9–1. Event Entry Slip for Track and Field Meet Participants.

Before the start of each event, the clerk of course or "heat arranger" calls for the individual entry slips. For example, prior to the 100-yard dash, he collects all individual 100-yard dash slips. The number of heats is determined by dividing the number of lanes into the number of entries. After arranging and announcing the first heat, a track supervisor takes the slips for that heat to the head judge or timer who records the places and times of the winners. In no way does this preclude pre-conditioning workouts. It is a tremendously efficient method of handling large numbers of track entries. There is no possibility of a forfeit because participants must be present to fill out the entry slip. (This individual entry procedure is equally effective in swimming, cross country, and wrestling, or any other activity in which entries can be accepted moments before it begins.)

Another heat-arranging procedure involves lining up all entrants according to height. For example, in the 220-yard dash, there are eight track lanes and 32 participants. After lining up according to size, participants "count off" by fours. Number 1's run in the first heat, 2's in the second, 3's in the third, and 4's in the fourth. Runners line up in their heats behind the starting line and are ready to run as soon as their heat is announced. Arranging heats according to size provides a good distribution of fast and slow runners. It may be necessary to switch the heats of some team members so that all do not run in the same heat.

Scoring in intramural track meets should be liberal, awarding points to as many participants as possible. Two scoring methods used are scoring all events including relays according to the point scale 10, 8, 6, 4, 2, 1 or scoring 6, 4, 3, 2, 1 in all events except the relays which are assigned values of 12 8, 6, 4, 2.

Several variations may be devised for intramural track meets. In field events such as the long jump and high jump, team points can be assigned for achieving certain distances. Each team is represented by the same number of contestants, and points are awarded to each participant who reaches specified heights or distances. The reverse method is also used with points assigned to contestants who fail to survive the trials, and the team with the least number of points is the winner.

The long jump can be conducted on a "match play" basis. For example, the number one jumper of Team A is matched against the number one jumper of Team B; number two of Team A against number two of Team B; etc. One point is awarded to the winner of each match jump. Team points are totaled to determine the long jump winner, and they may also be incorporated in the point totals to determine the overall track meet winner.

Another variation adds all team members' standing long jump distances and compares the total with the opposing team's total. After A jumps, teammate B places his toes at the heel marks of jumper A and jumps in the same direction. Each team member jumps in this manner as do members of other teams. The team that jumps the greatest distance wins. This type of comparison eliminates measuring distances.

Indoor Meets. Intramural indoor track and field meets are conducted similar to outdoor meets with the exception that events must be adapted to local facilities. Some institutions have curved running tracks in gymnasiums with enough floor space for a 50-yard straightaway. Others have access to a field house with an eighth-mile track or a comparable running area.

Relay races may be included as a part of the indoor meet, but in some programs they are conducted as a separate activity. To add interest to the event, the first four relay teams may be scheduled to run in a race premilinary to a varsity indoor track meet.

INDOOR TRACK MEET

FIELD EVENTS

1. Pole vault ....7:00 P.M.
2. High jump ....7:00 P.M.
3. Shot put ....7:00 P.M.
4. Long jump ....7:00 P.M.

TRACK EVENTS

1. 60-yard dash, trial heats ....7:30 P.M.
2. One-mile run ....7:50 P.M.
3. 60-yard dash, finals ....8:00 P.M.
4. 70-yard high hurdles, trial heats ....8:15 P.M.
5. 440-yard dash ....8:30 P.M.
6. 70-yard high hurdles, finals ....8:40 P.M.
7. 70-yard low hurdles, trial heats ....8:50 P.M.
8. 880-yard run ....9:05 P.M.
9. 70-yard low hurdles, finals ....9:15 P.M.
10. Relay ....9:25 P.M.

Swimming Meets

A swimming meet is easier to conduct than a track meet because only one event is contested at a time. However, to run an efficient meet requires detailed planning and almost as many officials as a track meet. Preliminary events are usually scheduled for one or two evenings with the finals on the following evening.

Officials consist of a referee, starter, finish judges, diving judges, clerk of course, take-off judges, timers, scorer, and inspector of turns and swimming form. For intramural meets, the varsity coach or other experienced official may assume the duties of more than one of these. For example, the coach may serve as the referee, starter, take-off judge, inspector of turns and swimming form, and one of the diving judges. Varsity swimmers and intramural assistants may be utilized as timers, finish judges, and scorers.

Swimmers for the finals are selected on the basis of time and place of finish in the time trials. Two finish judges and three timers should be assigned for each lane. Some meet directors forego finish judges in the preliminaries, relying on timers to determine who swims in the finals and use both timers and judges for the finals. Picking places in a swimming or track meet can be very difficult, particularly in short distance races. There are times when this task is troublesome for experts. Thus, it is advisable to secure experienced personnel whenever possible. Some mechanical computerized scoring devices have been devised that record the contestant's time and place on a totalization board.

There is usually a wide-range of ability in intramural diving. Divers perform their required and optional dives on the one-meter board. The total number of dives depends on the ability of the divers, but it is usually not more than 11 or less than five. As an example, two dives are required such as the plain front and plain back with three dives optional. Dives are divided into five categories: group one, forward dives; group two, back dives; group three, reverse dives; group four, inward dives; and group five, twist dives. Another method is to draw the compulsory dives from several or all of the foregoing groups and insist that voluntary dives represent at least three or four different groups. For intramural purposes, it may be desirable to simplify the procedure further by requiring a plain front dive and three optional dives.

Three judges should be appointed to evaluate the diving. If five judges are used, high and low awards should be canceled. Dives are judged on the following ten point scale: very good = 10, 9.5, 9 points; good = 8.5, 8, 7.5, 7 points; satisfactory = 6.5, 6, 5.5, 5 points; deficient = 4.5, 4, 3.5, 3 points; unsatisfactory = 2.5, 2, 1.5, 1, 0.5 points; completely failed = 0 points. The sum of the three awards is multiplied by the degree of difficulty for a particular dive to obtain the total value. The diver with the highest point total wins the event.

The following scoring chart serves as a guide for assigning team points in an intramural swimming meet:

LANES	MEDLEY AND FREESTYLE EVENTS	OTHER EVENTS
4	10–6–4–2	5–3–2–1
5	12–8–6–4–2	6–4–3–2–1
6	14–10–8–6–4–2	7–5–4–3–2–1

If all participants are timed, twelve places may be assigned points according to the following scale: Individual events: 8–6–5.5–5–4.5–4–3.5–3–2.5–2–1.5–1; Relays: 16–14–11–10–9–8–6–5–4–3–2–1.

It is advisable to limit swimmers to participation in any three events. Conditioning periods should be encouraged, and if necessary, distances should be shortened to accommodate the abilities of the participants. Suggested events for an intramural swimming meet are as follows:

1. 200-yard medley relay (four swimmers on a team; each swims one-fourth of the distance continuously: first, backstroke; second, breast-stroke; third, butterfly stroke; fourth, a stroke other than these three)
2. 50-yard freestyle
3. 50-yard butterfly stroke
4. 50-yard backstroke
5. 100-yard freestyle
6. 50-yard breakstroke
7. One-meter springboard diving

8. 100-yard individual medley (the first one-fourth distance is the butterfly stroke; the second one-fourth, the backstroke; the third one-fourth, breakstroke; and the last one-fourth, any stroke other than the first three)
9. 200-yard freestyle relay (four swimmers on a team, each swims 50 yards continuously)

Gymnastic Meets

Gymnastic meets are generally arranged according to a schedule similar to track and swimming. Events usually include floor exercise, side horse, rings, long horse, parallel bars, and high bar. Judging the routine for each piece of apparatus is similar to judging diving.

Four judges evaluate each performance according to a scale based on 10.0 points for a perfect routine. Each routine is evaluated in terms of difficulty, maximum 3.4 points; combination, maximum 1.6 points; and execution, maximum 5.0 points. Of the four awards, the highest and lowest are eliminated and the average of the two middle numbers is the performer's score. Gymnastic coaches and varsity team members provide an excellent source of judges for intramural meets.

Each team may be limited to a maximum of three or four entries per event. The best three scores for each team comprise the team's performance in each event. Scores for all events are then totaled to determine the team winner. Recognition may also be given to the best individual performance for each event as well as to the individual who scores the highest number of points for all events.

Other Meets

Other activities may be organized on a meet basis such as football and baseball field meets, described in Chapter 7, sports festivals, field days, sports days, and speed skating. The latter is held indoors or outdoors, depending on available facilities, and consists of long and short distance races, relays, and novelty events.

ROUND ROBIN TOURNAMENTS

As the name implies, "round" robin participation involves every entry playing all other entries an equal number of times. If everyone plays each other once, it is a single round; twice, a double round; and less than once, a partial round. This form of competition is also known as the league or percentage plan.

The round robin is used extensively in intramurals because it provides for maximum participation and produces the most valid winner. One of the disadvantages is the amount of time required to complete a round robin involving a large number of entries. To offset this disadvantage, some tournament directors schedule partial round robins. This means that teams only play a portion of the round equal to the amount of time available. With this arrangement, the league winner is not a true champion.

A more desirable method is to divide large numbers of teams into smaller leagues and schedule the respective league winners for a championship playoff. This does not produce a valid champion, but the winner is more representative than one of a partial round robin.

To illustrate the advantages of subdividing leagues, the following examples are given. If 16 teams enter a basketball tournament, 120 games must be scheduled to complete a round robin. If time or facilities are not available to play this many games, 2 leagues of 8 teams may be scheduled. This breakdown requires 28 games for each league or a total of 56 games. Each team plays 7 league games whereas a 16-team league requires each team to play 15 games.

The 16 teams may also be subdivided into 4 leagues of 4 teams each. This arrangement requires playing 6 games in each division or a total of 24 games for the 4 leagues. The number of games played by each team is reduced to 3.

League Standings

The results of round robin play are expressed in the form of league standings as shown below. These indicate the relative positions of each team, games played, games won and lost, percentages of games won of the total number played, and the games behind. Standings are maintained throughout the round robin, and the team that has the highest percentage of wins at the end of tournament play is the winner. For checking the accuracy of won and lost records, the sum of the won column should equal the sum of the lost column, and at the completion of the schedule, each column should total the number of games played.

Determining Percentages. Percentages for league standings are figured by dividing the number of games won by the number of games played. The division is carried three places to the right of the decimal.

$$\text{Example: } \frac{\text{Games Won}}{\text{Games Played}} = \frac{7}{9} = .778$$

For computing tie games, they are either not considered as games played or a tie is valued as a half game won and a half game lost. The percentage of a team with 7 wins, 2 losses, and 1 tie is .750 (7.5 ÷ 10).

The method of listing percentages in league standings, e.g., .778, is actually incorrect. The combination of 7 wins and 2 losses by the Beavers in the example below means they have won 77.8 percent of their games. Traditionally, the decimal point is placed two numbers to the left of where it should be.

Point systems are sometimes utilized to identify the relative positions of teams in a league. Two points are awarded for each victory, 1 point for each tie, and 0 points for a loss. A team with 7 wins, 2 losses, and 1 tie is assigned 15 points. The one with the greatest number of points at the end of the round robin is the winner.

A variation of this method is to divide the total number of points received if all games had been won into the number of points that were actually earned on the basis of the team's performance. Using the above example, the percentage would be .833 (15 ÷ 18).

SOFTBALL LEAGUE STANDINGS

TEAM NAMES	GAMES PLAYED	GAMES WON	GAMES LOST	PERCENT-AGES	GAMES BEHIND
1. Bulldogs	9	9	0	1.000	—
2. Badgers	9	8	1	.889	1
3. Beavers	9	7	2	.778	2
4. Bobcats	9	6	3	.667	3
5. Baboons	9	5	4	.556	4
6. Broncos	9	4	5	.444	5
7. Bears	9	3	6	.333	6
8. Buffalos	9	2	7	.222	7
9. Beagles	9	1	8	.111	8
10. Barnacles	9	0	9	.000	9

Number of Games Behind. Listing the number of games a team is behind the leading team in the league adds interest to the round robin. Games behind are figured by adding the differences in wins and losses between two teams and dividing this sum by two. In the softball league standings above, the Bulldogs won 9 games and lost none, and the Bobcats' record is 6 and 3. The difference in wins is 3, and the difference in losses is 3. Three plus 3 equal 6 and 6 divided by 2 is 3; therefore, the Bobcats are 3 games behind the Bulldogs. This same procedure may be used in determining how many games a team is behind any other team that has a higher position in the league standings. A mathematical formula for determining the number of games behind is as follows:

$$\frac{(W_1 - W_2) + (L_2 - L_1)}{2} = \text{Games Behind}$$

Another figure of interest to those participating in round robins or leagues is the "magic number," the combination of wins and losses needed to eliminate a team from winning the championships. The magic number is figured by determining the number of games remaining for the first place team, subtracting from this number the difference between the losses of the first place team and another team, and adding one game to eliminate a possible tie. For example, Team A has 19 games remaining and has lost 54 while Team B, in second place, has lost 65 games. The difference in losses is 11, which subtracted from 19 is 8, plus 1 for the possible tie, results in a magic number of "9." Any combination of Team A wins or Team B losses totaling 9 would eliminate Team B's chances of winning the championship.

Breaking Ties. A potential disadvantage of round robin tournaments is that after playing a full schedule of games, two or more teams may finish with identical won–lost records. When this occurs, one of the following methods must be utilized.

1. If time is available, schedule playoffs between or among the tied teams. This is without question the fairest method.
2. Allow ties to stand and name co- or tri-champions if the tie involves first place.
3. Resolve two-way ties by crediting Team A with a higher position because it defeated Team B, the other tied team, during league play. However, this has an element of unfairness to the extent that Team B defeated a team which in turn had defeated Team A during the regular season.
4. Flip a coin or use some other method of chance to decide a winner.
5. Use the point differential system described below.

Two- or three-way ties may be broken according to the differences in teams' scores, a procedure which takes into account offensive and defensive ability. Subtracting the difference between the sum of the offensive points and the sum of the defensive points results in a plus or minus factor. The team with the highest plus factor is awarded first place or the highest place if a tie does not involve the number one position. For example, Teams A, B, and C are in a three-way tie for first place in a six-team basketball league. According to the tabulation below, Team B has a plus factor of 13 and is awarded first place, Team A with a + 8 is assigned second place, and Team C with a − 1 is given third place.

Round Robin Calculations

Before drawing up a round robin tournament, the total number of rounds and games for a complete round robin schedule must be determined. These factors are not only necessary in the actual construction of the tournament, but also aid in calculating the number of officials and supervisors needed and the amount of time required to complete the tournament.

	TEAM A (w–4, l–1)	TEAM B (w–4, l–1)	TEAM C (w–4, l–1)
1st game scores	42–40	54–44	44–54
2nd game scores	41–38	38–41	50–47
3rd game scores	63–62	32–31	39–36
4th game scores	38–40	61–59	40–38
5th game scores	55–51	48–45	56–55
Total differential	239 − 231 = (+8)	233 − 220 = (+13)	229 − 230 = (−1)

Number of Rounds. The term "round" is used in the name of this tournament to indicate that a complete round or full schedule of games is played in which each team plays against all of the other teams. The other use of the term in tournament construction, the one used for purposes of this discussion, refers to a measurement of tournament progress or the degree to which the schedule or tournament has been completed. In a league, the first round is completed when each team has played its first game, unless a team has a bye, the second round when teams have played their second game, and so on. In a sense, a round indicates the number of playing dates or weeks in a schedule, if all teams in a round play on a given date or during the same week.

For round robins involving an uneven number of entries, the number of rounds is equal to the number of entries, and for an even number of entries, the number of rounds is equal to one less than the number of entries. For example, with 7 teams in a league, the number of rounds is 7, and for 8 teams, the number of rounds is 8 minus 1 or 7 rounds.

Number of Games. The following formula is used to calculate the number of games required to complete a round robin: $N (N − 1) ÷ 2$; N equals the number of entries. First, subtract 1 from the number of entries; then multiply this number by the number of entries and divide this figure by 2 to determine the number of games.

A word formula describing this procedure is as follows:

number of entries TIMES number of entries MINUS one

———

DIVIDED by two

EQUALS number of games

Example: Number of teams equals 6.

$$\frac{6\,(6-1)}{2} = \text{number of games}$$

$$\frac{6 \times 5}{2} = \frac{30}{2} = 15 \text{ games}$$

Another method for figuring the number of games is to record the number of entries in arithmetic progression, cancel the largest number and add the remaining numbers. Example for 6 teams:

1, 2, 3, 4, 5, 6 $1 + 2 + 3 + 4 + 5 = 15$ games.

Rotation Methods. The basic method for structuring round robin participation is the clockwise or counter-clockwise rotation system. Entries are represented by letters (A, B, C – a, b, c) or numerals (I, II, III – 1, 2, 3) and after these are properly rotated, team names are substituted for the symbols. They may be listed vertically or horizontally.

1 vs 2	1 6 5	
6 vs 3	vs vs vs	
5 vs 4	2 3 4	

One number remains stationary while all other numbers are rotated around it. The rotation may be clockwise or counter-clockwise, but the same direction must be used throughout the process. The numbers are rotated each round, until each team is paired with every other team. In the following example of 6 teams, 5 rounds or 5 rotations are necessary for a complete round robin. According to the previous formula, 15 games will be required with each team playing 5 games. In this illustration, number 1 remains constant and all other numbers are rotated clockwise.

ROUND 1	ROUND 2	ROUND 3	ROUND 4	ROUND 5
1 vs 2	1 vs 6	1 vs 5	1 vs 4	1 vs 3
6 vs 3	5 vs 2	4 vs 6	3 vs 5	2 vs 4
5 vs 4	4 vs 3	3 vs 2	2 vs 6	6 vs 5

For a double round robin, the rotation process is repeated. This may be desirable if there are too few teams in the league and time and facilities are available for more games. In a 6-team league, each team plays 10 games in a double round robin.

In constructing a round robin tournament for an uneven number of teams, the same rotation pattern is followed, but the word "bye" replaces one of the numbers. The word "bye" represents a nonopponent, and the team which has a "bye" does not play in that particular round. In the following plan, the word "bye" replaces number 6 and remains constant while all other numbers are rotated clockwise.

ROUND 1	ROUND 2	ROUND 3	ROUND 4	ROUND 5
1 vs 2	5 vs 1	4 vs 5	3 vs 4	2 vs 3
5 vs 3	4 vs 2	3 vs 1	2 vs 5	1 vs 4
4–Bye	3–Bye	2–Bye	1–Bye	5–Bye

Schedule makers save considerable time and effort by using tournament calculators, round robin tables, and instant scheduling forms, instead of working out a rotation plan each time a schedule is drawn. For the convenience of tournament directors, a calculator for three through thirty-two teams, round robin tables for three through sixteen teams, and instant scheduling forms for three through sixteen teams are included in Figures 15–1; 15–8, a–b; and 15–9, a–f. The round robin tables not only indicate the rotation pattern, but pairings have been adjusted so teams will play on each field, court, or lane an equitable number of times. For those who are involved in "home and away" scheduling, this factor has been incorporated in the schedules.

Graph Methods. There are several methods of developing round robin schedules with the use of graphs. Figures 9–2 and 9–3 are examples of the most common forms. Names of teams or their symbols are listed in the same order, horizontally on the top and vertically on the side. Teams scheduled to meet in the round robin are indicated by the intersecting lines. Types I and II in Figure 9–2 may also be used as schedule sheets by recording the score in the appropriate intersecting spaces. In Type I, scores are written across from the team names in two squares. The score is first listed and underlined in the winner's square (Bisons, 45–38) and then in the loser's square but not underlined (Broncos, 38–45).

Type II, cut diagonally, shows scores recorded in only one space. With this graph, it is necessary to record the name of the winning team (D) and the score (45–38). Using this procedure in the first graph, it is possible to adapt Type I for a double round robin, recording scores in the upper portion for the first complete round and listing the scores in the lower part for the second round. If the same teams are entered in two sports at the same time such as basketball and bowling, the upper part

TEAMS	BRONCOS	BOBCATS	BEAVERS	BISONS	BEARS	BADGERS
BRONCOS			38-45			
BOBCATS				52-48		
BEAVERS						
BISONS	45-38					
BEARS		48-52				
BADGERS						

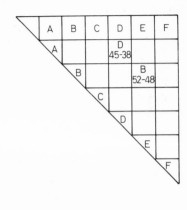

Fig. 9–2. Two Types of 6-Team Graph Round Robin Schedules.
TYPE I: Score Recorded Twice. TYPE II: Score Recorded Once.

may be used for one sport and the lower portion for the other. It is also possible to list the places, games won, games lost, and percentages in columns on the side of the graph.

These forms show which teams have won and lost, and the games remaining to be played. One of the disadvantages is that unless daily schedules are carefully drawn from the graph, there is a possibility that teams will not play regularly, perhaps meet each other more than once, or be scheduled to play two teams at the same time. These inconsistencies will not occur if the graph illustrated in Figure 9–3 is used.

Usually scores are not recorded on this type of graph, although it is possible to record them in the lower squares. The letters in Figure 9–3 represent teams or other entries, and the numbers indicate the round or

	A	B	C	D	E	F
A		1	2	3	4	5
B			3	4	5	2
C				5	1	4
D					2	1
E						3
F						

	A	B	C	D	E	BYE
A		1	2	3	4	5
B			3	4	5	2
C				5	1	4
D					2	1
E						3
BYE						

Fig. 9–3. 6- and 5-Team Graph Round Robin Schedules. (Left) 6 Teams.
(Right) 5 Teams.

the games which can be scheduled on the same date. This scheme provides a systematic pattern for scheduling games.

As an example, in the six-team graph, number 1 signifies that A plays B, C plays E, and D plays F on the same day or in the first round. In the five-team graph with byes, 1 indicates that A plays B, C plays E, and D draws a bye. It is not necessary for round 2 to follow 1 or to maintain any particular order as long as all rounds are played, but there is less chance for error if the schedule follows the logical progression of rounds: 1, 2, 3, 4, and 5. An alternative method is actually to list the playing dates instead of the numbers.

The type of graph round robin illustrated in Figure 9–3 may be designed for any number of teams by following these procedures.

1. List the names or symbols of six-teams horizontally and vertically, draw intersecting lines and block out each team's intersecting square.
2. Begin under the second team (B) on row A and write numbers consecutively from 1 through 5, one number less than the number of teams to be scheduled.
3. In row B, indent two squares and start the horizontal numbering with a number which is one higher (3) than the number immediately above it (2). *Do not record any numbers in the vertical F column.*
4. Continue the indentation and progression for subsequent rows. In carrying out the numerical progression, revert back to 1 after writing the highest number, in this sample, 5.
5. For the remaining numbers in the F column, list in descending order a number which is one greater than the first number in the row immediately above it. In the first graph, 2 is one greater than 1, 4 is one greater than 3, 1 is the next number in progression from 5, and 3 is one number greater than 2.
6. For an uneven number of teams, in this case five, follow the same procedures for six teams and list the word "bye" in place of the sixth team, F.

A triangular pattern of listing pairs can be extruded from the graph arrangement as indicated below:

A–B	A–C	A–D	A–E	A–F		A–B				
	B–C	B–D	B–E	B–F		A–C	B–C			
		C–D	C–E	C–F	*or*	A–D	B–D	C–D		
			D–E	D–F		A–E	B–E	C–E	D–E	
				E–F		A–F	B–F	C–F	D–F	E–F

With practice, it is possible to develop this triangular pattern without referring to a graph. As in the graph, Figure 9–2, a schedule of games must be made from the list of pairings.

Round Robin Variations

Several types of round robin variations can be arranged to add considerable interest for participants. Actually, the basic principle of round robin play is altered very little, the difference being in the scoring and method of determining league winners. In some instances it is possible to complete these tournaments in a few hours or one or two days.

Continuous Round Robin. The continuous round robin is suitable for activities in which scores can be compared such as bowling, golf, archery, horseshoes, rifle shooting, weight lifting, and free throw contests. In this variation, a complete round robin or a full season of competition takes place simultaneously in what is normally one playing date of the round robin. In bowling, for example, two teams may be scheduled to bowl on two lanes, but in reality, they compare scores with all of the other teams bowling on adjacent lanes. This procedure continues for as many weeks as would normally be required to bowl a round robin. If there are ten teams, the continuous round robin is extended over a nine-week period. On a 4-point scale (one point for each of three games and one for total pins), instead of the opportunity to win 4 points at one bowling session, a team may win as many as 36 points. League standings fluctuate considerably from game to game, and this sharpens the enthusiasm of the participants, particularly for those teams at the botton of the league who envision a higher position in the standings.

Play-'Til-You-Win Method. Another variation of the round robin is the "play-'til-you-win method." As an example, six players draw for positions in a round robin handball tournament. Play continues beyond the single round robin, if necessary, until one player wins five games, the number of rounds for six players, or 5 points, 1 point being awarded for each game won. Only one 11-point game is played per match instead of the usual two out of three 21-point games.

This tournament could be won by a player if he scored a victory in each of his first five games. However, it might be necessary to play part of a second round robin before a winner is determined, as shown in the following table. Art's won and lost record was 4 and 2 before winning his last game.

PLAYERS	GAMES PLAYED	GAMES WON	GAMES LOST	POINTS
Art	7	5	2	5
Bob	7	4	3	4
Cal	7	4	3	4
Don	7	3	4	3
Jim	7	3	4	3
Tom	7	2	5	2

The round robin may be continued to select additional places or a playoff can be held to break ties.

Approximately one and one-half hours are required to complete this tournament. In the illustration above, it is necessary for Art to play a maximum of 75 game points. This compares with 63 winning points in three regulation 21-point handball games. Depending on the condition and playing ability of the contestants, it may be necessary to complete the tournament on a succeeding day.

Lombard Tournament. The Lombard is a "quickie" or instant tournament variation of the round robin. It may be used for basketball, volleyball, touch football, softball, hockey, squash, handball, tennis, badminton, and table tennis. In basketball, an instant tournament can be organized by making up teams from participants informally shooting baskets on the gymnasium floor.

The length of an abbreviated game may be determined by dividing the regulation playing time by the number of teams. If courts are available, a centralized timing system may be used to time games on a straight running time basis. Assuming the length of a basketball game is 40 minutes and there are eight teams competing, the length of each game is five minutes. Each team plays every other team a five-minute game. The time required to play seven games is approximately equal to the time necessary for one regulation game.

After the round robin is completed, each team's points for seven games are totaled. Points scored by the opponents are also added, and this sum is subtracted from the offensive point total. The team with the highest positive differential wins. Another method of ranking teams is to count the won and lost records for the seven games played by each team. Additional competition may also be arranged by scheduling the first two or four teams in a playoff of regulation games for subsequent days.

ELIMINATION TOURNAMENTS

Elimination tournaments, also known as knock-out or match play tournaments, are based on the elimination of losing participants until only one team remains. Each game results in the elimination of the losing team or moving the loser to another division for a second chance at the championship or the opportunity to win a championship of lesser importance. There are two basic kinds of elimination tournaments, the straight or single elimination and the double elimination, and to these are added various consolations and participation combinations.

Single Elimination Tournament

The single elimination tournament is the simplest and most expedient method of determining a winner. Each time a game is played, the losing team is eliminated. This tournament is used to best advantage when there are numerous entries and limited time and facilities. It is not an objective measure of ability because the best team or player might lose in an early round due to an "off day." Similarly, the runner-up may not be the second best in the tourney for the reason that a better player or team might have been eliminated by the winner in an earlier match. The most undesirable element is the fact that many participants are eliminated early in competition, a violation of the intramural participation principle. Single elimination tournaments are recommended only when it is not feasible to use round robin and other more equitable forms of competition.

"Perfect Power of Two." In drawing up an elimination tournament, it is necessary to structure a geometric pattern that can be equitably divided, one proportionally reduced in size as teams are eliminated until the winner evolves. To accomplish this objective, the number of lines on which team names and byes appear must equal the perfect power of 2. Since two lines make up a bracket for one game, the number of brackets must likewise be comparable to a perfect power of 2.

The mathematical term "perfect power of 2" is defined as 2 multiplied by itself and each product subsequently multiplied by 2. The following tables illustrates the perfect powers of 2 involved in tournament structuring. Generally, it is not necessary to use more than 128 lines (2 raised to the seventh power).

PERFECT POWERS OF TWO

2^2 (raised to the second power) 2×2 . . . . = 4
2^3 (raised to the third power) $2 \times 2 \times 2$ . . . . = 8
2^4 (raised to the fourth power) $2 \times 2 \times 2 \times 2$ . . . . = 16
2^5 (raised to the fifth power) $2 \times 2 \times 2 \times 2 \times 2$ . . . . = 32
2^6 (raised to the sixth power) $2 \times 2 \times 2 \times 2 \times 2 \times 2$ . . . . = 64
2^7 (raised to the seventh power) $2 \times 2 \times 2 \times 2 \times 2 \times 2 \times 2$ = 128

For those who have difficulty understanding and applying this mathematical concept, the perfect powers of 2 will be referred to as tournament "magic numbers," not to be confused with those identified in the presentation on league standings. The magic numbers for tournament structuring are 4, 8, 16, 32, 64, and 128.

Number of Rounds. In a single elimination tournament, a round is each vertical series of brackets, and the term is used to specify tournament progress such as "all teams have played through the second round." A round with eight teams remaining is the "quarter-finals"; four teams, the "semi-finals"; and two teams, the "finals."

The number of rounds in a single elimination tournament is the power to which 2 must be raised as it relates to the number of entries. If the number of entries equals a magic number, the number of rounds is equal to the power to which 2 must be raised to equal that magic number. For example, if the number of entries is 16, 2 must be raised to the fourth power, and therefore, the number of rounds equals 4. When the number of entries is not equivalent to a magic number, the number of rounds is equal to the power to which 2 must be raised to equal the next higher magic number which exceeds the number of entries. For example, 28 entries require 5 rounds because 2 must be raised to the fifth power to equal the next higher magic number, 32, in excess of 28.

Number of Games. The number of games or matches in a single elimination tournament is one subtracted from the number of entries. The formula is $N - 1$, with N representing the number of entries. For example, if there are 16 entries, $16 - 1 = 15$ games; with 11 entries, $11 - 1 = 10$ games. The number of games in the first round of a single elimination tournament is equal to the difference between the number of entries and the next *lower* magic number.

Placement of Byes. When the number of entries is not equal to one of the magic numbers, it is necessary to fill out the geometrical pattern with nonopponents in the form of byes. This means a team which is paired with a bye automatically advances to the next round of play.

To calculate the number of byes in a single elimination tournament, the number of entries is subtracted from the next higher magic number. For example, if there are 11 entries, the next higher magic number is 16. Sixteen minus 11 equals 5, the number of byes. Figure 9–4 illustrates a single elimination tournament for 11 entries with 4 rounds and 5 byes.

Three principles of bye placement should be followed in structuring a single elimination tournament:

1. All byes must be listed in the first round.
2. When the number of byes is uneven, the extra bye is placed in the bottom half of the tournament.
3. Byes should be positioned symmetrically on the drawing sheet.

If there are 2 byes, 1 is placed on the bottom line and the other on the top line of the draw sheet. With 4 byes, 1 is placed on the bottom line, another on the top line, the third on the top line of the lower half of the tournament, and the fourth on the bottom line of the upper half of the tournament. Figure 15–2 specifies the number of byes for 3 through

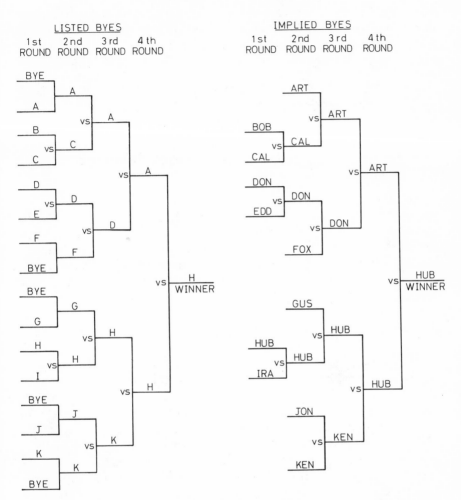

Fig. 9–4. Single Elimination Tournaments: 11 Entries. (Left) Listed Byes (5). (Right) Implied Byes (5).

64 entries and identifies the exact lines on which they should be placed. This ready reference table simplifies the construction of a single elimination draw sheet.

An elimination tournament draw sheet may be designed according to the listed byes or the implied byes method. For listed byes, entries and byes are positioned in the first round on the draw sheet. With implied byes, those receiving byes are not listed in the first round but are automatically advanced to the second round. In this case, the number of lines equals the number of entries. The implied byes method requires less space, but the draw sheet is more difficult to construct, particularly for inexperienced tournament directors. Figure 9–4 illustrates both methods, and additional listed and implied byes single elimination draw sheets for 3 through 16 entries are diagramed in Figure 15–5, a–f.

Assignment of Positions.   For assigning entries to the various brackets in the tournament, making up the pairings, several methods may be used:

1. Positions may be drawn by lot
2. Positions may be assigned in the order in which entries are received.
3. Positions may be designated on the basis of known player ability or team strength.

The first two methods should be used only when lack of information prevents distribution of tournament talent. If positions are decided by chance, there is a possibility that the best teams will meet in the first round. This further magnifies the disadvantage of elimination tourneys because the best teams will not be playing in the finals. Whenever possible, the best players should be equally distributed throughout the draw sheet, and the seeded entries should receive byes if any are assigned.

Double Elimination Tournaments

In a double elimination tournament, also titled "second chance" or "continuous consolation," a participant is eliminated after losing twice and every entry plays a minimum of two games. A team which loses its first game in the winners' division is rescheduled to play other losers, with the possibility of eventually winning the tournament. The winner of the losers' division plays the winner of the winners' division. If the winners' representative wins this game, the tournament is completed. If the losers' divsion team wins, each team has one loss and an additional game must be played to select the champion.

The double elimination tournament produces a truer champion than single elimination competition, but it is less valid than a round robin. It overcomes the disadvantage of a "bad game" or an unlucky draw, but it violates the participation principle in eliminating some teams as soon as two games are played and lost, while others play numerous additional games.

Number of Rounds.   For determining the number of double elimination rounds or playing dates, the procedure is the same as for single elimination tournaments with the exception that the number of rounds is multiplied by 2 and if an extra game is played, an additional round is added. If there are 10 entries, the number of rounds is 8 or 9. The tournament calculator in Figure 15–1 eliminates the necessity of laboriously applying formulas to calculate the rounds, byes, and games for round robin, single elimination, and double elimination tournaments.

Number of Games. The number of double elimination games or matches is derived by applying the following formulas with N representing the number of entries.

Minimum number of games to play = 2 (N − 1)
Mamixum number of games to play = 2 (N − 1) + 1

For 10 entries, the number of games is 18, [2 (10 − 1) = 18] or if an additional game is necessary, 19, [2 (10 − 1) + 1 = 19].

Placement of Byes. The placement of byes for a double elimination follows the same rules as for single elimination tournaments except that it is necessary to have byes beyond the first round of the losers' division; and although byes are symmetrically positioned, they may not be on identical lines, depending on the method of designing the draw sheets. There is less confusion for participants and more conservation of space if byes are implied instead of listed.

Double Elimination Patterns. There are two basic patterns for arranging double elimination tournaments, the back-to-back and over-under, illustrated in Figure 9–5. The first round of each method is basically similar to that of a single elimination tournament, although the bye positions may be slightly altered in the back-to-back method. In this pattern, winners' and losers' divisions are arranged back-to-back with the winners advancing to the right and losers following the broken lines and arrows to the left. This winner of the losers' category, Jon, follows the line of arrows to the front and plays the undefeated finalist, Cal. A second game is played if Jon wins since Cal would only have one loss.

The back-to-back method is less confusing in positioning losing teams because arrows indicate the route of play. Note the diagonal lines directing Edd to the bottom half of the losers' division and Gus to the upper half. Whenever possible, pairings in the losers' division should be arranged to prevent entries from playing each other a second time until the latest possible moment. This is accomplished by crossing losers from the top and bottom halves of the winners' division. Back-to-back double elimination draw sheets for 3 through 16 entries are illustrated in Figure 15–6, a–h.

In the over-under pattern, the losers' brackets are arranged under the winners' division. As entries lose, they are transposed to the losers' brackets, with the winner and loser finalists, Cal and Jon, meeting for the championship. The over-under method provides greater flexibility

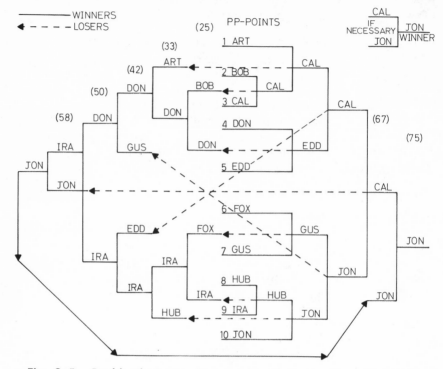

Fig. 9–5. Double Elimination Tournaments: 10 Entries, 18 or 19 Games. (Left) Back-To-Back Method. (Right) Over-Under Method.

for crossing losing teams, but properly inserting the losers into the lower division is sometimes confusing.

After the draw sheet has been constructed, lettering the lines to which losers are to be transferred aids in the transition from the winners' to the losers' division. In Figure 9–5, the loser of the Bob–Cal match is positioned on line C in the first round of the losers' division. Because of the excessive time factor and complexity of structuring them, double elimination tournaments are usually not used for more than 16 entries.

Semi-Double Elimination Tournament

In a semi-double elimination tournament competition begins on a double elimination basis and ends with single elimination. Entries are paired in an elimination pattern, with winners continuing in the winners' division and all first round losers plus losers in the second round who drew first round byes, playing in the losers' division. From this point in the tournament, all games in the winners' and losers' divisions are played on a single elimination basis. The winners of the losers' and winners' divi-

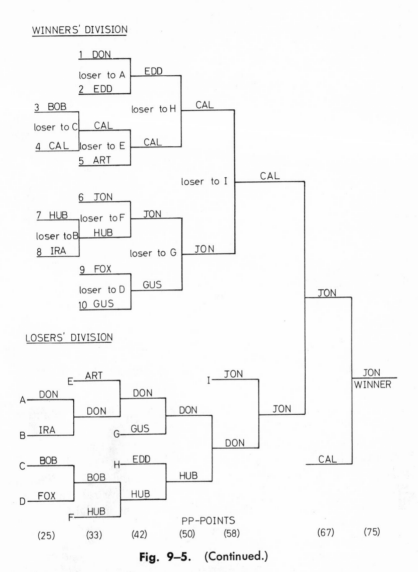

Fig. 9–5. (Continued.)

sions play for the championship. It may be structured according to the back-to-back or over-under method.

Figure 9–6 illustrates a back-to-back semi-double elimination draw sheet for 12 entries. The design of this type of tournament varies depending on who wins and loses in the first and second rounds. For example, if Deb lost to Fay in the second round, Deb would not move to the losers' division since her second match is beyond the double elimination phase of the tournament. Similarly, Bea, with one loss, does not

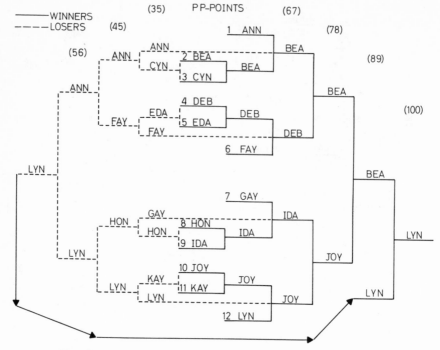

Fig. 9–6. Semi-Double Elimination Tournaments: 12 Entries.

play Lyn a second game after losing to her in the finals; the tournament is single elimination at this stage.

In a semi-double elimination tournament, each entry does not receive two losses, but all entries play a minimum of two games. It has the advantage of compensating for an "off game" in the initial stages of the tournament. This tournament design is desirable for selecting a winner among a large number of entries with limited time available.

Consolation Tournaments

Consolation tournaments are arranged in conjunction with single and double eliminations to offer opportunities for additional games to losers of the main tournament. They overcome the single elimination objection of eliminating approximately half of the participants in the first round. The minimum number of games for a consolation with a straight elimination is two, and a consolation with a double elimination is three.

The extent to which losers are included in a consolation draw ranges from the simplest form of first round losers and second round losers with first round byes, to a second place tournament which is just one game short of a double elimination tournament. Consolation tournaments may be designed to accommodate these minimum and maximum possibilities or to terminate at any round between these points. The tournament draws may be structured using back-to-back or over-under methods as shown in Figures 9–7 and 9–8. Some of the possible consolation combinations are presented in the following sections.

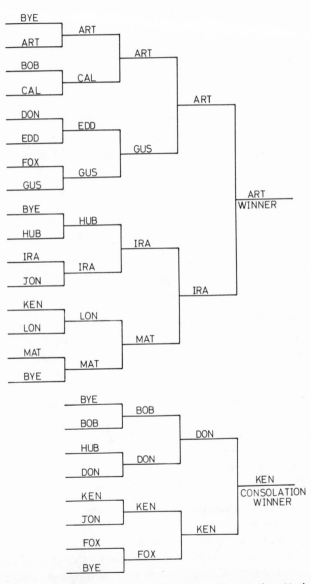

Fig. 9–7. Consolation Tournament: 13 Entries, Over-Under Method. (Top) Main Tournament. (Bottom) Consolation Tournament.

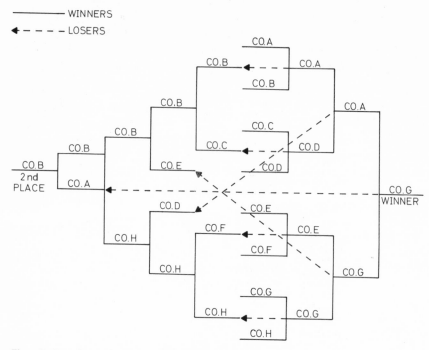

Fig. 9–8. Second Place Consolation Tournament: 8 Entries, Back-To-Back
Method.

Simple Consolation. The most common type of consolation tournament
includes all first round losers and second round losers who were assigned
first round byes. The latter situation exists only when the number of
entries is not equal to a magic number. In this case, it is necessary to
wait until byed entries play their first games before the consolation draw
can be completed. If the byed entries win, the losers do not enter the
consolation tourney because they played and won their first round games.

In the example shown in Figure 9–7, Hub received a bye in the first
round, then lost his first game, moving him to a position in the consolation division. However, Cal and Lon who lost to Mat and Art, two byed
players, do not play in the consolation because they won their first games.

Second Place Consolation. The second place consolation tournament
selects a second place winner in addition to the champion. All players
eliminated from the main tournament are eligible for additional competition. This type of consolation is similar to a double elimination tournament with the exception that the winner of the losers' division does not
meet the winner of the winners' division.

In the illustration, Figure 9–8, winners advance to the right in the main tournament and losers follow the broken lines and arrows to the left. Company G won this tournament and Company B finished in second place. Company A could be credited with third place and Company H with fourth place, or the teams could play off to determine third and fourth places. In this illustration, the back-to-back method is used, but as with all consolation structures, the over-under pattern is an alternate method.

Mueller-Anderson Playback. This continuous consolation-type playback incorporates a single elimination tournament, increases participation, ranks the teams or players, and usually requires no more rounds than a single elimination. Instead of being out of the tournament after a first round loss, players continue to play for a position among all of the entries. A comparison of the single elimination and Mueller-Anderson playback is shown in Figure 9–9.

In the single elimination tournament of 8 entries, the total number of games is seven with each player playing a minimum of one game. For the Mueller-Anderson playback, the total number of games is 12 and the minimum number of games is three. Both tournaments are completed in three rounds or playing dates.

Winners advance to the right on solid lines and losers move to the left on broken lines. Players are ranked in order from one through eight. The winner, Don, is first; Gus, the losing finalist, is second; Art and Fox, the losing semi-finalists, play for third and fourth; Edd and Bob, winners in the losers' division, play for fifth and sixth; and Hub and Cal, losers' division losers, play for seventh and eighth. Common practice for back-to-back structuring would place the winner of the losers' division in Cal's eighth position, but the match between Edd and Bob is shifted contrary to this pattern to facilitate ranking the players in consecutive order.

The playback design provides a better distribution of participation–performance points than the single elimination. Points in the playback are 75–68–61–54–46–32–25. For the single elimination, they are 75–58–42–25. Mueller-Anderson playback patterns for 4 through 12 entries are included in Figure 15–7, a–f.

Bagnall-Wild Tournament. The Bagnall-Wild tournament selects second and third place winners with reasonable accuracy. This method or variations of it is used extensively in wrestling meets where considerable importance is given to team points awarded to second and third place winners of each weight division. The theory is that the tournament winner may have eliminated a player that was better than the defeated finalist.

Contestants defeated prior to the finals by each of the finalists enter separate consolation playoffs. In the main tournament, Figure 9–7, Cal

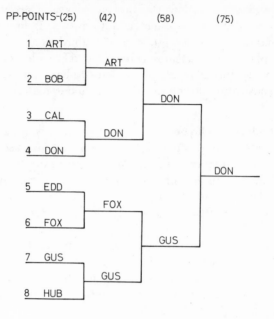

STRAIGHT SINGLE ELIMINATION
3 ROUNDS-7 GAMES
MINIMUM GAMES-1

PP-POINTS-(25)   (42)   (58)   (75)

1 ART
        ART
2 BOB
                DON
3 CAL
        DON
4 DON
                            DON
5 EDD
        FOX
6 FOX
                GUS
7 GUS
        GUS
8 HUB

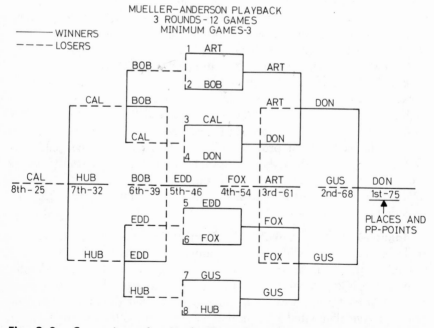

MUELLER—ANDERSON PLAYBACK
3 ROUNDS-12 GAMES
MINIMUM GAMES-3

————— WINNERS
— — — — LOSERS

CAL   HUB   BOB   EDD   FOX   ART   GUS   DON
8th-25   7th-32   6th-39 5th-46 4th-54 3rd-61 2nd-68 1st-75

PLACES AND
PP-POINTS

Fig. 9–9. Comparison of a Single Elimination Tournament and the Mueller-Anderson Playback Tournament.

156

and Gus were eliminated by the winner Art. As illustrated in Figure 9–10, Cal defeats Gus and plays Ira for second place, which Ira wins. If Ira had lost, he would automatically be assigned third place because he defeated all other players eligible for this position, namely, Mat, Hub, and Jon. Since Ira won, Cal plays Jon, the winner of those previously eliminated by Ira, and Jon wins third place. The disadvantage of this tournament is that the second and third place consolations cannot be scheduled until the main tournament finalists are decided.

Ideas for Intramurals. (1) To provide all teams with the experience of winning, arrange a last chance tournament among all of the intramural teams that did not win a game during the regular season's play. Continue to schedule the losers of this tournament until only one winless team remains. An appropriate award can be presented for their unique distinction. (2) After the first round of an elimination tournament, the winners advance to the second round, and the losers challenge each other or are scheduled to play one another for the privilege of entering the second round on an equal basis with the first round winners. After the second round is completed, the procedure is repeated for each additional round.

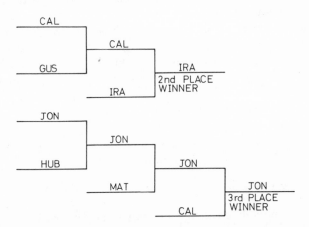

Fig. 9–10. Bagnall-Wild Portion of a Single Elimination Tournament.

CHALLENGE TOURNAMENTS

Challenge or perpetual tournaments are usually conducted over an extended period of time. No one is eliminated and at the completion of the tournament, players are ranked individually or by groups, depending on which challenge method is utilized. These tournaments are essentially self-administered in that participants schedule their matches and realign names of winning and losing players on the tournament. Participants attempt to gain a higher position on the board by challenging, defeating, and replacing other players. This form of participation is best suited for individual and dual activities such as tennis, golf, handball, paddleball, squash, archery, and horseshoes, but it may be adapted for team competition.

Challenge Arrangements

Participants' names and telephone numbers are recorded on paper board or similar material and attached to the tournament boards. These may be circular disks which hang on pegs or rectangular slips inserted into slots. Peg boards serve as excellent backing material for challenge tournaments.

Players may be positioned in the tournament according to (1) the order in which entries are received, (2) drawn by lot, (3) seeded on the basis of past performance or known ability, or (4) on the basis of rankings from an elimination or other type of tournament. When players are placed on the board according to ability, it may be advisable to put the best players at the bottom of the tournament and require them to work their way to the top.

After players are listed on the board, competition begins with players issuing challenges to other participants. If a challenger defeats a player in a higher position, the two players exchange places on the board; if the defender wins, positions remain the same. At the tournament termination date, the player in the number one position is declared the winner. A variation of this is to schedule the top four or five players in a round robin or elimination playoff.

Challenge rules vary according to the design of the tournament, but they usually include some of the following:

1. Challenges must be accepted and played within a specified period of time.
2. Players randomly challenge any player on the board.
3. Players challenge one or two positions above or one row above.
4. Players must challenge someone in their own row before challenging above.
5. Players challenge only those to their immediate right or left in the same row and the one above.
6. After losing, a player must accept a challenge from another contestant before reissuing one to the player who defeated him.
7. A new player may enter the tournament by challenging a player in the lowest position on the tournament board.

A messenger board may be located next to the tournament board for the convenience of players who wish to register challenges. The challenged player's name is listed along with a proposed date, time, and court for the match. As a matter of interest, provisions should be made for posting game scores.

There are several unique challenge tournament designs which provide interesting forms of competition. These include the ladder, pyramid and open pyramid, king or crown, funnel and upside-down funnel, round-the-clock, spider web, and record bump board, descriptions of which are presented in the following sections.

Ladder Tournament

This tournament receives its name from the design of the chart which resembles rungs on a ladder. The advantage of this tournament is that each player is ranked according to ability when it is completed. For this reason it is frequently used to select varsity squads in sports such as tennis, golf, and wrestling.

After entries are placed on the ladder, players issue challenges according to one of the challenge procedures outlined above. When a challenger defeats a defender, the two players exchange places. In Figure 9-11, if Cpl. King defeats Lt. James, King moves to fifth place and James replaces him in seventh place.

Ladders may be arranged in combination to accommodate additional entries. By arranging ladders side by side, as in Figure 9-12, horizontal and vertical challenging are permissible. The winners of each ladder may play for the championship. Another variation is to require players to progress numerically up the ladder from their place toward the number one position. This, in essence, is a vertical ladder divided into three portions.

Pyramid and Open Pyramid Tournament

The pyramid tournament (Fig. 9-13) ranks players by groups instead of individual ability except for the number one player. It offers greater flexibility in challenging, the rules of which are listed on page 158. A variation to the pattern is to number consecutively the positions on the tournament board from last place to first place, and issue the challenges numerically, comparable to the ladder arrangement.

The open pyramid provides another method of pyramiding winners. No names are on the pyramid board at the beginning of the tournament. Players issue challenges to other entries, and the winners are awarded a place on the bottom row of the pyramid. Contestants move to the row above by challenging and defeating a player on the same level, but this advancement is only possible when there is a vacancy in the row above. The first player to gain the top position is the winner. After all entries

1	SFC JONES	1
2	CAPT. SMITH	2
3	SGT. THOMES	3
4	SP/4 CLARK	4
5	LT. JAMES	5
6	COL. MOSS	6
7	CPL. KING	7
8	MAJ. WHITE	8
9	LT. COL. LAKE	9
10	SP/5 GEE	10

Fig. 9–11. Ladder Tournament: 10 Entries.

have been placed on the board, it is possible to extend the tournament by following the regular pyramid tournament rules.

King or Crown Tournament

The king or crown tournament (Fig. 9–14) is a combination of several pyramids. This tournament design can accommodate large numbers of entries. Pyramids are placed at different levels, the number depending on the size of the entry. After a participant reaches the top in one of the lower pyramids, he may challenge horizontally. By winning, he gains a position in the bottom row of the higher pyramid. The king or winner is the player who advances to and holds the top position in the uppermost pyramid at the end of the tournament.

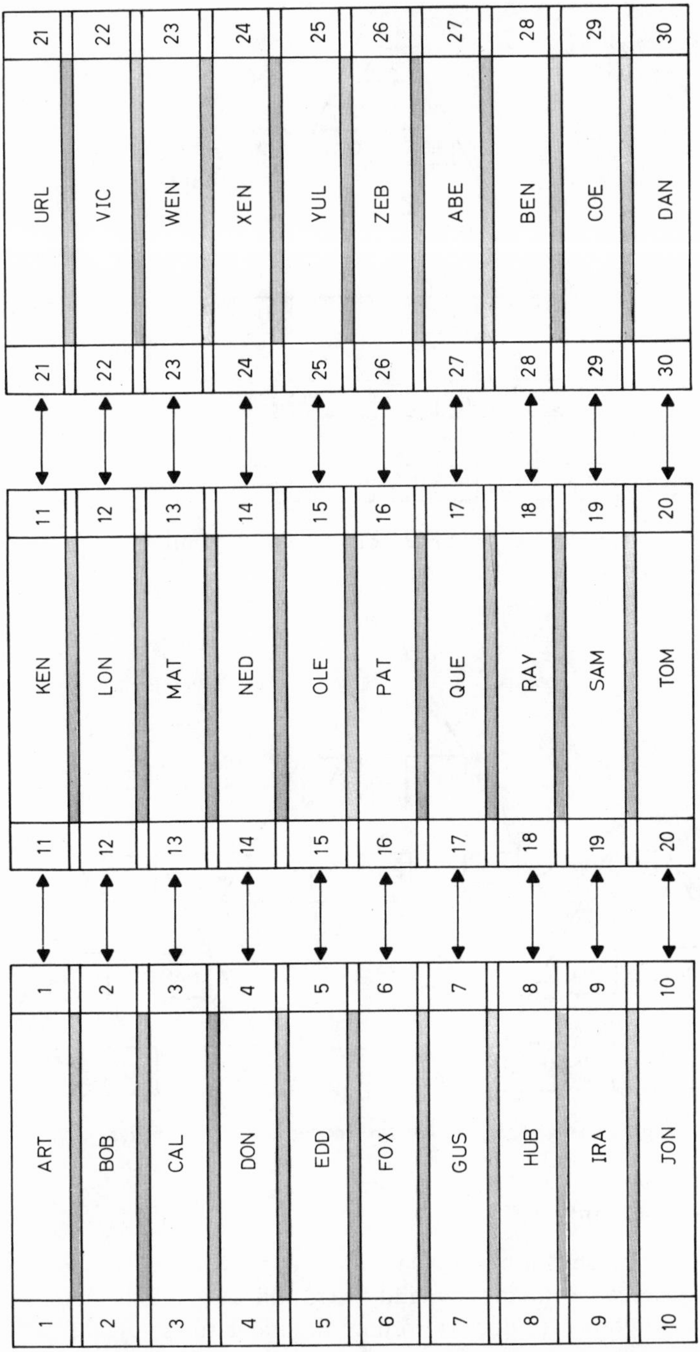

Fig. 9–12. Combination Ladder Tournaments Permitting Horizontal and Vertical Challenging.

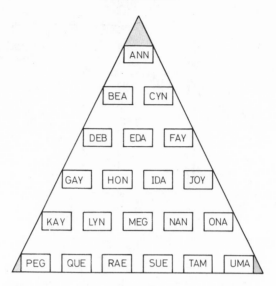

Fig. 9–13. Pyramid Tournament: 21 Entries.

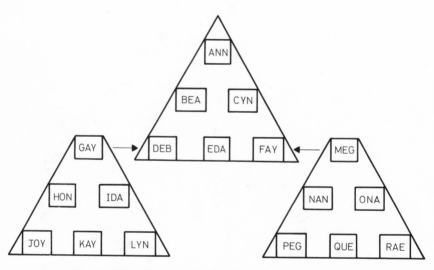

Fig. 9–14. King or Crown Tournament: 18 Entries.

Funnel Tournament

Funnel tournaments are combinations of pyramids and ladders. Players in the top section follow pyramid rules, and the bottom four players advance to the lowest position according to ladder rules. In this tournament, the objective is to filter through the funnel to the lowest place. In

Figure 9–15, Ann is the winner if that place is maintained at the tournament deadline.

This type of tournament provides for numerous entries and objectively selects the first four places in order of ability. More players may be ranked in the ladder portion by increasing the number of rungs. In the upside-down funnel tournament (Fig. 9–16), players advance to the top as in pyramid and ladder tournaments.

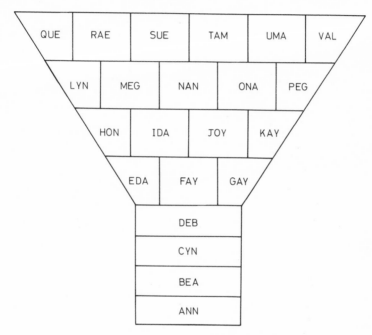

Fig. 9–15.   Funnel Tournament: 22 Entries.

Round-the-Clock Tournament

In the round-the-clock tournament (Fig. 9–17), participants are positioned at each o'clock number on the face of the clock. Rules may be set with one of these objectives for the winner: (1) the winner is the player who advances in a clock-wise direction and is in the 12 o'clock position at the tournament deadline, or (2) the winner is the first player to make one complete revolution to his original starting position. One of the usual challenge procedures may be selected.

The arrow on the clock is set to indicate the winning hour position or to designate the player who advances the farthest. Variations may be arranged in which several revolutions are required and more than 12 entries can be accommodated by using more clock faces.

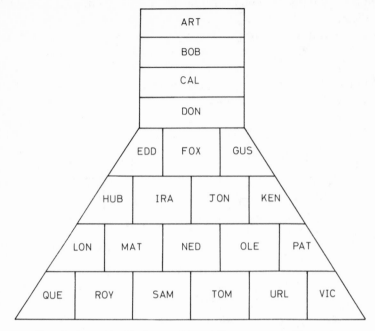

Fig. 9–16. Upside-Down Funnel Tournament: 22 Entries.

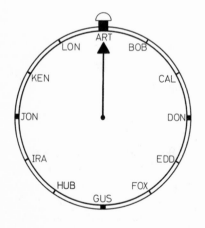

Fig. 9–17. Round-the-Clock Tournament: 12 Entries.

Spider Web Tournament

The spider web tournament illustrated in Figure 9–18, also known as the hexagon, is conducted according to the rules of the pyramid tournament. The object of the spider web is to advance to the center and hold that position. A disadvantage is that the player in the middle must ac-

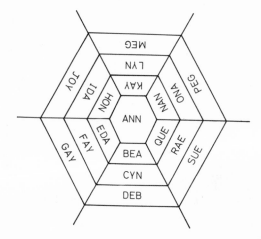

Fig. 9–18. Spider Web Tournament: 19 Entries.

cept numerous challenges from the six players in the inside hexagon. To reduce some of the pressure on this player, it is advisable to require players to play someone on their own level before permitting them to challenge the center position.

Record Bump Board Tournament

The record bump board tournament is one in which participants do not compete against each other but challenge records or scores appearing on the board. The name and performance of a competitor who breaks one of the listed records is placed in the appropriate position on the board, and the other names are adjusted in descending order, the last one being dropped from the board. This participation arrangement provides excellent motivation for track, swimming, Sigma Delta Psi, and other events graded on a time and distance basis. Figure 9–19 illustrates a track record bump board. If a contestant runs the mile in 4 minutes and 38 seconds, his performance is recorded in third place, Wilk and Feld shift to fourth and fifth, and Mati is dropped from the board.

Archery, bowling, rifle shooting, and golf are also adaptable to bump board scoring. For example, names of the top ten bowlers and their scores are listed on the board. A bowler who bowls the fifth highest scores moves into fifth place on the board and all bowlers below him are moved down one position with the last player being bumped from the board. Contestants bowl at any time in an attempt to gain a position on the board.

TRACK BUMP BOARD

EVENT	NUMBER 1	NUMBER 2	NUMBER 3	NUMBER 4	NUMBER 5
100 YDS.	DON WIESE 9.9	DAVE VAALER 10.1	JON OLSON 10.5	RON SMITH 10.7	DAVE JONES 10.9
220 YDS.	TIM MILLER 22.8	DICK KELLY 23.0	JOHN VELIN 23.4	KEVIN LEE 23.8	BOB SNOOK 24.1
440 YDS.	BRUCE GROTH 50.4	PAUL BENSON 50.8	DAVE REID 51.3	DON ASP 51.6	TOM KIREN 52.0
880 YDS.	DICK TROUT 2:00.0	RAY KROLL 2:04.1	KEN BARR 2:04.6	TED BEAN 2:05	DALE WARD 2:05.5
MILE RUN	JIM KING 4:34.0	GENE MYERS 4:36.5	JES WILK 4:39.2	LEE FELD 4:44.4	PHIL MATI 4:45.0
180 L. HURDS	MARK SHIM 20.6	TONY LUCS 21.3	BART ROOT 21.7	PAT BOND 21.9	LEN KERR 22.2
120 H. HURDS	DAN OLDS 14.8	JERRY MOLIN 15.4	BRAD THOR 15.7	LYLE FINN 15.9	RUSS WOOD 16.1
LONG JUMP	NICK MILES 22'8"	OTTO WISHY 22'1"	JOE NOWO 21'7"	CHET LAST 20'5"	NORM RICE 19'6"
HIGH JUMP	ROG SAND 6'0"	CURT LOE 5'7"	RICK KING 5'6"	AL BLAD 5'4"	MIKE HIRT 5'3"
SHOT PUT	JEFF HAYS 51'2"	LOU STANS 49'7"	VAN CUTTS 48'8"	SCOT BORD 46'2"	REX BOE 42'0"
POLE VAULT	BILL BEER 14'0"	DOUG HOLT 13'4"	PAUL SINS 12'6"	MILT SUGS 11'4"	FRED LOCK 10'8"

Fig. 9–19.   Track Record Bump Board Tournament.

Ideas for Intramurals. (1) Set aside a challenge court for sports such as squash or handball in which players must be willing to accept a challenge from anybody who wishes to play them. If two players are playing a game, a third player may challenge the winner who must accept it as soon as the current game is completed. Losers or other players may issue challenges to be played as soon as a game in progress terminates. The court should be labeled as a challenge court with rules posted on the door. This method provides competition without preliminary arrangements and encourages players to play with persons other than their usual partners. To this extent, it is a good mixer and allows for a flexible pattern of porgramming. In handball, a separate court for singles and another for doubles may be reserved for challenge competition. (2) A graph round robin form (Fig. 9–2) may be used for challenge-type competition. Individuals do not play their matches at exactly the same time, but rather challenge opponents according to pairings identified on the graph. The tournament is completed when all of the spaces are filled, and the participant with the best won and lost record is the winner.

INFORMAL-TYPE TOURNAMENTS

Informal-type tournaments are best suited to motivate participation in co-intramural and other less formal activities. It is not advisable to use them when the primary objective is the selection of a valid champion. Tournaments in this category are the marker, ringer, rotation, detour, and the telephonic, telegraphic, and postal comparisons.

Marker Tournament

The marker is also referred to as the tombstone or accumulative tournament. Teams or individuals attempt to reach a predetermined objective or goal, usually a certain score, time, or distance. Players total performances over a period of time, and the first one reaching the marker is the winner. Activities suitable for this type of tournament are golf, archery, bowling, track, swimming, free throw contests, horseshoes, and rifle shooting.

In swimming, a goal of 25 miles may be established either with or without a time limitation which restricts swimming to a specified period each day. Time limits assure a closer finish whereas no limitation undoubtedly produces a winner who is the best conditioned swimmer. For additional interest, relay teams can be formed to swim a mythical distance on the Mississippi River or similar water area. Laps can be equated to miles between two points on the river, and progress of the teams may be plotted on a map.

In bowling, a goal of 10,000 pins is set with restrictions on the number of lines bowled each day as well as the number of days per week. The first bowler to reach the 10,000 pin objective is the winner. In horseshoes, a player throwing the greatest number of ringers out of a specific number of rounds over an extended period of time is the winner. Similarly, the highest number of successful free throws out of a specific number of tries over a two-week period could determine the winner of the contest.

Ringer Tournament

In the ringer tournament, a modification of the marker, only the best scores over a period of time are totaled with the highest accumulation identifying the winner. For golf, each entry posts all hole-by-hole scores for every round as illustrated in Figure 9–20. At the end of the tournament, the lowest scores for each hole of all rounds are circled and added to determine the ringer score. The winner is the player with the lowest total, which in many instances may be considerably less than par. In

ENTRIES	HOLES																		TOTAL
1. ROY T.	1	2	3	4	5	6	7	8	9	10	11	12	13	14	15	16	17	18	
	—SCORES—																		
ROUND 1	⑤	4	5	6	4	5	5	4	⑤	④	4	5	6	4	6	5	3	5	85
ROUND 2	5	4	5	⑤	②	4	④	④	5	4	5	④	⑤	5	5	④	4	6	80
ROUND 3	5	③	④	6	3	④	6	5	5	5	5	5	6	8	⑤	6	③	③	87
ROUND 4	5	4	5	6	4	5	6	5	6	4	④	5	6	③	5	5	6	5	89
RINGER SCORE	5	3	4	5	2	4	4	4	5	4	4	4	5	3	5	4	3	3	(71)
2. BRUCE A.	1	2	3	4	5	6	7	8	9	10	11	12	13	14	15	16	17	18	TOTAL
ROUND 1	5	5	4	6	4	5	④	5	7	3	④	6	5	4	⑤	4	6	3	85
ROUND 2	6	④	4	7	③	6	5	⑤	5	4	6	6	⑤	5	5	3	④	4	87
ROUND 3	⑤	4	4	⑤	5	4	6	5	⑤	5	5	⑤	6	5	5	③	5	3	85
ROUND 4	7	5	④	5	3	④	5	6	5	③	4	6	5	④	5	3	4	③	81
RINGER SCORE	5	4	4	5	3	4	4	5	5	3	4	5	5	4	5	3	4	3	(75)
3. MIKE S.	1	2	3	4	5	6	7	8	9	10	11	12	13	14	15	16	17	18	TOTAL
ROUND 1	3	4	④	3	3	6	4	5	5	④	3	6	4	③	5	6	③	3	74
ROUND 2	4	4	4	4	3	④	5	3	5	4	4	④	4	4	5	④	3	2	70
ROUND 3	③	3	4	③	②	4	5	③	4	4	4	5	④	4	4	5	3	②	66
ROUND 4	3	③	4	3	4	4	④	3	④	4	③	4	5	3	④	4	3	3	65
RINGER SCORE	3	3	4	3	2	4	4	3	4	4	3	4	4	3	4	4	3	2	(61)

Fig. 9–20. Golf Ringer Tournament.

softball, basketball, and other team sports, the highest score among all teams for each round may be circled, and the one with the greatest number of points at the deadline is the winner.

Rotation Tournament

The rotation tournament is also known as the bridge tournament because it is frequently used in bridge and other card games. It is suitable for table tennis, volleyball, badminton, handball, squash, paddleball, and tennis. This tournament may be played on the basis of time rather than game points.

As an example, there are six volleyball courts, twelve teams, and one hour of playing time. At the end of each five-minute period, a whistle is blown, and teams ahead at that time rotate clockwise to the next court while losers remain on the same court. In Figure 9–21, if C is ahead when the whistle blows, it moves to court 3 and D remains on court 2. At the

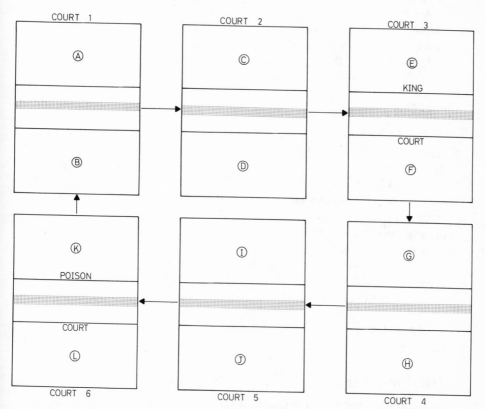

Fig. 9–21. Court Arrangement for a Rotation Volleyball Tournament.

end of the hour, twelve rounds have been played, and the winner is the team that has won the most rounds or partial matches.

A disadvantage of this tourney is that participants may meet each other more than once, depending on which ones win and lose. It has the advantage of being an instant tournament and provides excellent opportunities for socializing.

A variation is to designate one court as the "king" court and another as the "poison" court. Winners at the "king" court remain while losers go directly to the "poison" court. The tournament winner is the leading team occupying the "king" court when the final whistle blows.

Still another possibility requires changing partners. For example, in handball doubles, winners not only advance to the next court, but each winning player is paired with one of the losers. This means that players have new partners for each round. A tournament winner is the player who accumulates the greatest number of wins. It is also possible to use complete matches or games instead of time periods for this type of tournament competition.

A further adaptation is to schedule several different activities such as badminton, table tennis, deck tennis, aerial darts, and shuffleboard in adjacent areas, and to rotate the participants among the areas after a specified time period. Points scored in each activity are totaled to determine the winner of the rotation competition.

Detour Tournament

The basic purpose of the detour tournament is to provide practice games for losing teams, those who are in need of extra participation. The detour is best suited for entries equalling multiples of four such as 4, 8, 12, and 16 because uneven numbered groups result in unmatched practice games. An inverse scoring system is used in which one point is scored against a team for each loss. An undefeated team at the end of the tournament receives no points and is the winner.

After teams play the first round, the winners wait for the subsequent round while losers take time to play practice games. Winners and losers are then paired for the second round of regular games. Opponents should be assigned to prevent teams from meeting more than once. The practice procedure is followed after each round. Teams may be ranked in order with 0 points representing first place; 1 point, second place; 2 points, third place; etc.

Telephone, Telegraph, and Postal Tournaments

Participation by telephone, telegraph, or mail is particularly suitable for extramural activities wherein teams from one institution compete against others representing one or more institutions. Numerous activities may be utilized for this type of participation, but the most popular are bowling, golf, archery, swimming, track, Sigma Delta Psi, horseshoes, and free throws.

Competition is usually conducted simultaneously at the site of each participating unit according to pre-arranged regulations. After the contests are completed, each team reports the results via telephone, telegraph, or mail. When competition involves two teams, the scores are interchanged. If several units are entered, the results may be tabulated at a central location.

CLASSIFICATION AND EQUALIZATION METHODS

One of the most important elements in organizing intramural participation is the utilization of classification and equalization procedures. Participation, interest, and enthusiasm in intramurals are proportional to the opportunities for reasonably successful competition. If the participant loses consistently or loses by one-sided scores, he may turn from intramurals to some other form of recreation in which he can succeed to a satisfactory degree. Various methods of classfying and equalizing competition for teams and individuals are presented in the following sections.

Combination Tournaments

There are many potential combinations of tournaments which add interest to intramural participation. Some of them equalize competition by placing teams or individual participants in different classes. Examples are various combinations of round robins, eliminations, and playbacks.

Round Robin–Elimination.   In the round robin–elimination, teams are divided into leagues and play a complete round robin schedule. After completing these games, teams are assigned to classes for playoffs utilizing single or double elimination or Mueller-Anderson playback tournaments to determine the respective class championships. The number of classes depends on the number of teams in each league. If four teams are in each league, there are four classes: A, B, C, and D. Five team leagues result in five classes; six team leagues, six classes; and so on.

The illustration in Figure 9–22 shows the playoff arrangement for eight four-team leagues. At the completion of the round robin, undefeated teams from each league are placed in the Class A playoffs. Second place teams in each league are assigned to Class B playoffs; third place teams, to Class C playoffs; and fourth place teams, to Class D playoffs. Under this plan, teams compete against others of their own ability. For exam-

Fig. 9–22. Combination Round Robin–Elimination Tournament: (The Class A Won–Lost Records of 2 and 1; Third Place Teams,

CLASS C PLAY-OFFS   (Third place teams from each league)

CLASS D PLAY-OFFS   (Fourth place teams from each league)

Winner is the Intramural Champion. Second Place Teams Usually Have League
1 and 2; and Fourth Place Teams are Winless.)

ple, it is possible for a team to lose all of its round robin games, enter
the Class D playoffs with all other winless teams, and win the all-institutional Class D championship by winning all of its elimination games.
Too often these last place teams are not included in playoffs when they
perhaps have the greatest need for participation.

This method adds considerable interest for players of lesser ability
and consequently aids in eliminating forfeits. Playoff games between
Class A, B, C, and D champions are not recommended because the competition is unfair, particularly between Class A and Class D. Also, a good
team may intentionally lose to be assigned to a lesser class with the aim
of winning the overall championship.

In some programs, participants choose a class prior to competing on
the basis of a personal evaluation of their ability. These classifications
are referred to as Class A, B, C, etc., or by other names such as actives
and pledges, majors and minors, old pros, novices, and rookies.

Mueller-Anderson Playback—Elimination. A combination of the Mueller-Anderson playback and a single elimination tournament provides
classes for singles and doubles competition in single or double elimination
tournaments. For 16 entries, players play a minimum of three matches
and have an opportunity to win an all-institutional Class championship.
This method provides more participation and may be completed in the
same amount of time as a single elimination tournament.

Initially players are scheduled in a 4-entry Mueller-Anderson playback. Players may be assigned an opponent as soon as 2 entries are
received. After completing the four-player playback, all first place
winners, in Figure 9–23 Jack, Bart, Don, and Clair, are placed in a Class
A elimination playoff; second place winners, Class B; third place winners,
Class C; and fourth place winners, Class D. If there is an uneven number
of entries, byes must be placed in the elimination playoffs. Two rounds
are required for the playback and two additional rounds for the elimination playoffs, or a total of four rounds, the number required for a single
elimination tournament of 16 entries. This arrangement also provides for
a more equitable distribution of participation–performance points.

Mueller-Anderson Playback—Round Robin. Teams may be classified
for round robin leagues by following the playback pattern described
above. Teams compete in four-team Mueller-Anderson playbacks, and
the first place winners are scheduled in League I; second place, League
II; third place, League III; and fourth place, League IV. Figure 9–23
illustrates the procedure if Leagues I, II, III, IV are substituted for Class
A, B, C, D, and names of teams are substituted for the players. A round
robin is played in each of the leagues after which a single elimination
playoff may be scheduled similar to the one described under the heading
"round robin–elimination."

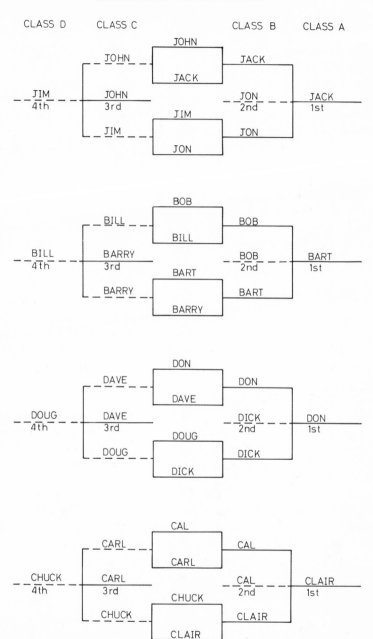

Fig. 9–23. Combination Mueller-Anderson Playback–Elimination Tournament: (First Place Playback Winners Enter the Class A Elimination Playoff; Second Place Winners, Class B; Third Place Winners, Class C; and Fourth Place Winners, Class D.)

Qualifying Rounds or Heats

A large number of entries may be reduced by holding one or more qualifying rounds or heats prior to final competition. This procedure is used in track, swimming, golf, bowling, archery, free throw contests, etc. In this type of qualification, each player is given an equal number of chances to participate in the preliminary rounds. A limited number of players with the best performances, preferably equal to a magic number or a figure limited by the facilities available, continue in the tournament.

Perhaps the most familiar use of qualifying heats is in track and swimming, where only the best performers advance to the finals. In golf, numerous players play in the qualifying rounds, but only the top 64 or 32 players or those who are under a specific cutoff score continue in the tourney. Another method of using the qualification plan is to place golfers in different flights on the basis of scores made in the qualifying rounds.

Age, Height, and Weight Classifications

One of the simplest methods of classifying participants is to establish age, height, and weight classifications individually or in combination. Among older participants, a weight classification frequently used is light-weight, under 150 pounds, and heavyweight, over 150 pounds. For example, 150-pound basketball is played where participants under 150 pounds play in one tournament and those over 150 pounds play in another. For younger age participants, a practical three-way classification is 100 pounds, 125 pounds, and unlimited, and a five-weight division is 80 pounds, 95 pounds, 110 pounds, 120 pounds, and unlimited. In sports such as wrestling, weight classes for each event are established by the rules.

Players may also be classified using a combination of age, height, and weight. The table in Figure 9–24 illustrates how these three criteria can be used to classify participants. Exponents are determined as follows: age—14 years, 3 months = an exponent of 29; height—63 inches = an exponent of 30; weight—126 pounds = an exponent of 20; and the sum of the exponents is 79. On the basis of this table, exponents may be grouped into various classes such as A, B, C, etc.

Seeding Participants

Seeding is a method of classifying participants in which the best players do not meet until the latest possible moment in the tournament. It is accomplished by positioning players so their early matches are against entries of lesser ability. The object, barring any upsets, is to have the

EXPONENT	AGE (yrs.-mos. to yrs.-mos.)		HEIGHT (inches)	WEIGHT (pounds)	EXPONENT
13	—	—	—	79-84	13
14	—	—	—	85-90	14
15	—	—	—	91-96	15
16	—	—	—	97-103	16
17	—	—	—	104-109	17
18	—	—	—	110-115	18
19	—	—	—	116-121	19
20	—	—	—	122-128	20
21	—	—	—	129-134	21
22	10-9	to 11-2	47 -down	135-140	22
23	11-3	to 11-8	47.5-49	141-146	23
24	11-9	to 12-2	49.5-51.5	147-153	24
25	12-3	to 12-8	52 -53.5	154-159	25
26	12-9	to 13-2	54 -55.5	160-165	26
27	13-3	to 13-8	56 -57.5	166-171	27
28	13-9	to 14-2	58 -59.5	172-178	28
29	14-3	to 14-8	60 -62	179-184	29
30	14-9	to 15-2	62.5-64	185-190	30
31	15-3	to 15-8	64.5-66	191- up	31
32	15-9	to 16-2	66.5-68		32
33	16-3	to 16-8	68.5-70.5		33
34	16-9	to 17-2	71 -72.5		34
35	17-3	to 17-8	73 -74.5		35
36	17-9	to 18-2	75 -up		36
37	18-3	to 18-8			37
38	18-9	to 19-0			38

APPLICATION:

AGE-	14 years, 3 mos.	= EXPONENT OF	29
HEIGHT-	63 inches	= EXPONENT OF	30
WEIGHT-	126 pounds	= EXPONENT OF	20
		SUM OF EXPONENTS	79

Fig. 9–24. Age, Height, Weight Classification Table. (Courtesy California Interscholastic Federation.)

two best players in the finals, the four best players in the semi-finals, the eight best players in the quarter-finals, and so on. If tournament directors could seed all players perfectly, it would be unnecessary to play the tournament.

Usually, not more than half of the entries are seeded, and in some instances, only one out of every four or one out of every eight entries may be seeded. However, if sufficient information about the ability of the players is available, all of them may be seeded to assure the most valid competitive results.

Seeded players should be assigned tournament byes. This procedure advances the best players to the second round and gives weaker players an opportunity to play in at least one match against players of lesser ability than the seeded players.

There are several methods of positioning seeded players on a draw sheet, but the one recommended here automatically assures the assignment of byes to seeded players if the byes placement method identified in Figure 15–2 is followed. With this arrangement, the first seeded player is placed on the bottom line of the tournament and the second seeded player is on the top line. The third seeded player is positioned on the first line of the bottom half of the tournament, and the fourth seeded player is positioned on the bottom line of the top half of the tournament. If players are correctly rated and play according to their ability, the number 1 seeded player meets 3, and 2 plays 4 in the semi-finals, with 1 defeating 2 in the finals for the championship.

Some directors follow a slightly different arrangement and give the first seeded player a greater advantage by reversing the placement of the third and fourth seeds. Number 4 is positioned in the same half of the tournament as 1, and 3 is in the same half as 2. This means that 1 plays 4 and 2 meets 3 in the semi-finals. In the interest of fair competition, it seems desirable to seed 1 and 3 in the same half and 2 and 4 in the other half of the tournament. Specific seeding placements for 4-, 8-, 16-, and 32-entry draw sheets are listed in Figure 15–3.

Handicap Procedures

Handicapping is a method of equalizing competition between opponents of unequal ability. Whenever possible, it should be used in conjunction with classification procedures. In some instances, participants with lesser ability do not enter competition unless there is a reasonable chance to defeat some of the other competitors. A handicap system provides points for the participants of lesser ability which enables them to defeat stronger opposition. Generally, basketball, baseball, football, and similar games are not handicapped. A nonhandicapped contest is "played from scratch."

There are several informal methods of handicapping. In racquet games such as squash and badminton, a good player receives a minus six handicap which means he must score six points before starting to score from zero. The poorer player may start the game with a plus six handicap, the size of the handicap depending on the difference in the ability of the players. For tennis singles, the better player may be required to cover the entire doubles court while his opponent plays within the singles boundaries. In badminton doubles, the good players may be allowed only one serve to every two serves by the poorer players. For handball, the better players may be restricted by not permitting any shots to touch one or both of the sidewalls.

Bowling Handicaps. Bowling and golf are examples of activities that are suitable for formalized handicapping. In bowling, an average is calculated by adding the total number of pins and dividing the sum by the number of games. The result is subtracted from a scratch score (170, 180, 190, 200) which should be approximately ten pins higher than the highest individual average in the league. A percentage of this difference is the handicap. The percentage may be 66 2/3, 70, 75, or 80 per cent, depending on the ability of the bowlers in the league. One hundred percent of the difference should not be given because the lesser percentage encourages every member of the league to bowl his best at all times.

For example, the average for 3,800 pins bowled in 25 games is 152 (3,800 pins ÷ 25 games). This average subtracted from 170 (scratch score) is 18. Two-thirds of 18 is 12. The 12-pin handicap is added to the bowler's score in each game. If a bowler rolls 158 in the first game, his score with handicap is 170. Twelve added to a second-game score of 144 is 156, and 148 plus 12 in the third game is 160. Averages are tabulated each week to assure up-to-date handicaps for each round of bowling. Handicaps may be figured on a team as well as an individual basis. Three individual handicap charts for 180, 190, and 200 scratch appear in Figure 15–9.

A variation for bowling handicaps is to use a scratch of 300. This provides a low average bowler with the opportunity of bowling handicapped games which approach the perfect score of 300.

Golf Handicaps. In golf, handicaps may be figured similarly to those of bowling. They may be calculated by averaging the scores of several rounds, subtracting par from the average score, and multiplying the difference by a percentage such as 75, 80, or 85. However, for precise handicapping, the United States Golf Association method should be utilized. In this system, the handicap is 85 per cent of the average of the lowest ten differentials. Ideally, the best ten of the last 20 scores should be used in the computation, but the number of differentials can be adjusted for as few as five rounds.

The procedures for calculating USGA handicaps are as follows:

1. Differentials are determined by subtracting the course rating, based on the USGA yardage rating system, from the scores of each round.
2. The ten lowest differentials of the last 20 scores are totaled and this sum is applied to the USGA Handicap Differential Chart (see

Fig. 15–11) which specifies handicaps for various ranges of differentials.

3. Handicaps are not assigned to players with fewer than five scores.
4. If fewer than 20 differentials but five or more are available, a supplementary table identifies the number of differentials to be used. Proceed according to the following steps:

   a. Determine the number of differentials.
   b. Compute the average of the differentials.
   c. Multiply the average by ten and apply the product to the USGA Handicap Differential Chart.

For medal or stroke play, the handicap is subtracted from the gross score to equal the net score. A player with a gross score of 92 and a handicap of 15 has a net score of 77. In match play, handicap strokes cannot be utilized at the discretion of the golfer, but must be subtracted in the sequence indicated in the score card handicap column. This procedure takes into account the varying degrees of difficulty of each hole. A nine-hole handicap chart, unofficially adapted from the USGA system, is illustrated in Figure 15–12.

Several one-round or one-day golf handicap systems, the Peoria, Callaway, and Horner, are used to equalize competition, particularly when previous scores are unavailable.

Peoria handicaps are based on six holes, chosen after all of the golfers have left the first tee. Preferably, these should represent two par 3 holes, two par 4's, and two par 5's. The total of the scores for the six holes is multiplied by 3, and par subtracted from the product is the handicap. As a modification, 80 per cent of this result may serve as the handicap.

Handicaps in the Callaway system are figured by applying the scores of each player to a chart which appears in Figure 15–13. Strokes on a specific number of the highest holes plus an adjustment, as indicated on the chart, are deducted for the handicap.

In the Horner system, all 18 holes are classified as birdies, pars, one over par, two over par, and so on. For golfers whose gross scores are 100 or less, the Horner system operates as follows:

1. Select the nine holes with the lowest scores.
2. Count the number of strokes over par for these nine holes to determine the differential.
3. Multiply the differential by 2.
4. Subtract this figure from the actual score to determine the net score.

For players scoring 101 or more, the procedure is the same with the exception that ten holes are used instead of nine. An application of the Horner system is illustrated for eight players:

SCORING CLASSIFI-CATIONS	PLAYERS							
	A	B	C	D	E	F	G	H
Birdies	1	—	—	—	—	—	—	—
Pars	7	2	9	2	3	1	—	1
1 Over	9(1)	12(7)	5	6(6)	7(7)	5(5)	5(5)	1(1)
2 Over	1	3	2	8(2)	3	7(8)	8(10)	4(8)
3 Over	—	1	—	2	4	5	3	4(12)
Gross Scores	82	93	91	100	101	106	110	136
Differentials	1	7	—	8	7	13	15	21
Handicaps	2	14	—	16	14	26	30	42
Net Scores	80	79	91	84	87	80	80	94

10

Point Systems:
Group and Individual

A properly designed and administered point system is an extremely important element in intramural programming. Valid systems measure intramural participation and performance comparable to the manner in which grades signify academic achievement. All games and athletic contests contain some type of scoring mechanism to denote the relative status of participants throughout the contest. A point system is an extension of this scoring concept, cumulatively applied to all activities in the program. The additional interest generated by these systems encourages participation in the program.

In each activity, points are assigned according to the order teams finish in tournament competition. Points for each activity are added throughout the year to give teams an indication of their competitive position among other units. The team or organization which earns the most points at the end of the last programmed activity wins the all-year championship. All-year winners usually receive permanent or rotating awards.

Not all intramural personnel agree with the point system principle. Opponents of point systems argue that participants cease to enter activities for pure enjoyment, and the major objective is to enter and win at any cost for the sake of earning points. To a degree, participation is forced rather than voluntary, violating a primary precept of intramurals. They contend that undue emphasis is placed on some activities because of the large number of points given while others are neglected with low point values or do not fit the pattern of the system.

Opponents also argue that motivation is artificial and perpetuates the notion that a participant must be recognized for everything he accomplishes. Furthermore, they object to the amount of time required to keep office point records up-to-date, particularly for an individual point system. Those in opposition believe that much time and effort would be saved if the point system were eliminated and that it would not reduce participation percentages.

Proponents insist that point systems encourage participation in new as well as established program activities. While enthusiasts participate without a point plan, many additional participants are included in the program as a result of a little added incentive. Not everyone has a wholesome attitude toward physical recreation, and therefore, a slight inducement is necessary to encourage those who may be hesitant about participating. Proponents further suggest that if participants gain beneficial sports experiences from intramural participation, a motivating device such as the point system is not only helpful, but most necessary.

Whether point plans are imperative to the success of intramurals or unnecessary, they are consistently used. When selected or constructed, they should coincide with the purposes of intramurals. If an inequitable point system is adopted, it creates many administrative problems which an intramural director prefers to avoid.

TYPES OF SYSTEMS AND DISTRIBUTION METHODS

Although point systems have comparable objectives, there are perhaps as many variations as the number of programs using them. Most systems have the same basic elements, but the items for which points are awarded produce many combinations. This is necessary in many instances because they must be adapted to local situations.

There are two general types of point systems: (1) one which includes only intramural activities and (2) another which is all-encompassing including intramurals, band, organization membership, committee work, debate, and scholarship. A review of the following items for which points are awarded gives some indication of the possible combinations of the two categories.

1. Scholarship: awarded for high grades and deducted for low grades
2. Publications: editor, business manager, staff members
3. Organizational membership: fraternities, clubs—additional points for officers and committee members
4. Membership in honorary societies
5. Debate and other speech activities
6. Band and instrumental groups
7. Choirs and glee clubs
8. Theatrical groups: actors, stage crew

9. Varsity sports squad members: additional points for letter winners, captains, all-conference, all-district and all-regional players
10. Intramural participants: additional points to winners
11. Intramural council meetings attendance
12. Sportsmanship
13. Physical fitness performances
14. Hygienic habits: posture, cleanliness

One of the most important considerations in establishing a good point system is to be certain participants have equal opportunities to earn points and that they be equitably distributed. It is difficult to justify the all-encompassing point system because there is too much subjective judgment involved for such items as sportsmanship, posture, and cleanliness. It is also doubtful as to whether bonus points attained by only one or two persons (e.g., the captain of a varsity team or a newspaper editor) should be awarded. These are undoubtedly more justifiable for individual rather than group point systems.

In addition to the numerous items for which points are assigned, the combinations are further complicated by the different methods of point distribution. Some of these procedures are briefly surveyed to indicate the types of plans used in intramural programming.

Comparative High–Low Order

After an activity is concluded, each participating group is assigned points according to its respective order of finish. The last place team receives one point; second from the last, two points; third from the last, three points; and so on, and the first place team is awarded points equal to the number of participating teams. When some activities are considered more important than others from the standpoint of interest and number of players on a team, they may be classified into major, intermediate, and minor categories. In this plan, the last place team gets one point for minor, two points for intermediate, and three points for major activities. All team positions are similarly multiplied by one, two, and three points. The group with the highest total for all activities at the end of the year is the all-year champion.

In some systems, points are assigned to only the first four places. The number of points may be 4, 3, 2, 1; 100, 80, 60, 40, or any other four-number combination. This method tends to throw the point system out of balance, because the emphasis is placed on winning one of the four top positions.

Another method used to equate activities and to assign points for comparative rankings is to multiply the number of games each team plays by the number of players required for a team and divide the product by ten. This factor is multiplied by the ranking of each team to give the number of points earned. As an example, eight volleyball teams are in a league with six players on a team and each team plays seven games. Six times 7 divided by 10 equals 4.2. This number multiplied by the ranking of each team results in 33.6 points for the first place team, 29.4 for second place, 25.2 for third place, etc.

Comparative Low–High Order

This procedure is the reverse of the high–low scheme and is similar to cross-country scoring wherein the team with the low total wins. The first place team receives one point and the last place team is awarded points equal to the number of participating teams. There are two disadvantages to this plan: (1) psychologically, there is a preference for having the team with the highest total win and (2) groups that do not enter must be assigned more points than the last place team or it would be advantageous not to enter activities. If this fact is not taken into consideration, groups not entering receive no points, and the winner is given one point.

Comparative Order Plus Entry Points

Teams receive points according to their place of finish as previously described and additionally earn points for entering the tournament. Each team is given 10 points for entering each activity or 30, 20, and 10 points for major, intermediate, and minor activities, respectively. One point may also be given to each individual who enters a sport such as track and swimming. In using the comparative low–high order method, it is necessary to subtract points instead of adding them for entering. The winner could easily end the year with a negative point total.

Comparative Order Plus Game Points

With this method, points are assigned for winning each game in addition to the points that are awarded for the order of finish. Any arbitrary number of points may be established for winning each game such as 2, 5, 10, etc.

Combination Plans

Point systems can be devised to include any part or all of the following distribution methods:

1. Comparative high–low or low–high order.
2. Points distributed to first, second, third, and fourth place teams or more if desired.

3. Entrance points for teams and/or individuals.
4. Points for winning each game.
5. Bonus points.
6. Points for major, intermediate, and minor categories.
7. Separate point plans for individual, dual, and team sports.

SELECTION OF A POINT SYSTEM

Because there are numerous point plans, perhaps no two exactly alike, it is necessary for an intramural director to give careful consideration to some of the positive and negative aspects before devising or adapting a particular system. A point scheme should be designed for the local situation and not selected because it is effective in another intramural program. Every effort should be made to choose a properly balanced plan that will upgrade the program and not one that will detract from satisfactory participation experiences. An inequitable point system can generate considerable ill-will among participants.

Insofar as possible, a point system should supplement the intramural program to the extent that it adds interest and encourages participation, but it should not be emphasized to the degree that it is the most important aspect of a participant's life. When a system gets out of focus, players are often encouraged to use any means, fair or foul, to earn points for their unit.

Both small and large organizations should have an equitable opportunity to accumulate the highest point total. At the same time, the number of entries or teams from a large group should not be restricted. An adjustment for more than one team from an organization can be made by only assigning points to the team that advances farthest in the tournament.

A point system should stress proper balance between participation or entering and performance or winning. If too much credit is given to entering, such as awarding points for more than one team or for each individual entering a track meet or swimming meet, there is a danger of forced participation and the possibility of harming someone's health. An organization sometimes penalizes its members to the extent of paying a fine if they do not enter a tournament in which points are awarded for every person entering. Pressure points should be eliminated from all point plans.

Points should not be assigned for negative participation such as forfeits and the use of ineligible players. If points were awarded for forfeits, groups might resort to bargaining for points on the telephone, particularly if the emphasis is on entrance points. One group might call another and suggest that they will forfeit to their opponents in handball this week if their opponents will forfeit to them in badminton next week. This results in telephone victories, participation points, and no participation.

Methods vary for handling forfeiture points. For each forfeit, a set number of points, perhaps ten, is subtracted from the total number of points earned up to that time; or the number of points the team would have won if they had played the game is eliminated; or no points are assigned for the activity in which the forfeit occurred. These same procedures are followed when a team uses an ineligible player.

A point system should not be complicated to the extent that it is difficult for participants to understand and too time consuming to administer. It should simply record an up-to-date ranking of teams after each activity is completed. When records are not kept up-to-date, the system loses its effectiveness. Often student managers are responsible for recording points.

It is advisable to strike a reasonable medium in determining the size of point figures to be used. Fractions such as ¼ or ½ and large numbers, 10,000 and 100,000, do not add to the simplicity of point administration. On the other hand, because points do not cost anything, it seems logical to use ten or 100 points instead of one.

When devising distribution methods, consideration should be given to assigning different point values to the various activities. These values are determined on the basis of whether the activity is individual, dual, or team; the number of players required for a team; the number of games played; and the number of teams or entries competing. Activities with different point values may be divided into groups or classes. Names used to identify these groups are unimportant, but if they are referred to as major, intermediate, and minor, it should be understood that these classifications do not mean one activity is more important than another. They are classified strictly on the basis of the above factors.

The distribution of points should be adaptable to all types of competition. The system should be applicable to meets, round robin, single elimination, double elimination, consolation, challenge, and combination tournaments.

A point system's stability is reduced if bonus points are assigned for such things as winning games outside the unit of participation, entering every event, or enrolling every member of an organization in activities. It is also doubtful if points should be awarded for items such as sportsmanship, which cannot be measured objectively. These elements are extremely important and are emphasized through sportsmanship programs, but the inclusion of subjective items and bonus points tends to reduce the validity of point systems. Awarding points in the same activity more than once during the year without making an appropriate adjustment in point values also reduces the system's equitability. In intramurals, attention must always be given to fair competition and this especially applies to point distribution methods.

Point plans should be designed so that it is unnecessary to enter every sport or to win every championship. Obviously, teams are required to enter most activities, but it should be possible to win first place in a few, finish reasonably high in several more, finish low in some, and perhaps not enter one or two. Ideally, year-end point totals should be relatively close, and the all-year winner should not be decided until intramural activities for the year are almost concluded. If a team is far in advance of other groups and a winner is determined early, or if there is a wide range of total point distributions, it is highly possible the point system is in need of adjustment.

Occasionally, a successful competitive point system encourages the intramural director to add new activities or too many point activities to the program. This produces pressure participation and excessively involved participants. The addition of new activities should not be discouraged, but it is doubtful if it is necessary for them to be offered on a point basis. The mere fact that an activity is excluded from the point system does not mean it is less important than those for which points are assigned.

Point systems for groups and individuals are beneficial or detrimental to intramurals in direct proportion to the adequacy with which they are selected and administered. As indicated above, some of the watch words are simplicity, equality, participation, performance, fairness, uniformity, adaptability, and conformity. To be effective, a point system must be continually evaluated to keep it in proper balance with the other phases of the program.

PARTICIPATION–PERFORMANCE POINT SYSTEM

An intramural point system is presented to serve as a guide for those who are responsible for selecting or developing one. The basic considerations previously summarized are incorporated in this participation–performance point system. It evaluates group or individual performances and is adaptable to any form of competition—leagues, meets, single elimination, double elimination, consolation, and challenge tournaments. There are four simple procedures involved in administering this system:

1. Refer to the minimum–maximum scale to identify the point range of the activities.
2. Determine the number of teams or places for which points are to be assigned.
3. Refer to the participation–performance point tables for the actual point distributions.

4. Record the accumulated point totals throughout the intramural year.

Minimum–Maximum Scale

The minimum–maximum scale categorizes activities into three divisions: (1) the minor division of 25 minimum and 75 maximum points, (2) the intermediate division of 35 minimum and 100 maximum points, and (3) the major division of 50 minimum and 150 maximum points. (See Fig. 10-1.) For grouping these activities, consideration is given to the number of teams involved, the number of players for each team, the competitive tournament used, and the number of games played. Teams that play a round robin schedule deserve more points than those competing in a one- or two-day meet. Also, a nine-player softball team should be credited with more points than a four-player tennis team. Teams entered in a round robin play more games than an equal number of teams participating in a single elimination tournament. Although these factors are relatively stable, it may be necessary to revise the scale according to local conditions.

If points are awarded in an activity more than once during the year, the minimum and maximum points must be adjusted. As an example, when points are assigned for bowling in the fall and again in the winter, the minimum–maximum scale may be set at 25–75, which equals half of the 50–150 points assigned for one league during the year.

Point Distribution

In the participation–performance point plan, the first place team in each activity receives the maximum number of points, and the last place team receives the minimum number of points. Teams finishing between are assigned points proportional to their place of finish. The size of the point interval between places is determined by the number of teams competing or the number of places to be awarded points. In the 50–150 scale, the interval for eleven places is ten: 50, 60, 70, 80, 90, 100, 110, 120, 130, 140, and 150. For twenty-one places, the interval is five.

The number of places to be assigned points sometimes produces intervals of fractions or decimals instead of whole numbers. These are eliminated by using equally distributed whole number intervals; e.g., 5 and 4. With twelve places in a 25–75 scale, the interval between first and second place is 5, second and third is 4, third and fourth is 5, etc.

Application of Points for Competition

The participation–performance system can be applied to any type of competitive structure which provides a ranking or grouping of teams or

ACTIVITY	MINIMUM POINTS	MAXIMUM POINTS
ARCHERY	25	75
BADMINTON	25	75
BASKETBALL (MAJOR)	50	150
BASKETBALL (MINOR)	25	75
BOWLING	50	150
CROSS COUNTRY	25	75
FENCING	25	75
FREE THROW CONTEST	25	75
GOLF	35	100
HANDBALL	25	75
HOCKEY	50	150
HORSESHOES	25	75
PADDLEBALL	25	75
RELAYS	25	75
SPEED SKATING	35	100
SOCCER	50	150
SOFTBALL (FAST PITCH)	50	150
SOFTBALL (SLOW PITCH)	50	150
SWIMMING	35	100
TABLE TENNIS	25	75
TENNIS	35	100
TOUCH FOOTBALL	50	150
TRACK	35	100
VOLLEYBALL	50	150
WATER POLO	25	75
WRESTLING	35	100

Fig. 10–1. Participation–Performance Point System: Minimum–Maximum Scale.

individuals. Examples of these applications are presented in the following sections.

Leagues and Meets. The distribution of points for a bowling league (round robin) and a track meet is shown in Figure 10–2. Points are comparably distributed for leagues and meets, but in this example, bowling is assigned points according to the 50–150, major division scale and track is in the 35–100, intermediate category. The participation–performance plan permits an organization to enter any number of teams,

BOWLING LEAGUE

	TEAMS	WON	LOST	PERCENT	POINTS
1.	ALLEY OOPS	45	15	.750	150
2.	KING PINS	41	19	.683	143
3.	FOUR FRAMES	38	22	.633	137
4.	KEGLERS	35	25	.583	130
5.	CLEAN SWEEPERS	33	27	.550	123
6.	BOWLING BELLES	32	28	.533	117
7.	PIN SPLITTERS	30	30	.500	110
8.	GUTTER BALLS I	29	31	.483) TIE	100
9.	LUCKY STRIKES	29	31	.483)	100
10.	APPROACHABLES	28	32	.467	90
11.	BOWL WEEVILS	27	33	.450	83
12.	SPLITFENDERS	26	34	.433	77
13.	WHOLLY ROLLERS	24	36	.400	70
14.	POCKET POUNDERS	23	37	.383	63
15.	GUTTER BALLS II	21	39	.350	57
16.	LEAGUE LEADERS	19	41	.317	50

TRACK MEET

	TEAMS	PLACE	POINTS
1.	LIMBO A.C.	1	100
2.	BRAND X	2	96
3.	DAILY DOZEN	3) TIE	89.5
4.	MUDDERS A.C.	3)	89.5
5.	DROP OUTS	5	83
6.	ALL STARES	6	78
7.	MEDICARE A.C.	7	74
8.	ROAD RUNNERS	8	70
9.	VERGELTUNGSWAFFE	9	65
10.	FIGHTING SAINTS A.C.	10	61
11.	GREYHOUNDS	11	57
12.	SUPREME SIX	12	52
13.	SCHOLARS A.C.	13	48
14.	STRIDERS A.C.	14	43
15.	LANE STRADDLERS	15) TIE	37
16.	SPEED DEMONS	15)	37

Fig. 10–2. Participation–Performance Point Distribution. (Top) Bowling League. (Bottom) Track Meet.

but only the one which advances the farthest earns points. In a sense, there is an advantage of entering more than one team in that the additional teams may serve as a defensive mechanism preventing others from earning points. Extra teams also reduce the size of the interval.

In bowling, the Gutter Balls received 100 points for finishing in a tie for eighth place. The Gutter Balls' second team finished in fifteenth place and received no points although they are listed for 57 points. In the accumulative point tables, the Gutter Balls' organization is credited with only 100 points. To establish the correct interval, it is necessary to list all teams, including those which represent the same organization.

In this illustration, the second Gutter Balls' team did not provide much of a defense in preventing other teams from earning points. While they were winning 21 games, they also lost 39, which may have assisted other teams in gaining a higher position in the standings. The second team's effectiveness in restricting the advancement of other teams depends on whether its victories were against the top teams in the league and those which may have accumulated high point totals in other activities.

In case of ties in the standings, the number of points assigned to these positions is added, and the total is divided by the number of teams tied. In the track meet (Fig. 10–2) the Daily Dozen and Mudders A.C. are tied for third place. The points assigned to third and fourth place are 92 and 87. The sum of these numbers is 179, which divided by 2 equals 89.9. Each of the tied teams receives 89.5 points.

Some teams do not earn "meet" points in a track or swimming meet. In this instance, places can be determined by the number of participants representing each organization, or a tie can be declared among all "non-meet" point teams, and participation–performance points assigned according to the foregoing tie procedure.

Individual and Dual Competition.   It is not necessary to have all team competition with the participation–performance point system. For example, if three- or four-man teams are not used in activities such as tennis, golf, horseshoes, or paddleball, points may be given to the singles player or doubles players who advance the farthest. As is the case with teams, any number of individuals can enter, but only one singles player or two doubles players may earn points for the unit.

Single Elimination.   The touch football Class A, B, C, and D playoffs in Figure 10–3 illustrate how the participation–performance point system applies to single elimination competition. In the playoffs, touch football teams are classified on the basis of the round robin-elimination method. First place teams in each four-team league are grouped in Class A, second place teams in Class B, third in Class C, and fourth in Class D. Losers of the first round in Class D receive the minimum points of 50. The winner in Class A is awarded the maximum points, 150, with other teams earning points proportional to their final position in the playoffs.

It should be noted that the winners of one class are awarded as many points as the losers in the first round of the class immediately above. The Doves earn 100 points for winning Class C, as do the losers in the first round of Class B. It seems reasonably logical to have a winning team in one class earn as many points as the teams losing their first game in the next higher class.

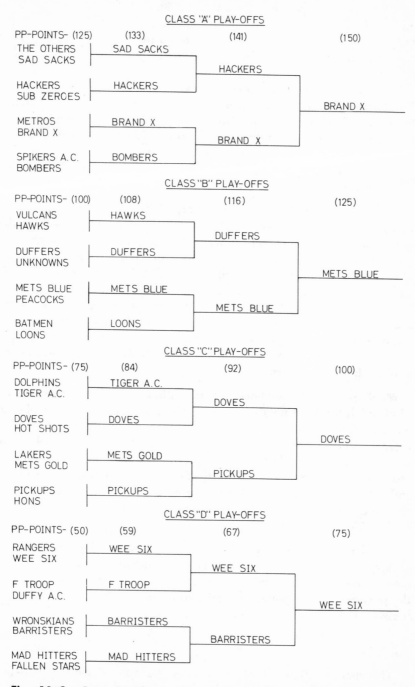

Fig. 10–3. Point Distribution for Touch Football Elimination Playoffs.

Note also that the Mets have two entries, the Blue team in Class B and the Gold team in Class C. The Gold team did not receive 84 points, but prevented the Lakers from advancing to the 84-point bracket. Since the Blue team advanced farthest, it earned 125 points in the Class B play-offs.

For single elimination tournaments not divided into classes, points are listed across the bottom or top of each round, and teams or participants losing in a round receive the listed number of points. Applying points to a single elimination tournament is illustrated in the top half of Figure 9–9. The winner Don received 75 points; the loser of the finals, Gus, 58; Art and Fox, the two semi-final losers, 42; and the four losers in the first round, Bob, Cal, Edd, and Hub, 25.

Double and Semi-Double Elimination. The same general pattern of applying points for single elimination tournaments is applicable to double and semi-double elimination tournaments. In some instances, more than one loser in the same round receives the same point totals, and in other rounds only one is assigned points. Point distributions for back-to-back and over-under double elimination tournaments are shown in Figure 9–5. For the over-under tournament, points appear at the bottom of the brackets because participants are eliminated in the losers' division.

Point arrangements for a semi-double elimination tournament are listed in Figure 9–6. These points are distributed similarly to the back-to-back double elimination tournament.

Mueller-Anderson Playback. This continuous playback tournament is ideal for distributing points because each of the contestants is ranked in order of finish. There is no need for participants in the same round to receive identical point totals. In the bottom half of Figure 9–9, points for an eight-team Mueller-Anderson playback tournament are as follows: first—75, second—68, third—61, fourth—54, fifth—46, sixth—39, seventh—32, eighth—25. For a single elimination tournament of eight participants, the distribution is: first round—25, second round—42, third round—58, and the finalist—75.

Challenge Tournaments. Participation–performance points may also be applied to challenge tournaments. For example, in a funnel tournament, players receive individualized points for the ladder portion and for the pyramid section, points are assigned to groups of individuals in each horizontal row.

Point Totals

The chart in Figure 10–4 contains an example of participation–performance all-year point totals. There are twenty-one sports in this illus-

LEGEND
□ - WINNERS
D - DROPPED
O - NO ENTRY
F - FORFEIT
I - INELIGIBLE PLAYER

TEAM	PLACE	TOTAL POINTS	TRACK	TENNIS	GOLF	SOFTBALL	BASEBALL	SWIMMING	WRESTLING	VOLLEYBALL	SQUASH	FREE THROWS	ICE HOCKEY	BOWLING	BASKETBALL (B)	BASKETBALL (A)	PADDLEBALL	RIFLE SHOOTING	HORSESHOES	HAND BALL	TABLE TENNIS	TOUCH FOOTBALL	CROSS COUNTRY
NO NAMES	15	1375	65	87	35	100	106	67	55	131	25	38	94	119	46	88	25	57	31	0	50	112	44
LIMBO A.C.	13	1401	100	0	76	94	119	44	59	100	65	35	112	100	43	81	28	61	25	31	28	144	56
NERVOUS RECS	8	1445	52	83	88	69	112	63	51	106	75	0	138	69	25	138	0	96	28	42	44	106	60
15TH STREETERS	11	1412	92	D	84	50	150	90	96	56	48	52	106	112	71	50	52	65	0	28	47	138	25
BRAND X	10	1424	96	43	72	150	50	0	47	144	52	65	56	106	0	131	69	48	62	45	72	50	66
ATROPHIEDS	4	1525	61	92	80	112	69	86	43	94	45	69	62	138	68	56	62	52	35	38	69	131	63
FIGHTING SAINTS	9	1432	83	52	96	56	131	40	67	75	55	31	131	I	39	125	65	100	55	72	75	56	28
SAD SACKS	17	1358	87	57	47	144	56	95	39	125	38	45	88	62	0	144	55	0	38	35	31	119	53
PUSSYCAT A.C.	7	1474	74	39	92	62	144	49	88	62	69	42	119	56	36	119	31	74	58	48	56	62	50
MENTAL MIDGETS	12	1404	35	61	43	106	125	58	84	69	35	62	100	144	50	62	42	70	69	25	53	125	47
ROOKIES A.C.	5	1495	39	100	39	75	62	35	100	50	31	58	150	88	61	100	58	92	52	55	60	81	31
EASY RIDERS	2	1572	70	78	67	88	100	81	92	112	62	28	81	81	64	106	45	87	65	52	63	75	75
UNTOUCHABLES	1	1602	78	48	100	81	94	54	35	138	75	25	125	94	54	69	72	78	48	69	25	150	40
GREYHOUNDS	14	1400	57	96	63	125	88	81	80	88	28	55	81	125	32	75	35	35	42	65	F	100	37
PICKUPS	16	1372	48	70	55	81	81	0	76	88	72	48	75	50	57	75	48	83	72	58	37	94	34
MORTICIANS	3	1536	65	65	59	131	138	77	63	81	48	72	131	50	29	150	38	43	75	62	66	69	72
BAND AIDS	6	1482	43	74	51	119	75	63	76	150	43	72	69	131	75	94	38	39	45	75	40	88	69

Fig. 10-4. Participation–Performance Point Totals.

tration, and if every sport is entered, the maximum number of points is 2250 and the minimum 760. The seventeen teams averaged 1512 points.

The Untouchables won the all-year championship with 1602 total points. They won championships in touch football and golf, and finished last in table tennis and the free throw contest. Easy Riders, the second place team, won three championships but failed to compile enough points in other sports to overtake the first place team. The Morticians won third place, although a team was not entered in track. It is also significant that the Atrophieds finished in fourth place without winning a champion-ship. The last place team, Sad Sacks, ended the year with 1358 total points, just 244 points behind the first place total.

Point Tables

If point systems are refigured each time a tournament is conducted, the chance of error increases, intervals may vary each time, and it is time consuming. For these reasons it is advisable to use point tables which list point distributions. Participation–performance point tables for major, intermediate, and minor categories are available in Chapter 15, Figures 15–14, 15–15, and 15–16. When the number of places for which points are to be assigned is determined, selection of the correct listing in the table reveals the number of points for each position. These point tables further simplify the administration of the participation–performance point system.

INDIVIDUAL POINT SYSTEMS

Individual point systems are similar to group systems, and in many instances, the methods of point distribution are used interchangeably. However, they are not used as extensively as group plans. Group systems have greater continuity from year to year than individual schemes. Intra-mural organizations maintain their identity over an extended period of time, whereas individuals leave the program after a few years. Organiza-tions can compare point standings from year to year, but these traditions cannot be established among individual point plans.

A carefully planned and administered individual point system creates interest and encourages participation in intramurals. Participants are in-terested in knowing their relative competitive standing among other individuals. Participation points are given for being members of a team and taking part in nonteam activities, and performance points are awarded if their team wins or if they win in individual competition. An individual point system serves as a stimulus for participation in the following ways:

1. Participants are encouraged to belong to a team resulting in the formation of more teams.
2. Interest is created in noncompetitive activities and provides an incentive for the individual to seek physical recreation apart from the group.
3. Participants are encouraged to obtain an overall knowledge of activities rather than specializing in a few.
4. Students enroll in physical education classes or join sports clubs to learn basic skills which enhance their opportunities for success in intramurals.
5. All-encompassing plans encourage participation in all institutional activities, not just intramurals, thus broadening the learning experiences of each participant.
6. Participants are individually recognized, whereas only a few persons gain recognition playing on a championship team.

The individual point system serves as a basis for making awards to either one or several of the top ranking performers. Presenting awards only to first place team members overlooks the skilled participant who belongs to an organization which does not field a strong team. Although he competes faithfully with his unit for several years, there is little opportunity for recognition because of the team's lack of success. The individual plan enables a deserving participant to gain recognition regardless of team success. Awards in the form of trophies, plaques, medals, blankets, numerals, and letters are presented to all-year individual winners.

Record keeping for individual point systems is more detailed than for group plans. Managers or clerical assistants frequently assume the responsibility for this detail. The problem of recording individual points is reduced if the intramural staff furnishes individual and group scoring charts to units for their bulletin boards. Team managers keep the records up-to-date so each member knows the ranking of his organization and his personal participation–performance record. The intramural clerical staff maintains a similar record which is available to every unit manager for checking purposes.

In establishing an individual point system, it is necessary to observe precaution to assure effective administration and desirable outcomes. The basic considerations discussed earlier in this chapter apply to individual as well as group plans.

Individual scoring systems are used for only intramurals or for all activities, and they are based either on team participation, individual participation, or a combination of these methods.

Team Scoring

In the team plan, points are assigned to individuals according to their team's performance. However, if the participant does not take part in all games, he receives points in proportion to the number of games he plays. As an example, if his team earned 100 participation–performance points in softball and he only played in one of ten games, ten points or one-tenth of the total is credited to his account.

Another plan does not consider the number of games played by each member, but gives blanket point coverage to all team members. The first four teams receive 5, 4, 3, and 2 points, respectively, and all others receive 1 point. Individuals are assigned the same number of points as those earned by their team. This avoids excessive record keeping with the same totals transferred from the team chart to individual records. If major and minor classifications are used, the number of points is doubled for those in the major category.

Individual Scoring

This plan does not take into account results of team play. Consideration is given only to the individual's participation and performance. Points are awarded for performances in track, swimming, wrestling, handball, paddleball, squash, tennis, table tennis, horseshoes, badminton, archery, bowling, free throws, golf, fencing, and rifle shooting or any other activity in which he competes individually. The participation–performance point system or a similar method of distribution may be used for awarding points. In addition, entrance points can be assigned for participation on teams and for participation in noncompetitive activities. Individual plans frequently include items which are measured subjectively such as sportsmanship, dependability, posture, and health habits.

Combination Scoring

Combination team and individual plans measure participation and performance in team games as well as individual, competitive, and noncompetitive activities. This plan is more effective than either of the above schemes for determining an individual's overall rating in intramurals. While the team scoring method promotes strong group spirit for sports such as track, swimming, and wrestling, it gives a team member who does not contribute "meet" points to the team total, the same rating as the individual who wins place points in one or more events.

Through individual point systems it is possible to rank not only participants but also organizations. For example, points for individuals are awarded and recorded. Group rankings are then determined by adding together the total points earned by individual members of each group.

Sigma Delta Psi Point System

Another type of point system designed for self-testing activities is used in Sigma Delta Psi, the national honorary athletic fraternity. In these tests, certain standards are established which the participant tries to attain. He earns points not only for attempting to pass the tests and for passing them, but also for successful performance beyond the minimum requirement. The Sigma Delta Psi point system does not measure the individual's performance against an opponent, success as a member of a team, or the number of participations, but it evaluates his ability to compete against predetermined standards.

A maximum of 100 points is awarded for achievement at the top of the scale in each activity, and a minimum of one point is given at the bottom of the scale. Test results which fall between these limitations are assigned proportional points. If the student is tested in twelve activities, the maximum total points is 1200.

For individual competition, a participant accumulates points according to his performances in each self-testing event. The person with the highest total for all activities is the winner. For group competition, each organization enters any number of competitors, but only the top ten individual totals apply toward the team championship. The organization accumulating the highest total for the top ten individuals is the winner. It is also possible to name all-around individual winners as well as individual winners for each event. Sigma Delta Psi requirements and scoring tables appear in Appendix C.

11

Rules and Regulations

Before anything can exist, some limitations must be created to identify its existence. Every organization, program, business, educational institution, etc., must have rules and regulations, a code of operation, or it cannot function, and so too it is true of intramural programs. Although some participants may feel that rules and regulations are an infringement on an individual's rights they are absolutely and undeniably necessary for intramural programming.

There is a reluctance on the part of some individuals to accept this fact. Many of them would prefer to see rules abolished or changed to favor their point of view. Others believe that rules are made to be broken and proceed to challenge them to see if they are breakable.

To the contrary, rules are not created for these purposes, but rather to serve as a guide for enjoyable intramural participation. The spirit of the rules should be constantly emphasized, and participants should know, understand, and support the limitations established by them. The intramural program is voluntary, and those who wish to participate must be willing to pay the small price of accepting the rules. Others who are unwilling to uphold them are under no obligation to participate, and they may be well advised not to do so.

Players should not only abide by the rules, but also enlist the support of all other team members. They should attempt to understand an implement the philosophy that anyone who violates the rules and wins, realistically has not won at all. Their cooperation will result in a better intramural program for everyone.

Game rules, eligibility rules, disciplinary procedures, and health and safety regulations are reviewed in this chapter.

GAME RULES

Game rules apply specifically to each individual activity. They prescribe patterns of action and conduct to which players must conform. Those who most skillfully perform the required actions are identified as the winners of the rules.

Modifications of Rules

One of the unique aspects of intramurals is that games can be made extremely flexible through rules modifications. Rule books are generally written for highly skilled athletes and regulation facilities. For intramurals, it is often necessary or desirable to alter the pattern of play to fit the local situation. These changes involve shortening playing times, limiting distances, reducing or expanding the number of players, changing the equipment, and modifying the style of play. This type of adaptability challenges the intramural director's creativity, and when properly applied, modifications increase the potential of intramural games.

Rules and some modifications of the principal games played in intramural programs are presented in Chapter 7.

Officiating Game Rules

The dualistic nature of games is such that each competitive side attempts through offensive and defensive maneuvers to restrict or place the opposition at a disadvantage. This type of conflict occasionally causes rules violations which may be relatively neutralized by compensatory adjustments specified in the rules. Games must be officiated to identify these infractions and to administer the appropriate equalizing action. Many intramural games such as golf, bowling, tennis, and handball are self-administered, but other team games and meets require the services of officials.

Quality officiating is perhaps the most important element of the competitive phase of intramurals. A corps of game officials, referees, umpires, scorekeepers, and timers, not only administer events and games according to the prescribed rules, but also assist in controlling player eligibility by reporting inconsistencies. Numerous game rules protests are prevented through good officiating.

Selection of Officials. Officials may be selected from varsity athletes, physical education majors, or other individuals who have an interest in sports officiating. All candidates should be properly trained in rules interpretation and officiating techniques. This may be accomplished through interpretation meetings, clinics, and written and practical examinations. Films, slides, and video tape recordings on the various phases of officiating may be utilized for these purposes. In some programs, the intramural staff organizes an intramural officials' association to carry out this educational training program.

Volunteer officials are used in some programs to administer intramural contests. Varsity players may also be assigned with the cooperation of the coach who usually encourages this experience, because it enables players to become better acquainted with the application of rules to game situations. Another method is to require each participating team to furnish an extra player who serves as the referee. These individuals do not officiate at the games involving their teammates, but are sent to an adjoining field or court, and in turn two extra players from another area are assigned to work their game. The most satisfactory arrangement, however, is for the intramural staff to train and assign a corps of game officials.

Payment of Officials.   If at all possible, officials should be paid for their services. Payment at a rate slightly above average wages enables the intramural staff to secure qualified candidates, and they can be required to assume greater responsibility. If officials are not paid or are paid a meager fee, they may assume their work is unappreciated and be less accountable for efficient performances.

Incentive pay scales may be incorporated to encourage improved officiating. Inexperienced officials can be paid the minimum wage, and those who excel in performing their duties may be raised to a higher pay rate. Officials may be assigned to work several games in one day because playing times are usually reduced.

Game officials should wear distinguishing uniforms such as regular referee shirts or T-shirts lettered with the words "Intramural Official." Inexpensive bibs made out of black and white striped material, which slip over the head and tie around the waist with two apron strings, are also available. These can be worn over jackets or sweaters on cold days and over T-shirts on warm days for indoor officiating. Sometimes officials are permitted to keep their officiating uniforms as extra compensation.

Rating of Officials.   It is advisable to rate game officials and to assign the ones who most consistently give the best performance. Those whose names appear at the top of the list should be permitted to work as frequently as they wish. A rating list provides competition among officials and encourages each one to do his best.

Team captains, intramural supervisors, and other staff members should cooperate in rating officials. A form similar to the one shown in Figure 11–1 can be completed by each team captain at the end of the games.

```
┌─────────────────────────────────┬─────────────────────────────────┐
│      I-M  OFFICIALS'            │                                 │
│      RATING  FORM               │  LINESMAN                       │
│  REFEREE                        │                                 │
│                                 │    Knowledge of Rules      3 2 1 0 │
│    Knowledge of Rules    3 2 1 0 │    Impartiality and Fairness  3 2 1 0 │
│    Impartiality and Fairness 3 2 1 0 │ Ability to follow the ball or play 3 2 1 0 │
│  Ability to follow the ball or play 3 2 1 0 │ Consistency in making calls  3 2 1 0 │
│  Consistency in making calls  3 2 1 0 │        OVERALL  RATING          │
│        OVERALL  RATING          │  3-Excellent           2-Good   │
│  3-Excellent          2-Good    │  1-Fair                0-Poor   │
│  1-Fair               0-Poor    │                                 │
│                                 │  TEAM_____ │
│  UMPIRE                         │                                 │
│    Knowledge of Rules    3 2 1 0 │  CAPTAIN_____ │
│    Impartiality and Fairness 3 2 1 0 │                                 │
│  Ability to follow the ball or play 3 2 1 0 │ DATE OF GAME_____ │
│  Consistency in making calls 3 2 1 0 │                                 │
│        OVERALL  RATING          │  COMMENTS:_____ │
│  3-Excellent          2-Good    │  _____ │
│  1-Fair               0-Poor    │                                 │
└─────────────────────────────────┴─────────────────────────────────┘
```

Fig. 11–1. Officials' Rating Form. (Left) Front. (Right) Back.

Although it is logical to assume that losing captains rate officials lower than winning ones, raising some doubt about their validity, trends of weak and strong points emerge over a period of several games. Ratings minus team designations should be made available to officials so they may follow their progress.

Sportsmanship Rating of Teams. Game officials should also rate teams on sportsmanship. The philosophy behind sportsmanship is that each player should react to officials and opponents with the same respect and consideration he wants to receive from them. Unsportsmanlike conduct is usually a sign of emotional immaturity, and one of the desired outcomes of intramural participation is that players learn discipline and self-control.

In rating teams on sportsmanship, officials should consider the stability of the team, acceptance of the rules and regulations, respect for their opponents and attitude toward officials. After formulating a general opinion of the team's conduct, the official should give an overall rating based on the following scale:

3–No difficulty
2–Occasional verbal disagreement
1–Unreasonable comments, complaining, arguing
0–Abusive language, chronic complaining, violent protesting

In this plan, teams with a "0" rating or several "1" ratings are requested to explain their actions and to show cause why they should not be dropped from the intramural program.

Critics of a two-way, officials–sportsmanship rating system may argue the validity of these ratings. The real value comes from the fact that poor officiating and unsportsmanlike conduct are constantly brought to the attention of officials and players. An official is more concerned about doing a good job if he knows he is being rated on his performance, and he has less tendency to loaf and to argue needlessly with players. Similarly, a team will be more cautious in their actions if these may result in their suspension from the program. Rating teams on sportsmanship in each game is more effective than telling them at meetings that good sportsmanship is important.

Conduct of Players

Sometimes participants develop the misconception that games involving body contact should be played in a manner that results in excessively rough play, unsportsmanlike conduct, and injured players. This attitude may particularly evolve as intramural directors attempt to stimulate program interest by increasing the competitiveness of the activities. As competition increases, officiating must be more strict to control player actions in the games.

Intramural contests should always be conducted in an environment of sportsmanship and understanding. Players must respect officials and members of the opposite team regardless of the severity of competition. All games require participation within reasonable common sense limits. Conduct outside of these limitations should not be tolerated or the program will deteriorate.

The following rule assists in maintaining the standards of acceptable conduct: Any participant who fights, strikes another individual, in an intramural contest, automatically suspends himself from further intramural participation. When this rule is invoked, it is advisable to make the suspension indefinite until the violator makes a commitment to accept the decisions of game officials and the "give and take" of competition. Games consist of errors made by players and officials, and when an enforcement is made, it usually results in displeasure for the offending players. However, games must be accepted for what they were intended to be and not as each individual would prefer to play them.

ELIGIBILITY RULES

In intramural programming, rules must be devised to define who is eligible to participate and under what circumstances. Eligibility rules relate to both individuals and organizations and are so categorized in the following sections.

Emphasis should be placed on equality of participation and simplicity because participants cannot be expected to know a large group of intricate rules and interpretations, many of which may be unenforceable. Eligibility rules should be periodically evaluated to determine applicability, and enforcements must be made equitably. If exceptions are made to the rules, there may be some doubt as to the need for them.

Individual Eligibility

Rules in this group apply to participants regardless of their affiliation. Some of them are more appropriate for intramurals in educational institutions, but they may be adapted for use in other programs.

Scholarship. Originally intramural programs were strict with regard to scholarship eligibility, and candidates had to fulfill requirements similar to those for varsity sports. Before participating, an individual had to be certified by the proper school authorities. The clerical work involved in preparing eligibility lists proved burdensome to the extent that the practice was discontinued.

A subsequent step was to prohibit students on probation from participating in intramurals. However, where large enrollments were involved, much effort was required to check the status of all the players and generally this practice, too, was found to be impractical and undesirable.

Most intramural programs follow the rule that any persons enrolled in an institution or affiliated with it are eligible to take part in intramurals. In large colleges and universities, there may be some restriction on the minimum number and kinds of credit to control individuals who may wish to enroll in correspondence or extension courses just to be eligible for intramurals.

From an intramural standpoint, there is no logic in depriving individuals of needed exercise and recreation. It would seem more advisable to encourage them to participate in wholesome physical recreation programs rather than in some of the other forms of entertainment and amusements that are available to them. One of the arguments in favor of intramurals is that participants are able to study better after recreating. Some studies indicate a positive correlation between scholarship and intramural participation.

Participation Limitations. Usually players are limited to playing on one team in the same activity. However, some directors grant special permission to play on two teams in the same sport provided teams represent different units of participation. Also as a protection against overexertion in some activities, individuals are limited to a certain number of events, such as three or four, in track and swimming.

Allowing players to play on two teams causes scheduling difficulties if the teams involved are scheduled to play at the same time. This is a problem if team A is scheduled to play against team B and several of the players on both teams also play on other teams. Theoretically there could be thirty-six scheduling conflicts if A and B were to play each other in a softball game.

Another drawback of an individual being a member of two different teams is that they may meet in the playoffs. When submitting entries, requiring players to designate which team they will play with in the playoffs eliminates this potential conflict.

Letter Winners. Varsity lettermen are usually prohibited from competing in sports in which the awards were earned. This restriction may also apply to transfer athletes who receive letters from other institutions.

Within small programs, there is a reasonably clear-cut distinction between abilities of an intramural and varsity player. In institutions with large enrollments, there is a wide range of ability and differences are not as clearly defined. Numerous individuals participating in intramurals may possess the skills to make the varsity squad, but do not try out for varsity teams because they must work, are too busy pursuing a professional degree in engineering, medicine, law, or dentistry, lack confidence in themselves, or were not recruited. Because of the lettermen's rule, some transfers who have earned varsity awards elsewhere are ineligible for intramurals and yet are not as skilled as some of the players in intramurals. It seems somewhat unjust to prohibit these persons of lesser ability from participating as a result of earning letters in small schools.

In some programs, all letter winners are barred from intramural participation and in others, the rule is liberalized to make them eligible on a limited basis. Some intramural personnel feel the use of lettermen is legitimate, particularly if intramural competition is organized on a Class A, B, C, D basis. Class structuring provides opportunities for above average, average, and below average ability participants to experience reasonable success at the various levels of competition.

Since it is humanly impossible for an intramural staff to categorize the ability of participants by observing them in action, it is necessary for each director to establish lettermen rules that will result in the greatest benefits for the greatest number of individuals. Several ideas are suggested which may be utilized to overcome this problem:

1. Allow only one letterman to be a member of an intramural team or permit only one actually to play in a game at any given time.
2. Require lettermen to wait one year, or other stated period of time, after varsity competition before being eligible for intramurals.
3. Arrange special leagues composed of lettermen.
4. Permit lettermen to play in graduate and faculty leagues.
5. Bar local varsity lettermen and those who attended institutions of comparable size.

Varsity and Freshman Squads. Members of varsity and freshman squads are barred from intramural participation in sports in which they are competing and usually from other intramural activities unless the coach registers his consent with the intramural staff. Procedures vary for this rule depending on the coach and the program. Some varsity coaches do not want their candidates to play in intramurals because of potential injuries, or because they feel squad members get enough exercise and should spend extra time studying. Others do not object to participation in less strenuous activities such as bowling, table tennis, or free throw contests.

One of the major problems with this rule is determining the status of players dropped from varsity and freshman squads. Early in the season squads are usually very large, and it is customary for coaches to make a number of cuts until a limited number of candidates remain. If varsity and intramural seasons are conducted simultaneously, enforcement of this rule places a hardship on candidates not clearly of varsity caliber, but whose enthusiasm caused them to try out for the team. This difficulty may be partially avoided by scheduling intramural activities to start later than varsity practices. With this procedure, the rule does not go into effect until varsity and freshman squads are reduced. However, the delay is not always possible on account of limited playing facilities and other extenuating circumstances.

A possible solution to this problem is to bar players who are retained on the varsity and freshman squads after the first game has been played. There are two reasons for choosing this deadline. First, coaches should know by this time which players are to be retained on the squads; second, it is not advisable to prolong the time limit because dropped squad members cannot be transferred to intramural teams without disrupting the latter's competition. The appearance of newcomers on a team after it has been organized may cause resentment on the part of regular members who would be subsequently asked to serve as substitutes.

Coaches should provide a list of squad members considered to be varsity caliber and potential letter winners. The posting or distribution of such lists gives each player a definite varsity or nonvarsity status. For freshman squads not playing scheduled games, a specific cut-off date may be established such as four weeks after practice officially begins.

Another problem involves the exceptional athlete who has not earned a letter but becomes scholastically ineligible for the varsity, and transfers who are ineligible for competition for one year because of the residence rule. A suggested regulation covering this category is that athletes who are scholastically ineligible for intercollegiate competition and freshman participation, and transfers who are ineligible to compete intercollegiately due to the residence rule, are not eligible to participate in the intramural sports of their specialty.

Athletes in this category may subsequently decide not to go out for varsity sports, but until a determination can be made in consultation with varsity coaches, they should remain ineligible for intramural participation. In some programs, these exceptional athletes are intramurally ineligible by a rule which states that the intramural staff, in cooperation with varsity coaches, may exercise authority to bar from intramural participation any individual of varsity caliber who is not out for varsity competition.

Professional Athletes.   Eligibility rules regarding professional athletes in sports such as football, baseball, basketball, and ice hockey usually consist of one of the following:

1. Permitted to play without restrictions.
2. Barred from all intramural sports.
3. Restricted from participating only in the sport in which they are professional.

If professional players are allowed to participate, a star pitcher in baseball or goalie in ice hockey can be responsible for easy victories to the point that opponents become discouraged. On the other hand, the rule that bars a former professional from all sports is not in harmony with the principles of intramurals. It prevents, for example, a professional baseball player from participating in sports such as soccer, handball, and volleyball, games entirely unlike baseball. The third rule of restricting participation only in their professional sport seems to be the most equitable. In some instances, this rule may be liberalized depending on the degree of professionalism. Many athletes may try out for professional leagues but never make the grade or may play in the lower classes or semi-professional leagues. These individuals are usually permitted to participate in intramural programs.

Organizational Eligibility

In addition to eligibility rules for individuals, special rules are necessary to prescribe limits of participation among the various units in the program. An example is restricting transfer of members from one organization to another. These are referred to as organizational eligibility rules, some of which are described in this section.

Dormitory Units. Participating units in dormitories usually consist of floors, houses, blocks, precincts, etc., and a problem arises when individuals move from one unit to another. One solution is to require them to play with the house or floor from which they moved until the end of the season, quarter, or semester.

Another conflict arises when members of fraternities–sororities reside in dormitories. Participants may be given the privilege of declaring their loyalty to the fraternity–sorority or the dormitory. Once the decision is made, it cannot be changed in the middle of the season but at a logical break in the schedule, e.g., the end of the quarter or semester.

Fraternities–Sororities' Units. It is not uncommon in some educational institutions to find individuals belonging to two fraternities–sororities, social or academic and professional. During pre-professional training, they are eligible for academic fraternities–sororities and after being admitted to professional programs, they become eligible for professional fraternities–sororities. The rule suggested above for members of fraternities–sororities living in dormitories may be applied to this situation, namely, that members must decide in which fraternity–sorority they will participate and may not change the choice until the end of the quarter, semester, or the like.

In some programs, pledges are not permitted to participate on fraternity or sorority intramural teams, and in others they are eligible because they are regarded as bona fide affiliates of the organization. Sometimes a pledge never becomes an active member of the fraternity or sorority. Another possibility is that in the midst of the championship playoffs, a fraternity–sorority pledges an individual of outstanding athletic ability to assist them with the chances of winning. A rule which prevents the latter situation requires pledges to be identified before the first game is played to be eligible for that particular activity.

Independent Units. Independent teams are usually restricted from "raiding" other units because it tends to disrupt group loyalty. These teams have a wide range of players from which to choose, whereas organizations are restricted to players from their own group. Members of residence halls, fraternities, sororities, etc., must compete with their own organization unless it does not have a team or they are released to play with independent groups.

League Classifications. Major and minor or Class A and B leagues are sometimes established to permit players to choose a level of competition suitable to their ability. Some organizations enter teams in each category and rules must be devised to control the interchange of players between leagues. One method is to require players to maintain identity with a given team, and another permits the interchange of Class B players to the Class A league at any time on the assumption that they have a right to graduate to a higher classification. However, this rule does not permit the transfer of a Class A player to a Class B team. The restriction in the latter case is aimed at dropping good players to the subordinate league when the Class A team is out of the running and the Class B team is a championship contender.

Ideas for Intramurals. Require individuals to sign a player's contract, 4″ x 6″ size, which commits them to play with a specific team. They are the property of that team until traded or released. The team manager, player, and intramural office are given copies of the contract.

Eligibility Forms

Organizational lists, team rosters, eligibility statements, and parental approvals are forms used to control eligibility of intramural participants. A description of each follows.

Eligibility Lists. A roster of eligible players should be on file in the intramural office before the season or activity begins. Organizations submit their membership lists at the beginning of the year, and teams turn in their rosters as a part of the entry form. With this procedure there is no overlapping of players, each group maintains its identity, and teams know who comprises the opposition's personnel. In some programs, new names may not be added after the original list is submitted, whereas in others, eligible players may be added at any time provided they have not played on another team in the same activity.

Eligibility Cards. An excellent method of placing responsibility for eligibility on individual players is to require each player to sign annually an eligibility card similar to the one shown in Figure 11-2. Frequently, violators of the rules imply that they would not have broken the rule if they had known about the rule and its interpretation. When a participant signs an eligibility card, he certifies that he knows and understands the eligibility rules and agrees to abide by them. Before signing the card, he is requested to read a summary of the rules on the reverse side, a sample of which is the following:

I-M Points of Reference

1. I have had a medical examination within the past two years and consider myself physically fit for participation in a vigorous sports program.

Date_____

Intramural Eligibility Card

NAME_____ TEL. NO._____
      PRINT   (Last)   (First)   (Initial)
ADDRESS_____ ZIP_____

TEAM OR ORGANIZATION_____

    This certifies that I know and understand the Intramural Eligibility Rules. In the interest of promoting a better program, I agree to abide by the rules without exception. On the basis of this pledge, I request permission to participate in the Intramural Program. It is my understanding that failure to comply with these rules will suspend me from I-M competition and a record of this negligent conduct will be placed on file.

_____
(Signature)

**Remember—A team which violates the rules and wins,
realistically hasn't won at all!**

Fig. 11–2. Intramural Eligibility Card.

2. I am a day school undergraduate student taking at least five credits.
3. I am a day school graduate student taking at least three credits.
4. I am a faculty member taking at least three credits.
5. I am a night school student carrying the equivalent of five day school quarter credits.
6. I will play on only one team (my original team) in a sport.
7. I am a bona fide member of the organization which my team represents.
8. I am a collegiate letter winner and/or professional athlete and have special certification for intramural sports participation.
9. I am a varsity or freshman squad member and my coach has granted permission for participation in intramural sports other than the intercollegiate sport for which I am a candidate.
10. I was a varsity or freshman squad member but quit before the fourth week of practice.
11. I am a varsity candidate but am not on the squad this year due to scholastic deficiencies or the transfer rule. Therefore, I am not eligible for the intramural sport involved.
12. I am not out for freshman practice because I failed to pass the predictability test and therefore am ineligible to participate in the sport for which I intended to be a candidate.

Parental Approval. In some elementary, junior high, senior high school and collegiate programs, written approval or consent of parents is secured before students are eligible to participate in intramurals. This procedure is also followed for some extramural participation. (See Fig. 13–4.) Blanket consent forms may be secured for the entire year or permission for each activity may be required as it is scheduled. Although this type of permission does not absolve the intramural staff from their responsibilities regarding legal liability, parents appreciate being consulted about the activities of their children.

VIOLATIONS AND DISCIPLINARY PROCEDURES

The intramural staff should follow a strict course of action with regard to intramural rules infractions. Laxity in rendering and administering decisions encourages players to follow a path of least concern. It is impossible to teach responsibility to participants if rules are not adequately enforced. Some intramural personnel know of illegal players in the program and do nothing about it unless a protest is registered. They believe participation is paramount and rules and regulations should be leniently administered. If this philosophy is valid, it is doubtful if there is need for any rules.

The intramural staff should solicit the complete cooperation of team managers, players, supervisors, and game officials in controlling eligibility. They should be encouraged to report inconsistencies to the intramural office to free the program of violators. The intramural director's goal should be to conduct activities on such a high level that the participant's pride in the program will not permit him to violate the rules. Participants must be made aware of the effect rule infractions have on themselves and the program, and they must understand that they are in the most strategic position to eliminate them.

Some rules infractions requiring corrective measures are the following:

1. Playing under an assumed name
2. Playing for more than one team in the same sport
3. Being a letter winner and withholding the fact
4. Misrepresenting a score
5. Being a member of the varsity or freshman squad
6. Using players who are not eligible for the program
7. Unsportsmanlike conduct

Disciplinary procedures vary with intramural programs, but the following list is an indication of some of the methods used for violations of the above types of infractions:

1. Forfeiture of the game or games in which the ineligible player participated.
2. Removal of team participation–performance points for the activity in which the player was involved.
3. Disqualification of the individual from intramural participation for a specified period of time such as one quarter, one year, or the remainder of the season.
4. Barring teams or organizations from competition for a specified period of time.
5. Indefinite suspension from the program if violations are repeated.
6. Recording violations on the individual's permanent record.

For suspensions, individuals or organizations may be reinstated when they show a willingness to support the basic purposes and principles of the program.

Occasionally, units develop negative patterns of participation including submission of late entries, tardiness for games, forfeits, and use of ineligible players. The intramural program is designed for those who wish to enjoy the activity experiences it provides. Those who persist in exhibiting a negative attitude toward the program should be asked to refrain from participation, particularly after they have been counseled and given extended opportunities to change their mode of operation. This type of participation detracts from the positive aspects of the program, and an intramural director has an obligation to protect the interests of those who participate within the rules and regulations of the program.

Protests

Quality officiating and efficiently supervised activities reduce the number of protests to a minimum, but a few are an inevitable part of intramural programming. Officials misinterpret the rules and participants unintentionally violate eligibility rules or do so with the self-assurance that the situation will not be uncovered. Only protests involving eligibility of players and those based on misinterpretation of playing rules should be accepted. Protests based solely on an official's judgment such as a fair or foul ball, strike or a ball, should not be considered. Failure of an official to apply proper rules to a given situation or to impose the correct penalty for a violation is protestable.

Players must notify officials that the game is being played under protest as soon as this type of discrepancy occurs. Sometimes protests can be immediately resolved by referring them to a mature, experienced field or court supervisor. Protests so made and overruled by a supervisor may be appealed to a protest board or the intramural staff.

Eligibility protests should be submitted as soon as the ineligible player is discovered. However, there is generally no time limit after which an ineligible player becomes eligible, and he should be disciplined no matter what the time sequence is following the act. Other protests are usually made within 24 hours after the game is played. (Refer to the protest form in Fig. 11–3.)

Protests are usually reviewed by the intramural staff or a protest board. It is necessary to collect all information regarding the case by discussing the matter with representatives of each team, the officials, supervisors, and the person or persons directly involved in the act. After hearing all of the evidence, a final decision must be made.

Protest boards consisting of three, five, seven, or more members may be appointed or elected. Membership may include representatives from the intramural staff, participants, and varsity coaches. One of the disadvantages of a board is that some protests require immediate action to prevent delays in scheduling subsequent games. Members of the protest board are not always available for emergency meetings, and for this reason, many directors prefer to resolve protests by holding hearings attended by members of the intramural staff and representatives of groups related to the protest.

Team or Unit Managers

Team or unit managers are important keys to successful intramural participation. They play an extremely important role in controlling eligibility and in setting the tone for acceptable conduct in games. Managers assume the responsibility for the eligibility of all players on their teams. To clearly establish this accountability, it is advisable to require them to sign a statement similar to the one shown in Figure 8–2, to the effect that they know the eligibility rules, understand them, have checked the eligibility of all of their players, and accept full responsibility if any discrepancies are discovered. Unless this procedure is followed, managers may plead ignorance of the rules when questioned about the eligibility of their players.

The following letter summarizes duties of team managers and identifies the importance of their roles in intramural programming.

A Letter to Intramural Managers

Dear Mr. Manager:
    Please accept our appreciation for serving as the manager of your intramural team. You may not fully realize how important your assignment is, but the intramural program could not function without your assistance. You will play the extremely important role of "contact man" or intermediary between the intramural staff and the members of your team. You will not only influence the lives of numerous individuals but your cooperation will have a direct bearing on the success of the overall intramural program.

INTRAMURAL PROTEST FORM

TEAMS_____VS_____

PROTESTING TEAM_____DATE PROTEST FILED_____

DATE OF GAME_____TIME OF GAME_____FIELD OR COURT_____

PLEASE CHECK (X)

_____ Protest based on eligibility of participants

_____ Protest based on an official's misinterpretation of a playing rule

_____ Protest based solely on an official's decision involving accuracy of
      judgment which is not protestable - submitted for information only
----

                          -GAME SITUATION-

FINAL GAME SCORE_____WINNER_____

SCORE AT TIME OF PROTEST_____TEAM LEADING_____

INNING_____PERIOD_____QUARTER_____TIME REMAINING_____

DESCRIBE THE INCIDENT AS ACCURATELY AS POSSIBLE:

_____

_____

_____

_____

_____

_____

_____

_____

_____
                  (Write on reverse side if necessary)

_____   _____
    Manager of Protesting Team   Intramural Supervisor or Official

Fig. 11–3. Intramural Protest Form.

The following suggestions for successful managing are given to assist you with your responsibilities:

1. Do not overanticipate the interests of your group. For example, at the beginning of a season it may appear that there is enough interest to enter three teams. Perhaps it would be wiser to enter only two teams, keeping in mind that in addition to studies there will be many other interests competing for the participants' time and attention.
2. Study the game and eligibility rules of intramural participation. Just as a game must have playing rules, the intramural program must have eligibility rules or it could not exist. Use a common sense approach to these rules. From time to time, members of your team may tempt you to set them aside, but remember that according to absolute standards, a team really does not win when it violates the rules.
3. Give some attention to sportsmanship. All games must be conducted within reasonable common sense limits. Some of the contact sports inevitably involve excessively rough play on the part of a few players. This kind of conduct cannot be tolerated, and as the leader of your team you can set the tone for sportsmanship attitudes. Insist on an honorable victory or none at all.
4. Learn to respect decisions of game officials. Like all human beings, including players, officials make honest errors. Competitive games must be played within a framework of errors. Try to accept the fact that they do not officiate with the idea of looking for difficulty but merely administer the game according to their understanding of the rules.
5. Avoid forfeits. They are detrimental to your team and completely demoralizing to the entire intramural program. Intramural participation is based on a cyclical pattern. When a team enters, it requests participation. If one party fails to carry out its obligation, the cyclical pattern breaks down and the time, attention, and effort of a number of individuals is completely wasted. Try to present this logical approach to the members of your team and abide by it.
6. Visit the Intramural Office frequently to familiarize yourself with program procedures.
7. Enter your teams in the desired sports prior to the closing dates and be sure that all team members are eligible and appropriately certified.
8. Notify team members of the time, place, and date of all scheduled contests and be at the playing area a few minutes prior to the scheduled time. Tardiness is a weakness which can be overcome easily with a little extra effort.
9. Avoid postponement of games, but, if it is absolutely necessary, contact the intramural staff and your opponents to make immediate arrangements for rescheduling the game.
10. Intramural games are generally scheduled the same night each week. Try to arrange other activities of your group around this schedule to prevent conflicts.
11. Write or print the first and last names of your players on the

scorecard. Sometimes the newspaper fails to give a team appropriate publicity because of the lack of first names.

12. Maintain your assignment throughout a minimum of one year. Changing managers in the middle of the program does not provide the continuity which is necessary for successful participation.

Remember that it is possible to be successful even if your teams do not win all of the games. Every reasonable effort should be made to win within the spirit of the rules. However, in sports contests it is absolutely impossible for all teams to win all of the games, all of the time. Be realistic and try to understand that games are designed to produce winners and losers. The purpose of a loss is to provide incentive for making a future gain. The most important element in sports participation is the attitude with which you and your players win and lose.

A team is only as good as its leadership. If you are sincere in carrying out the responsibilities of your managerial position, you will gain experience in leadership and organization that will contribute to other phases of your life. The same fundamental principles of success involved in managing intramural teams will apply in your postgraduate world.

The intramural staff is ready to be of assistance to you in carrying out your very important responsibilities. Do not hestitate to call us about any matter, insignificant as it may seem to be. We hope you and your team enjoy participating in the intramural program.

Most sincerely,
The Intramural Staff

HEALTH AND SAFETY

Intramural personnel must be constantly conscious of integrating sound health and safety practices into the various phases of program administration. Frequently, quantity programming occupies the attention of over-zealous intramural leaders to the neglect of the participant's welfare. Provisions must be made for medical evaluations, protective equipment, and properly maintained facilities to reduce potential hazards of participation.

Medical Examinations

Most intramural programs require medical examinations before participants are eligible to take part in activities. These examinations are given by local community doctors or by institutional health service physicians. The practice varies, with some programs requiring an examination every year, others every two years, and still others only upon entering the institution. Those following the latter procedure usually request special examinations for strenuous activities such as wrestling or as a follow-up of a serious injury or illness.

Various limitations of participation are made on the basis of medical evaluations: (1) no restriction; (2) no swimming, due to sinus or other respiratory conditions; (3) no strenuous activities such as wrestling, track, basketball, and touch football; (4) adapted activities only; and (5) no activities. The classification is noted on the individual's health record and on a permit card issued for his personal possession. In some programs, these permits must be shown to supervisors before participants can take part in activities. Another method is to publish a list of individuals with classifications of two or higher which can be checked by team managers to determine the health eligibility of their players.

Still another approach to the question of medical eligibility is to maintain that individuals are responsible for their own health and safety. Since the program is voluntary, participants are liable for determining the limits of their health status and participating accordingly. If intramural departments require medical examinations, they are accountable for preventing participation without examinations. No requirement places the responsibility on participants. Some of the legal questions are yet to be resolved in these matters.

Safety Procedures

Legal liability cannot be established unless negligence is proven and negligence can be avoided if safety provisions are constantly applied in program planning and administration. It is estimated that approximately 50 per cent of all injuries could be avoided if proper precautions were utilized. Injuries occur because of hazardous playing areas, inadequate equipment, inappropriate medical evaluation, improper supervision and officiating, and lack of conditioning.

All facilities must be inspected regularly and systematically. Padding should be installed on gymnasium walls and around poles or projecting obstacles which may serve as a source of potential injury. Gymnasium floors should be checked for traction, particularly after a dance or other social function. Playing fields should be level, free from holes, metal plates, and when multiple purpose softball—touch-football fields are used, softball bases and plates should be removed for the football season. Areas should be sufficiently large so teams are not required to play in crowded situations, nor should they be scheduled to play out of doors during inclement weather. If fields are adjacent to each other, as in softball, ample room should be provided to avoid collisions between players of each field.

The intramural program should provide quality playing equipment and maintain it according to standards of excellence. There is a tendency for participants to play with less protective equipment when they furnish

INTRAMURAL INJURY REPORT

NAME OF INJURED_____TEAM_____

ADDRESS_____TEL. NO._____

DATE OF INJURY_____TIME OF INJURY_____

COURT_____FIELD_____OTHER AREA_____

WEATHER AND FIELD CONDITIONS_____

_____

_____

NATURE OF INJURY_____

_____

_____

DESCRIPTION OF THE INCIDENT_____

_____

_____

_____

_____

ACTION TAKEN_____

_____

_____

_____

SUGGESTIONS FOR PREVENTION_____

_____

_____

_____

_____
WITNESS OR ATTENDANT

FILE THIS REPORT IN THE I-M OFFICE - ROOM 123 INTRAMURAL HALL.

Fig. 11—4. Injury Report Form.

their own or use second-hand substandard materials. Providing special equipment for specific positions such as baseball catchers and hockey goalies greatly minimizes injuries. Issuing track shoes for meets offers better traction for runners and reduces the number of falls caused by gymnasium shoes on cinder surfaces. Some programs are experimenting with soft rubberized headgears for football and ice hockey.

Area supervisors should be in attendance at all scheduled intramural contests and in gymnasiums, swimming pools, and field areas for self-directed activities. Players wearing glasses should be required to wear eye guards unless the lenses are unbreakable. Game officials must be made aware of their important role in controlling injuries. Strict officiating can reduce the number of injuries caused by unnecessary roughness. Rules of the games may also be modified to eliminate potential injurious situations. Participants should be encouraged to engage in a conditioning program before participating in intramurals, particularly for the strenuous sports of wrestling, track, and cross country.

If possible, intramural trainers should be in attendance when intramural activities are conducted or as a minimum requirement, supervisors must be trained in first-aid procedures. A training or first-aid room should be available for treating intramural participants. Emergency procedures must be clearly identified and posted in activity areas. They should be common knowledge to all supervisors and officials. These procedures should include the provision of emergency transportation for critically injured persons. It is advisable to install a telephone, two-way radio, or other communications system in the field and court areas for summoning emergency assistance. When injuries occur, a complete report should be filed in the intramural office (see Fig. 11–4). Although it may be impossible to eliminate all injuries, every effort should be made to minimize them.

12

Publicity and Recognition

PUBLICITY

Every phase of intramural programming—facilities, equipment, units of participation, activities, scheduling, tournament structuring, point systems, rules and regulations, awards, etc.—may be provided, but unless potential participants know about all of these arrangements, the program cannot be successful. Publicity is the catalyst which moves the program. It is the means by which the "intramural image" is created and constantly kept before those who are within the exposure range. It aids in conveying the concept that the program is designed for the benefit and enjoyment of all participants.

The existence of a company in the business world depends on its ability to develop and distribute products successfully. The best merchandising techniques are used to sell them to consumers. Every effort is made to produce quality products because of the realization that they tend to sell themselves through satisfied customer word-of-mouth advertising. In addition, vast advertising campaigns are conducted to inform the public about these quality materials. In a sense, an educational program consists of buying and selling, in the minds of people, old and new impressions, relationships, and methods of doing things in an ever-changing society.

Although the concept may not be educationally palatable for some, these same business principles relate to intramural programming. Every intramural director must understand that an efficiently administered, quality program results in satisfied participants, and satisfied participants are the best program advertisers. After a pleasant intramural experience, individuals encourage others to share these same kinds of experiences.

To publicize the program, repetition, a fundamental principle of advertising, must be utilized. The intramural "story" must be told over and over, using every available method. Participants should be informed about what is going to be done before it begins, what is being done while it is happening, and what has been done after it has been completed.

A key to successful intramural publicity is the use of participant names whenever possible. There is a magnetic effect when people read their name in print, and if given a choice, they prefer to read about themselves rather than others.

COMMUNICATION MEDIA

Media used to distribute information about the intramural program are listed in the following paragraphs. Although some may be more effective than others, all of them can be used to advance the intramural image. A variety of methods must be used to perpetuate the repetitive principle.

Newspapers

Newspapers, local and regional, are an important source of intramural publicity. Schedules, scores, game stories, feature stories, entry deadlines, and intramural columns are forms of newspaper publicity. Want ads may also be used to advantage in announcing a particular event.

Continuity is most necessary for effective newspaper publicity. If schedules and game results appear regularly every day, participants will rely on this source of information. It is important for them to be able not only to follow the progress of their own games, but also to compare the results of other contests. If schedules and results are reported sporadically, the publicity will not have the same impact.

Occasionally, intramural personnel experience difficulty in getting publicity in student newspapers. Some student writers try to compete with local newspapers and forget their responsibility to print the news of the school community. The sports' editor may be more interested in varsity coverage or may not be able to find reporters to write intramural copy. Student reporters may choose to cover daytime events rather than intramural games which are played during the late afternoons and evenings. Some reporters prefer varsity practices and games because they receive a vicarious thrill from associating with the star players on varsity teams.

Where this situation exists, some directors value newspaper publicity to the extent that they pay reporters to write intramural stories. In other programs, staff members or part-time assistants are charged with the responsibility of program publicity. There may be an additional problem of getting the news printed after the copy has been written. Personal conferences with the editors are advisable to review the mutual problems involved. Participant letters to the editor can be helpful in focusing attention on the lack of publicity. Some intramural personnel find it is advantageous to publish their own intramural newspaper.

Newsletters and Daily Bulletins

Mimeographed or multilithed newsletters and daily bulletins are an effective means of creating and maintaining program interest. A two- or three-page newsletter can be published periodically reporting game scores, team standings, and stories. Because there are usually no space limitations, all activities can be reported in more detail, using numerous names, than is normally possible in newspaper articles.

A banner title such as "Intramural Communiqué," cartoons, and double columns with unique headings add to the attractivenes of the newsletter. Different newsletters may be published for various phases of the program —faculty activities, sports clubs, extramurals, and co-intramurals—or one which includes all activities. If newsletters are consistently produced and distributed, participants sometimes prefer them to limited newspaper publicity.

Daily bulletins are equally effective for notifying participants of intramural events of the day. These may be posted in strategic locations or distributed to each individual.

Announcements and Notices

In institutions with public address systems, daily announcements can include information about intramural activities. It is an excellent method for reminding students of the various schedules or for postponing events in case of inclement weather. Intramural notices may also be read in home rooms, study halls, and assemblies. Required physical education classes may also serve as a place where students are notified about intramural events.

Mimeographed or dittoed notices can be circularized among all participating units. Bulletins, schedules, and notices can be made more attractive with sports figures and unique lettering arrangements. This type of notice may be prepared in the form of a monthly calendar, identifying the dates of future activities and describing some of these events in detail on the reverse side. Organizations can easily be encouraged to post attractive materials on their bulletin boards.

Bulletin Boards

Neatly arranged, properly maintained bulletin boards are essential for comprehensive intramural publicity. Preferably, they should be lighted and located where they will be readily visible to the participants. These places include the lobbies of intramural indoor facilities or entry ways to outdoor areas. In dormitory-type living units, they can be positioned to be read by persons waiting in meal lines. Portable bulletin boards are also useful for displaying information in the activitity areas.

Schedules, notices, charts, diagrams, tournament draw sheets, posters, and pictures may be posted on bulletin boards. Neat, easily read materials with individual headings for the various activities should be displayed. All items should be attractively arranged and tacked down at four corners to keep them flat against the board. No one item should remain on the board for an extended period of time, and game results and league standings must be kept up-to-date. Disorganized, ill-kept bulletin boards may give the impression that the program is run in a similar manner.

Photographs of winning teams and participants in action are excellent display materials. Some departments have their own photographic equipment including a darkroom and maintain picture files for publicity purposes. In some institutions, the print shop or art department assists in designing and making attractive bulletin board materials.

Posters

Program posters should be displayed in activity areas or in various public buildings in the community. Limited numbers may be professionally designed or they can be mass produced for widespread distribution.

Posters should simply answer the five W's: Who, What, Where, When, and Why. Brief, catchy phrases are more effective than long, wordy descriptions. Too much information detracts from the poster and it may not be read. Attention-getting pictures or designs should be placed in the upper left-hand quarter of the poster because this is the point at which a reader's eyes automatically focus. Every program has a few individuals with artistic talent who can make designs for posters. (See Figs. 12–1 and 12–2.)

Designing comic program characters and adopting themes are ideal methods for attracting attention. For example, "Gym Nasium says, 'The man who is wise will exercise.'" Slogans, samples of which are listed below, can be used as a part of the poster or displayed individually throughout the facilities to add program interest.

SAMPLE SLOGANS

PROGRESS TROUGH PARTICIPATION
THE ONLY LOSER IN INTRAMURALS IS THE NONPARTICIPANT
PARTICIPATE OR PERISH

WHO: EVERYONE EXCEPT VARSITY AND FRESHMAN
BASKETBALL PLAYERS AND BASKETBALL
LETTERMEN

WHAT: BASKETBALL ROUND ROBIN TOURNAMENT FOLLOWED
BY ELIMINATION PLAYOFFS FOR CLASS A,B, C,
AND D CHAMPIONSHIPS

WHEN: BEGINNING TUESDAY, JAN. 6 FROM 6:30 TO 10:30 p.m.

WHERE: INTRAMURAL GYMNASIUM BASKETBALL COURTS I, II,
III, AND IV

WHY: RECREATION, COMPETITION, PHYSICAL FITNESS,
SUCCESS AND FAILURE EXPERIENCES

PROGRESS THRU PARTICIPATION

ENTRIES NOW OPEN
SUBMIT THEM TO THE INTRAMURAL
OFFICE RM. 123 INTRAMURAL HALL

Fig. 12–1. Intramural Basketball Tournament Poster.

Fig. 12–2. Intramural Judo Club Poster.

MAKE FORFEITS INELIGIBLE FOR THE PROGRAM
PROPER PARTICIPATION PREVENTS POOR PERFORMANCE
ENTER–PARTICIPATE–CONTRIBUTE–BENEFIT
HAVE YOUR TEAM ON TIME, READY TO PLAY, EVERY TIME
ENJOY PARTICIPATING IN A BETTER PROGRAM BY ELIMINATING FORFEITS
INTRAMURALS FOR EVERYONE AND EVERYONE FOR INTRAMURALS
AN HOUR A DAY DEVOTE TO PLAY
DO YOUR BIT TO STAY PHYSICALLY FIT
PARTICIPATION IS AN EFFECTIVE DETERRENT TO DETERIORATION

Commercial concerns make attractive activity posters, tournament draw sheets, all-purpose charts, and periodic calendars. The posters have drawings of players performing specific activities with additional space for writing details about the event. Information is recorded with write-on, wipe-off grease pencils, and they can be reused many times.

Intramural Handbooks

Most departments publish an annual intramural handbook for distribution to all potential participants. Some institutions publish a handbook which combines information about physical education, intramurals, and other student activities. Usually it is one small pamphlet, but a few departments publish separate handbook information for each unit of participation. Others have developed unique calendars which contain program information on the back of each monthly page.

Intramural personnel have established an "exchange of ideas" program through the interchange of intramural handbooks. It is standard operating procedure for a director to send a handbook in return for one received from another program.

The average size of a handbook is approximately five inches by seven inches. Some directors prefer this size or smaller because team captains or managers carry them in their pockets and use them as a ready reference. A survey of handbooks indicates the following contents:

1. Messages from the president, superintendent, dean of students, athletic director, intramural director, and student chairman of intramurals
2. Departmental organization
3. Departmental personnel, building schedules, office room numbers, and telephone numbers
4. Yearly calendar
5. Activities calendar with starting dates
6. Activities in the program
7. Constitution and by-laws of the intramural councils or associations
8. Rules and regulations covering eligibility, protests, forfeits, entry fees, and postponements

9. A map and listing of indoor and outdoor facilities
10. Health and safety information
11. Description and distribution of awards
12. Intramural officials' association
13. Point system and point tables
14. Pictures of intramural staff, winning teams, and game action
15. Entry procedures
16. Co-intramural, extramural, and sports club activities
17. Tournament draw sheets identifying winners
18. Team captain's or manager's responsibilities
19. Participation records—number of teams, games, forfeits, participants, and participations
20. All-Star teams
21. Faculty program
22. Summer session program
23. Winning teams and players' names from previous year
24. Team champions from previous years
25. Comparison of team point tables indicating present year's place and previous year's finish
26. History of the intramural program and unusual happenings
27. Special events such as open houses, faculty-student nights, and sports festivals
28. Information about practices, informal workouts, and challenge games
29. Requirements of Sigma Delta Psi
30. Slogans and quotations

Manager's Manual

The manager's manual or workbook differs from the intramural handbook in that it has more specific information relating to each unit of participation. Material is arranged chronologically to aid the team manager in entering and managing intramural teams for the entire year. The systematic arrangement of entry blanks and activity regulations enables him to follow the program by checking the date and turning to the proper page in the manual. Manuals are looseleaf folders or notebooks which permit addition of tournament schedules.

The introduction contains the philosophy of a good manager, emphasizing qualifications, responsibilities, and suggestions on how to have more effective intramural participation (see page 214). There is also an explanation of the student's role in eliminating forfeits, preventing ineligibility situations, and promoting good sportsmanship. In addition, the following items are included:

1. How to submit entries
2. How to rate officials

3. How to register protests and postpone games
4. Explanation of the point system with point tables
5. Dated entry blanks for each sport
6. Summary forms for recording individual and team participation
7. Rules and regulations for each sport arranged in the order to be contested

Manager's manuals may be checked out to team representatives at the beginning of the year and returned when the last intramural activity is finished. The same manuals can be used the following year by inserting up-to-date material.

Yearbooks

Most yearbooks contain a section on intramurals with names and pictures of selected participants. In some instances, they may feature a complete pictorial review of the intramural program. When annuals contain records of graduates, intramural activities and honors are usually included.

News Releases

The intramural director, institutional news service, or public relations department can send formal letters and photographs to home town newspapers of members of a championship team giving pertinent information about the team's performance. Items of interest such as team name, scores of games, and numbers of teams and individuals participating should be included. Local home town newspapers often appreciate receiving this type of information.

Radio and Television

In some school systems, student radio stations and educational television units may be used for publicizing intramurals. Some student stations produce periodic intramural radio programs and broadcast entire intramural championship games. Additionally, spot announcements about entry deadlines and future events are made. Special intramural programs or film clips of intramural activities can be shown on educational television. Local community radio and television may also be interested in carrying intramural sports information.

Orientation Programs

Orientation programs are designed to welcome incoming participants and acquaint them with the facilities and program of the intramural

department. Skits, films, slides, and presentations by staff members encourage students to take advantage of intramural opportunities.

After a brief introductory program, individuals may be divided into
groups for actual participation in one or more activities. These events
should be conducted informally for immediate enjoyment, although
"quickie" tournaments may be arranged.

Orientations packets are usually presented to these persons, and a
four- or six-page intramural folder should be included. The folder may
briefly describe the program of intramurals, emphasizing the activities
and procedures for entering. It is more economical to circularize all
students with this abbreviated information than to provide everyone with
an intramural handbook. Subsequently, the enthusiastic ones can procure
handbooks by requesting them at the intramural office.

Films and Slides

A 15–20-minute film or set of slides may be produced describing the
various phases of the intramural program. If a local sports commentator
or personality narrates the film or a tape synchronized with the slide
presentation, it adds considerably to their effectiveness. These can be
shown at orientation programs or to community groups. By using an
automatic projector and a daylight screen, slides may be repeatedly
shown without a projectionist.

Other Media

Several other, perhaps less direct, methods listed below may be used
for publicizing intramurals.

1. Sports equipment or awards exhibited in display cases.
2. Portable displays developed for use at conferences and conven-
   tions.
3. Permanent boards listing intramural records posted in various
   facilities' locations.
4. Intramural materials displayed on nondepartmental bulletin
   boards.
5. Intramural games scheduled preliminary to varsity games, cross
   country meets conducted between halves of a football game, and
   relay championships run off during varsity track intermissions.
6. Open houses, sports clinics, and festivals.
7. Jerseys advertising intramurals provided free of charge or sold to
   participants at cost.
8. Trophy exhibits in building lobbies.
9. Cups, plaques, banners, ribbons, and trophies displayed in living
   units.
10. Awards worn by participants such as sweaters, jackets, T-shirts,
    belt buckles, tie clasps, and watch chains.

SYMBOLS OF RECOGNITION

There is little doubt that enjoyment of participation is the primary incentive for participating in intramurals; in a sense, participation is an award in itself. But there are numerous opportunities for participants to experience success in intramurals, and they should be recognized for these achievements. Success stimulates attempts to gain additional success, and intramural recognition supports this concept. These kinds of experiences encourage them to attain bigger and more important goals in intramurals as well as in other phases of their lives.

Recognition of achievement is accomplished through awards, all-star selections, performance records, and publicity accounts. Some persons regard these measures as promotionally superfluous and insist that participation should be strictly for the love of the activity. These individuals fail to remember how meaningful it is for a young person to be recognized for his achievements. A convincing method of determining how youths value awards is to let them decide which ones will be presented.

In this competitive world, comparisons are made beginning at an early age, and recognition is given throughout life for superior or even improved performances. Parents give special favors to their children for good behavior. In education, academic recognition exists in the form of valedictorians, scholarships, fellowships, research grants, and membership in honor societies. In business, employees are given promotions, salary increases, and bonuses for efficient work performances. Presenting intramural symbols of recognition conforms to the pattern of our existence. To eliminate these forms of recognition is to live unrealistically in a real world.

Awards Considerations

Some factors should be noted regarding the judicious use of awards. A distinction must be made between awards and rewards. Awards should be regarded as symbols of achievement and not as rewards for participation. Participants usually enter tournaments for the enjoyment of playing and not specifically for the potential award. The award is not given because the individual participates, but rather to denote a certain level of success.

In general, awards are presented to a team as a whole, members of a team, or to individuals participating without team affiliation. The performance of the group determines the type of awards plan to be followed. Large team trophies or similar awards are presented to groups that have a common residence or appropriate place to display them. In some programs, small individual trophies or medals are given to each member of the winning team and to winners of individual and dual activities.

Individual and team trophies should be awarded, but if it is a question of one or the other, individuals should be recognized. The award will be more meaningful, even if it is smaller, if it can be displayed in the participant's residence and taken with him wherever he lives. Large team trophies cannot be divided among the members, and personal identification is not as permanent as it is with individual awards.

A rotating award listing the names of annual winners is sometimes utilized. Permanent possession is gained if it is won a specific number of times such as any three years or three years out of seven. A group retaining the rotating award for one year receives a smaller trophy as a memento of its achievement.

The value of awards is increased if they are personalized by engraving names of individual champions, teams, and/or team members on them. Some delay may be caused by this process for the reason that names cannot be known until the championship is won. If given a choice between a slight delay or prompt delivery, participants prefer the delay in exchange for more personalized awards.

Awards should not be expensive or extravagant. It is illogical to spend too much money for awards if funds are limited for other phases of the program. The award should always reflect the symbolism of achievement, not the monetary values of a prize. In some instances it may be necessary to limit the number of individual awards presented to a particular team. If the team uses numerous substitutes, they may be given the privilege of buying additional awards.

Much of the value of awards is lost if they are not promptly distributed. There is no time when recognition means more to the participants than immediately following the championship. Individuals and teams are always anxious to display the fruits of victory. Undue delay may result in indifference not only to awards, but to the program in general.

Types of Awards

There are many different types of recognition symbols. Some are practical in that they may be worn or used by the participant in his daily endeavors, while others are primarily for display purposes. Whichever type is selected must be adapted to the framework within which the local program operates.

Trophies and Cups. Trophies made of wood, plastic, bakelite, and metal are available in a wide range of styles and designs. Most trophies have emblematic figures attached to depict the sport for which the award is won: for example, a bowler in position to roll the ball, a tennis player set to serve, or a swimmer in starting position. Plate areas may be used for inscribing team and player names. Some of the practical trophies are pen holders, desk sets, clocks, calendars, ash trays, lighters, and thermometers.

Cups are made of metal with silver, gold, and bronze plating. In addition to the usual inscriptions, they can be further personalized by incorporating the seal of the institution or organization.

Inexpensive plastic cups and trophies, less costly than medals, may be used for "on the spot" presentations. A figure denotes the activity, and information such as date, team, and level of championship may be typed on a band or plate. Some of these are very attractive in silver, gold, or bronze and, from a display standpoint, are more desirable than medals for individual awards. Small wooden trophies with figures and appropriate metal space for engraving are also effective awards.

When activities are grouped into major, intermediate, and minor categories or teams compete at different levels of competition; i.e., Class A, B, C, and D, it is advisable to equate the size of the award to correspond with the significance of the activity or level of competition. A team winning the championship in basketball after playing twelve games deserves a larger trophy than one winning a one-day bowling tournament. If attention is not given to different gradations, it is possible for a team to receive a larger trophy for a Class B championship than for a Class A championship. Examples of sizes are as follows: the All-Year trophy may be 25 inches high; All-Unit Class B basketball trophy, 16 inches; All-Unit Class C trophy, 14 inches; and All-Unit Class D trophy, 12 inches.

Medals.   The three most popular types of medals are: (1) small, solid balls, shaped like a football, basketball, or baseball; (2) large, flat medals with sport designs reflected in strong relief, some including suspended ribbons; and (3) small, flat medals worn as charms. They are made with gold plate, silver, and bronze finishes. Usually gold medals are presented to first place winners, silver to second, and bronze to third. It is customary to engrave the name of the league, division, year, winning team, and player on the back of the medal. Some departments design medals for exclusive use in their own programs.

Trophy Boards.   Individual and group winners may be permanently recognized by displaying trophy boards or framed placards on gymnasium, office, or lobby walls or along hallways. Names of sports are painted or burned on these boards, and various winners' names are inserted at subsequent times. The industrial arts department may be requested to design and make these awards to minimize expense.

Plaques.   An award which can be substituted for a cup or trophy is the wall plaque or shield. A medallion with an emblematic figure identifying the sport in which the award was earned is attached to the plaque. It is possible to buy separate medallions and make the plaques, the art working being arranged by students or professionals. This type of symbol has greater durability than cups and trophies.

Monogram Letters. Monograms represent a combination of an intramural letter and numerals of the year in which the award is won. School, class, or organization colors may be used. When an individual wins this award in two or more years, the distinction can be noted by placing two or more stars, bars, or chevrons on the monogram. This award may be given on the basis of winning a required number of points in the individual point system, or it may serve as a means of recognizing winners in other phases of the intramural program.

Class Numerals. Intramural numeral awards may be presented identifying the year in which a winner's class graduates. They may be awarded with sweaters, jackets, blankets, or jerseys, or departments may provide only the numerals with recipients furnishing the latter. Embroidered emblems may be incorporated with the numerals to make them more attractive.

Ribbons and Pennants. Ribbons may be designed in different colors to correspond with the order of finish—first, second, third—of winning teams or individuals. Names of the activity, institution, and winner are printed on the ribbons. Organizational colors may also be used for the lettering and ribbon material. An economical method of providing ribbon awards is to purchase large quantities of material, and instead of printing events and dates on the ribbon at the time of purchase, the information can be typed on the ribbon as needed. In addition to ribbons, cloth pennants and banners in school colors can be made with the assistance of home economics personnel.

Certificates. Paper or cloth certificates may be issued to winners of intramural competition. (See Figs. 12–3 and 12–4.) This form of recognition can also be used to identify members of all-star teams or outstanding individual performances. These may be comic or other unique certificates. An example of the content of one presented to members of a last place team is the following:

> This is to certify that John E. Jones, a member in good standing of the Pin Busters bowling team, is entitled to all privileges of a last place team. Your team was considered the strongest in the league because it held up all other teams. The only reason you didn't go up was that everyone knocked you down! BUT WAIT 'TIL NEXT YEAR!!!!

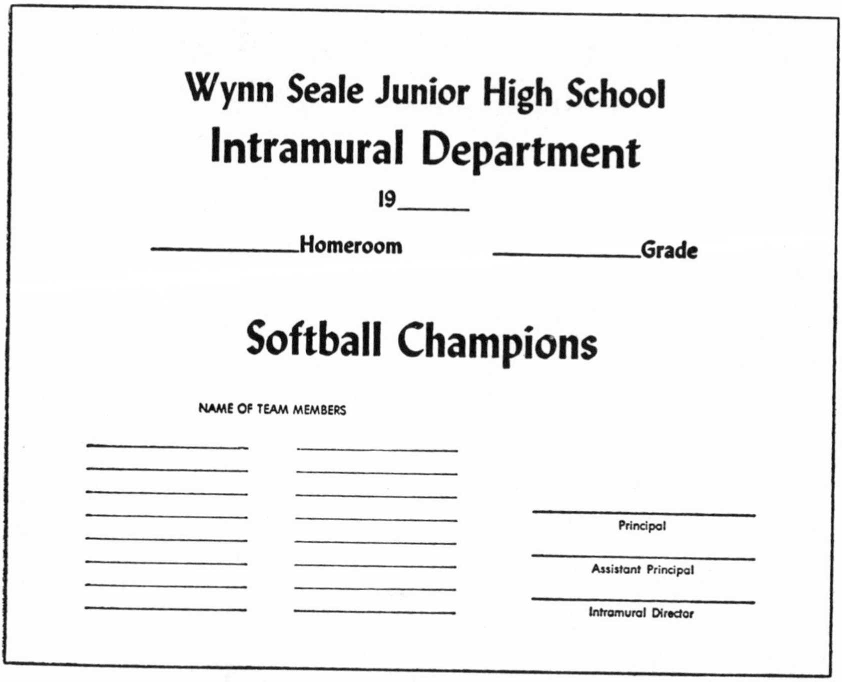

Wynn Seale Junior High School
Intramural Department

19_____

_____Homeroom   _____Grade

Softball Champions

NAME OF TEAM MEMBERS

_____   _____

_____   _____

_____   _____

_____   _____   _____
                                  Principal

_____   _____   _____
                                  Assistant Principal

_____   _____   _____
                                  Intramural Director

Fig. 12–3. Junior High School Intramural Award Certificate. (Courtesy Wynn Seale Junior High School, Corpus Christi, Texas.)

Additional Awards.   Awards such as blazers, sweaters, jerseys, T-shirts, scarfs, and blankets, although somewhat expensive and less frequently used, are very much appreciated by the recipients. Distinctive emblems, insignia, monograms, or numerals may be attached to these awards. They are usually presented for the most important honors in the intramural program, the All-Year or All-Institutional Championships and the outstanding intramural athlete of the year.

Other awards less noticeably worn are small emblems, keys, pins, necklaces, bracelets, belt buckles, cuff links, and tie clasps. Each of these awards can display the figure of the activity in which the participant distinguished himself, organizational insignia, or a distinctive design of the intramural program.

Presentation of Awards

The degree to which intramural recognition is effective is often determined by the manner in which the honors are bestowed. Presenting awards at an auspicious occasion instead of in the intramural office pro-

Fig. 12–4. Intramural Honor Award Certificate. Courtesy University of Michigan Intramural Sports Department.)

vides additional recognition over and above the award. For this reason, annual intramural award banquets are most desirable. In addition to the presentation of awards, the program may include speeches by local sports notables and other dignitaries, sports films, and entertainment.

An annual award's picnic attended by all intramural winners of the year is equally effective. With the outdoor atmosphere it is possible to conduct activities such as races, relays, stunts, games, and novelty contests. A program similar to the indoor banquet may be arranged, but generally the emphasis is on a more informal gathering for presentation of awards, fun, and food. If banquets or picnics are not utilized, arrangements may be made to present awards at assemblies or convocations.

Other Forms of Recognition

There are several other, perhaps less obvious, methods of recognizing intramural achievement. Photographs of each championship team may be given to the members. Cameras which photograph and instantaneously develop pictures in one process are useful for this purpose. Including pictures and names of the various winners in the intramural handbook and yearbook also gives credit to outstanding players.

Publicity accounts of intramural games in the newspaper provide daily recognition for individual performances. Printed programs for championship games with players' names, positions, season records, and past winners provide additional prestige to final games. Still another method of denoting achievement is the establishment of all-time, yearly, and seasonal records for each activity. These may be published in the handbook or newspaper, posted on bulletin boards, and recorded on special record boards in the gymnasium.

Another form of recognition is the selection of all-star teams, a procedure which is followed in many intramural programs. If all-star teams are chosen, it is advisable to utilize a large selection group. The intramural staff, officials, and sports writers of the newspapers should be consulted. When choices are determined by a sizable vote, there is less chance of a good player being overlooked.

Ideas for Intramurals. A series of designs can be developed for five or six different individual trophies or medals, only one of which is to be presented during a given year. The different styles and designs avoid duplication for those individuals who win awards in successive years.

13

Extramurals and
Sports Clubs

EXTRAMURALS

As indicated in Chapter 1, extramurals (intermurals) include competition between participants representing two or more educational institutions, community recreation centers, industrial organizations, military units, or other groups which compete outside of their defined program boundaries or immediate geographical areas. Broadly conceived, extramurals include interscholastic and intercollegiate athletics. However, in an educational setting, not all extramurals can be classified as interschool or intercollege because a team representing one institution may play against a local industrial or other community amateur team. Contrary to varsity athletic programs, extramurals usually include all individuals regardless of abilities or skills and require fewer practices to prepare for competition.

In many institutions, extramurals are an outgrowth of intramural programming and are sponsored and supervised by the intramural staff. Some programs and departments are titled "Intramural–Extramural." Because of limited financial resources, intercollegiate and interscholastic athletic programs cannot provide extensive varsity experiences for all men and women students. The extramural program, therefore, serves the important function of fulfilling the participation void between intramurals and varsity programs. It is conceivable that properly expanded intramural and varsity programs could eliminate extramural competition, in its present state, but contemporary programs are too far from ideal to make this concept a reality.

Types of Extramural Participation

Extramural and co-extramural events take place at the site of one of the opponents, or each participating unit utilizes its own facilities, and results are compared to determine a winner. Several categories of extramural participation are identified below:

1. Intramural championship teams or individuals play their counterparts from other institutions or enter district, regional, and national tournaments.
2. Sports clubs and other organizations issue challenges to and accept them from extra-institutional groups. They sponsor or travel to invitational tournaments such as sports days, play days, and sports festivals.
3. Individuals with exceptional ability but not necessarily representing intramurals or any formally organized group compete extramurally in sporting activities.
4. Individuals or organized groups take part in postal, telephonic, and telegraphic competition in which extramural results are reported and compared via these communications media.

Sports Days. Sports days are conducted with the emphasis on teams maintaining identity with their own institutions. Greater or lesser importance in terms of competitiveness may be attached to sports days, depending on the method and purpose of organization. In some situations, teams represent their own schools with the primary purpose being sociability rather than determining a champion, although scores may be recorded for additional interest. Other sports days are organized with the specific objective of deciding winners.

The competitive-type sports day or sports festival frequently involves intramural champions from one institution competing against intramural winners from another, or champions of several schools meet at a central location to determine the best players in various events. Sports festivals may be scheduled for each season or only once during the year. The site of the festival may be rotated annually among participating units.

Expenses for awards, officials, and equipment may be shared, or if the festival is rotated, the host institution may assume financial responsibility. Sports consists of basketball, softball, touch football, bowling, volleyball, handball, table tennis, golf, wrestling, tennis, and other activities which can be organized on a team basis. A point system is used to determine the festival winner. As an example, five points may be awarded to the first place winner in each event, four points to the second place winner, three to the third, two to the fourth, and one to the fifth.

Regulations of some sports festivals permit the use of all-star teams for each activity instead of intramural champions. This practice is questionable because it promotes divided loyalty within organizations and affects the units of participation in the intramural program. When all-star teams are chosen, participants are encouraged to further personal objectives rather than the interests of the team. In an effort to make the all-star squad, a basketball player may concentrate on becoming high point man in every game and overlook the importance of team play. Selection of intramural champions has the advange of providing added incentive for participation and performance for the reason that teams know they will represent their institution if they are the winners.

Play Days. The major objectives of play days or field days are participation, enjoyment, and sociability. They are organized most frequently in elementary, junior, and senior high school programs. This extramural activity is similar to the sports days program except teams are organized at the play day site. They are designated by colors, names, or other symbols, and members of each team represent several institutions in attendance. Play days include all individuals regardless of ability, whereas the tendency in sports days is to favor skilled players in that each participating unit wants to be represented by its best team. The events of the day are usually followed by a picnic, party, or banquet. Play days and sports days afford excellent opportunities for participants to plan and administer the activities with the guidance of staff members.

Arguments Against Extramurals

There is disagreement among intramural personnel as to the acceptance of extramurals, particularly highly competitive forms, as a part of intramural programs. However, recent trends indicate extramural participation is increasing, primarily caused by the growing sports club movement.

One of the major arguments against extramurals is that the development of intramurals is negatively affected. Programs become imbalanced when time, facilities, staff, equipment, and finances are applied to the participation of the few rather than the many. These same persons argue that good intramural programs eliminate the need for extramurals.

Others opposed to extramurals insist they are intercollegiate or interscholastic in nature and should be administered as varsity programs rather than as a part of intramurals. Opponents further suggest that extramural programming is thrust onto an already overburdened staff and results in inadequate administration of both intramurals and extramurals. Consequently, items such as travel, liability, and supervision are frequently left to the participants. Competition is frequently inequitable when arranged by these inexperienced persons. They argue that extramural participation cannot be justified unless the program can be administered in the best interests of the participants' welfare.

EXTRAMURALS AND SPORTS CLUBS

Arguments for Extramurals

Proponents of extramurals agree that proper administration is paramount to successful programming. Their primary contention is that many participants with varying degrees of ability who cannot make varsity teams are afforded experiences similar to those received by varsity squad members. Extramurals include more activities than interscholastic and intercollegiate programs, thus providing an even greater range of opportunities for more individuals. Some feel extramurals are an excellent answer to those who object to interscholastic competition at the elementary and junior high school levels. Extramural events are held less frequently, involve fewer practices, and no league championships, objections of those who oppose varsity competition for young age groups.

Some intramural directors favor extramurals as an incentive for intramurals. A few extramural meets each year are highlights of the intramural program and encourage players to seek improved performance so their team can be represented in these activities. This type of stimulation adds interest to intramurals and encourages more participation.

The need for expressing recreational interests is so great that some students will organize extramural competition with or without staff approval and support. Proponents suggest that it is only logical to exercise jurisdiction over extramurals instead of having students represent the institution in an unofficial capacity.

Administrative Considerations

When extramural activities are conducted, it is advisable to establish sound programming policies and procedures. Examples of these administrative guidelines are reviewed in the following sections.

Management. Extramural activities should be under the aegis of the intramural staff or similar unit in the institution, and ideally, all program ingredients should be provided. Some extramurals, particularly sports clubs, are administered with the assistance of the participants. In fact, many of them are primarily student organized and operated with minimal staff supervision. Limited staff finances, facilities, and equipment are frequently minimized by supplementary assistance from participants. An extramural or intramural–extramural advisory committee composed of participants and staff members should be established to assist with program supervision.

For purposes of administrative control, the application form in Figure 13–1 should be utilized. This form may be used by organizations desiring to sponsor extramural events or by intramural staff members who have

APPLICATION FOR SPONSORING AN EXTRAMURAL EVENT

DATE_____, 19____

NAME OF EXTRAMURAL GROUP_____

NAME OF EVENT_____

DATE(S)_____SITE_____

PARTICIPANTS INCLUDING INTRA AND EXTRA INSTITUTIONAL_____

_____

PURPOSE OF EVENT_____

_____

_____

_____

FINANCIAL ARRANGEMENTS, IF ANY:

　　　　ESTIMATED EXPENDITURES　　　　　　　ESTIMATED INCOME

_____　　　_____

_____　　　_____

_____　　　_____

_____　　　_____

　　　　　　　　　　　　BALANCE_____

FACILITIES ARRANGEMENTS_____

_____

_____

　　　　　　　　　　　　　　　　　　　_____
　　　　　　　　　　　　　　　　　　　　SIGNATURE OF APPLICANT

- -

APPLICATION APPROVED ON _____, 19___ BY_____
　　　　　　　　　　　　　　　　　　　　　INTRAMURAL-EXTRAMURAL DIRECTOR

Fig. 13-1. Application Form for Sponsoring an Extramural Event.

the responsibility of organizing extramural activities. When extramurals involve a specific game between two institutions, it is advisable to prepare a written contract similar to the one in Figure 13–2. These written agreements signed by representatives from each participating unit can avoid potential misunderstandings and conflicts.

EXTRAMURAL SPORTS CONTEST CONTRACT

THIS AGREEMENT, MADE AND ENTERED INTO THIS 15th DAY OF March, 19 __, BY AND BETWEEN Universal University INTRAMURAL-EXTRAMURAL AUTHORITIES AND THOSE OF Colossal College OR THEIR DULY AUTHORIZED AGENTS, STIPULATES:

FIRST: THE Soccer TEAMS REPRESENTING THE ABOVE NAMED INSTITUTIONS SHALL PLAY A GAME OF Soccer AT Brookdale ON October 1, 19 __, AT 2:00 P.M. AND AT Riverstown ON October 15, 19 __ AT 2:00 P.M.

SECOND: OFFICIALS FOR THESE GAMES SHALL BE AGREED UPON AT LEAST ONE MONTH PRIOR TO THE CONTESTS AND THE EXPENSES OF SAME SHALL BE PAID BY THE HOME TEAM.

THIRD: THESE GAMES SHALL BE PLAYED ACCORDING TO THE OFFICIAL RULES OF SOCCER.

FOURTH: IF EITHER EXTRAMURAL TEAM FAILS TO FULFILL THIS CONTRACT, THE TEAM REFUSING TO PLAY SHALL FORFEIT THE CONTEST TO THE OTHER TEAM.

FOR: UNIVERSAL UNIVERSITY   FOR: COLOSSAL COLLEGE

_____   _____
TEAM MANAGER   TEAM MANAGER

_____   _____
FACULTY ADVISOR   FACULTY ADVISOR

_____   _____
INTRAMURAL-EXTRAMURAL DIRECTOR   INTRAMURAL-EXTRAMURAL DIRECTOR

Fig. 13–2. Contract for an Extramural Sports Contest.

Finances.   The extent of financial support for extramurals must be dependent upon the source and amount of funds available for the total intramural program. Extramural expenditures should not unduly restrict participation by the masses in intramurals. Some programs follow a working principle of using not more than ten per cent of the intramural program operation budget, excluding staff salaries. Preferably, a separate budget for extramurals should be established.

Funds are used for equipment, supervision, entry fees, officiating, and transportation in amounts determined by total resources and needs. In some programs, participants pay all or a portion of their travel expenses. Because of cyclical interests and needs of groups, annual budgetary allotments must be flexible.

Transportation.   The number of trips per sport and the distance to extramural sites are usually restricted. The fatiguing effect of excessive travel may have a tendency to limit the performance and enjoyment of participation. Extramural activities are more effective if participating units are located in a reasonably close geographic area. It is also advisable to schedule competition on weekends to reduce the amount of time missed from classes.

Ideally, transportation should be provided by commercial bonded carriers or institutional vehicles, but participants frequently provide their own expenses and mode of travel. Participants should not be permitted to travel unless accompanied by a representative of the faculty. A written application should be submitted by groups desiring approval for extramural travel. (See Fig. 13–3.) Occasionally, extramural competition is scheduled to correspond with the varsity schedule, and extramural teams are transported with varsity teams.

Liability and Insurance.   In some extramural programs, minors must file a written parental or guardian consent and release before being eligible to participate. Through these forms, parents or guardians grant permission for their children to participate in approved extramural activities and release the institution from potential claims for injuries incurred during extramural participation. Individuals over twenty-one years of age are sometimes required to sign a liability release in their own behalf. (See Fig. 13–4.) Some programs only follow this procedure for activities which are considered to be hazardous or which involve travel.

Many institutions have blanket insurance programs covering participation in all activities including extramurals. High school and NCAA athletic insurance plans usually include extramurals. Insurance premiums are paid from institutional funds or by participants in the form of activity fees. Injuries of visiting and local participants are sometimes treated by the medical services of the institution.

APPLICATION FOR APPROVAL OF EXTRAMURAL TRAVEL

DATE_____, 19____

NAME OF EXTRAMURAL GROUP_____

DESTINATION_____

DEPARTURE: DAY_____ DATE_____ HOUR_____

RETURN: DAY_____ DATE_____ HOUR_____

STAFF MEMBER ACCOMPANYING GROUP_____

    ADDRESS_____ TEL. NO._____

HOST AT DESTINATION_____ TEL. NO._____

LODGING ARRANGEMENTS_____

_____

MODE OF TRANSPORTATION_____

IF BY AUTOMOBILE, IDENTIFY DRIVER(S):

    NAME_____ ADDRESS_____ TEL.NO._____

    NAME_____ ADDRESS_____ TEL.NO._____

    NAME_____ ADDRESS_____ TEL.NO._____

    NAME_____ ADDRESS_____ TEL.NO._____

_____   _____

   SIGNATURE OF APPLICANT   SIGNATURE OF ADVISOR

- -

APPLICATION APPROVED ON _____, 19___ BY _____

                                      INTRAMURAL-EXTRAMURAL DIRECTOR

Fig. 13–3. Application Form for Approval of Extramural Travel.

PARENTAL-GUARDIAN CONSENT AND RELEASE

I, **Jon A. Wilson**, BEING THE PARENT OR DULY CONSTITUTED GUARDIAN OF **Richard Wilson**, A MINOR, AGE **17**, AND A STUDENT AT UNIVERSAL UNIVERSITY, DO HEREBY CONSENT TO HIS OR HER PARTICIPATION IN UNIVERSITY APPROVED EXTRAMURAL ACTIVITIES. I HEREBY RELEASE THE TRUSTEES OF THE UNIVERSITY AND ALL OR ANY OFFICERS, FACULTY, AGENTS, STAFF, STUDENTS, OR ORGANIZATIONS OF SAID UNIVERSITY, FROM ANY RESPONSIBILITY OF LIABILITY FOR PERSONAL INJURY SUSTAINED BY HIM OR HER FOR ANY PROPERTY DAMAGE CAUSED BY HIM OR HER DURING OR BECAUSE OF HIS OR HER PARTICIPATION IN ORGANIZED EXTRAMURAL ACTIVITIES.

DATED THIS **15th** DAY OF   SIGNATURE *Jon A. Wilson*
September, 19—.   ADDRESS **7171 North Oaks Ave.**

                                                    St. Anthony, Minnesota

NOTE: ALL MINORS MUST FILE THIS RELEASE IN THE INTRAMURAL-EXTRAMURAL OFFICE BEFORE PARTICIPATION IN EXTRAMURAL ACTIVITIES.

Fig. 13–4. Parental or Guardian Consent and Release Form.

When extramural participants are transported by institutional vehicles or commercial carriers, accident and liability insurance is not a problem. However, if participants are transported in automobiles owned by students or staff, it is advisable to require minimum insurance coverage. In some instances, this problem is resolved by requiring all extramural participants to maintain low cost accident and liability insurance for extramural travel. Group policies written by commercial companies are available for this purpose.

SPORTS CLUBS

The basic organization of sports participation in European countries is the community sports club in which individuals of all ages and all levels of ability assemble to further their interests in a particular activity or phase of sports. Club members play within the group and against club teams representing other communities. Activities are administered by voluntary coaches, managers, and officers. Community facilities are utilized, and equipment and other club expenses are funded by membership dues.

This European concept is spreading in the United States through the formation of numerous sports clubs in educational institutions. Participants band together to share their interests in sporting activities. Sports clubs are essentially self-administered and self-instructed; to this extent, they follow the free university principle. Instructors, coaches, or supervisors may be employed or volunteers, but much of the instruction consists of club members exchanging knowledge and experience with each other.

In addition to instruction, events such as tournaments, trips, and social activities take them beyond the limits of the classroom. Some individuals prefer this type of association because it provides enjoyable participation without the regimentation and pressures of daily practices. The requirements of club membership are flexible and blend with the demands of a heavy academic study schedule.

Organization

Sports clubs elect officers, select faculty advisors, and determine their own membership which may include men and women, graduate and undergraduate students, faculty and nonacademic staff, and alumni. Occasionally, a few members are chosen from the community because they possess specific knowledge or skills that are valuable to the group. Some clubs operate according to written constitutions and by-laws while others function less formally, even to the exclusion of officers. Activities are financed by membership dues, special fund-raising projects, and funds from institutional sources.

More sports clubs are affiliated with intramural programs than with any other single unit. Others administering sports clubs are varsity athletic departments, physical education departments, student unions, student affairs departments, and recreation coordinator's offices. Administrative assistance ranges from complete or partial support in the form of finances, facilities, equipment, and travel to minimal arrangements for facilities and equipment. Other services may be provided such as secretarial typing and mimeographing, office space, telephone, and file cabinets. Because of the ingenuity and enthusiasm of club participants, a limited amount of initial support is sometimes all that is needed to move them in the direction of self-sufficiency.

Competition

Club competition is organized intramurally, extramurally, or in a combination of both. Some clubs stress instruction and participation within the group and never compete with anyone outside of the immediate locality. Others have as their primary objective extramural competition with similar interest groups, although they engage in intraclub practice and competition to prepare for these events. A few desire to attain varsity status and attempt to establish creditable records to further their cause.

Sources of extramural club participation include other educational institutions, play days, sports days, YMCA's, athletic clubs, industrial organizations, community recreation centers, military units, and regional and national competition such as NCAA, NAIA, and AAU tournaments. When engaging in extraclub participation, the extramural administrative procedures and forms outlined earlier in this chapter involving travel, liability, insurance, etc., should be followed.

Types of Clubs

A sports club can be formed to promote any interest, but soccer, judo, karate, bowling, archery, gymnastics, weight lifting, skiing, and badminton are among the most popular. Activities listed below indicate the types of sports clubs that are in existence.

archery	gymnastics	Sigma Delta Psi
aquatics	handball	skating
badminton	hiking	skiing
barbell	horseback riding	sky diving
baseball	horse polo	soccer
basketball	horseshoes	softball
bowling	ice hockey	sports car
bridge	judo	square dance
broomball	karate	squash
camping	lacrosse	surfing
canoeing	lifesaving	swimming
catalina	modern dance	table tennis
chess	mountaineering	tennis
cricket	orchesis	tobogganing
cross country	outing	track
curling	paddleball	trampoline
cycling	polo	volleyball
diving	riflery	water polo
fencing	rodeo	water safety
field hockey	rod and gun	water skiing
fishing	rowing	weight lifting
flying	rugby	white water canoe
folk dance	saddle	wrestling
football	sailing	yachting
glider or soaring	scuba and skin diving	yoga
golf	self-defense	

Although sports clubs may present administrative problems and of necessity must be limited because of restricted finances, facilities, and equipment, they play a very important role in providing sports experiences for many individuals. The sports club movement is gaining in popularity and formation of these clubs should be encouraged whenever possible.

14

Co-Intramurals, Special
Programs, and Evaluation

Co-intramurals, special programs, and evaluation are additional essentials of intramural programming. Most programs include co-intramural and co-extramural activities, and some directors organize special faculty programs, and events such as sports carnivals, open houses, clinics, and aquatic shows.

CO-INTRAMURALS

At one time, women were not allowed to attend institutions of higher learning, and not too many years ago, men seldom witnessed a women's gymnasium class even though participants were conservatively costumed in long black stockings, full-sleeved middies, and full-length bloomers. Today, traditions have been dissolved to a degree that many physical education classes are taught on a co-educational basis, and community groups such as churches, camps, and social service centers are placing greater emphasis on recreation for mixed groups.

One of the most encouraging trends is the extension of this concept in the intramural program. Unfortunately, staff, facilities, and equipment are frequently inadequate to develop fully these kinds of activities. Co-intramural or co-recreation activities, sometimes referred to as Co-I-M or Co-Rec, involve men and women, boys and girls, and truly fulfill the principle of "sports for all." All members of the institution may participate—upper grades, lower grades, staff, faculty, and families. Both phases of intramural programming apply to co-intramural participation, but the primary emphasis is placed on the fun, spirit, and fellowship of mixed play as opposed to highly organized, strenuous competition.

Although there is a natural desire for individuals to know and understand the opposite sex, they may be cautious about taking part in activities together. Frequently, through application of adult standards, it is assumed that youths develop these associations naturally, but in reality, there may be few opportunities for them to establish these wholesome relationships. Misinformation during adolescent years widens the confusion, and they need programs that encourage mutual understanding.

Much of an individual's life consists of sharing responsibilities, socializing, and working with members of the opposite sex. One of the primary aims of education is to provide experiences which aid in making these adjustments, and co-intramural programs make a positive contribution to this educational process. The co-intramural program is a laboratory in which participants have opportunities to develop an appreciation for commonality and differences of interests and skills. The degree of social adjustment varies considerably with each individual, and a well-integrated program benefits all participants regardless of their personal stage of development.

Through co-intramural activities, participants gain poise and confidence in social relationships. They usually give more attention to their personal conduct in the presence of their counterparts. This reaction is somewhat automatic. Men, for example, frequently refine their choice of words when they are with women.

Individuals are reached through co-intramurals who may not otherwise participate. Some of them do not take part in competitive or informal activities with members of their own sex, but when given the opportunity to participate with their girl friends or boy friends, they enthusiastically enter the program. Such activities also bring together persons of like interests, thus establishing many new friendships.

Types of Activities

Co-intramural activities must be carefully chosen to produce the preferred benefits of co-participation. Highly competitive, body contact activities are not desirable for these programs. Activities should coincide with skills taught in physical education classes and those learned in other phases of the intramural program. Special emphasis should be given to activities which can be utilized in later life. A well-balanced program includes competitive and noncompetitive team, individual, and dual sports, and informal, outing, and social activities. Examples of some of these are the following:

archery	fencing	singing
badminton	folk dancing	skiing
billiards	golf	slo pitch softball
bowling	ice skating	sleigh rides
box hockey	outings	social dancing
bridge	paddle tennis	swimming
canoeing	riding	table tennis
checkers	rifle shooting	tennis
chess	record-listening sessions	tobogganing
croquet	roller skating	trampolining
curling	sailing	volleyball
darts	shuffleboard	

When men and women or boys and girls participate in activities of a moderately competitive nature, it is necessary to modify the playing rules. For team play, the membership of teams is usually divided equally between men and women with the men playing under various restrictions. Through creative imagination, staff members can devise numerous rules modifications for co-intramural activities, examples of which are listed below.

SWIMMING

1. To equalize competition in a relay, men swim in sweatsuits or nightshirts.
2. Boy–girl combinations swim in tandem with the girl leading, using her arms, and the boy holding her feet, kicking with his legs.

GOLF

1. Both players hit a ball from the tee, select one to be played, and alternate swings until the ball is in the cup.
2. Scores of men and women are combined in mixed doubles medal or stroke play.

TRACK

1. Boys and girls run separately in the 50-yard dash and points earned by each individual are added to the team score.
2. Relay teams consist of two boys and two girls running alternately.

SOFTBALL

1. Five girls and five boys are on each team.
2. A special, extra soft, large ball is used which travels farther when hit with an easy swing than with a power swing.
3. The pitcher must be a girl and the catcher a boy.
4. Girls and boys must take turns in the batting order.
5. Boys must bat opposite their regular way, i.e., righthanders bat left handed and vice versa.
6. Boys cannot steal bases or bunt.
7. A run can be scored from third base only on a hit ball.

VOLLEYBALL

1. Teams consist of four girls and four boys.
2. All serves must be underhand.
3. Boys cannot spike or drive the ball across the net.
4. Each ball must be returned with a slight arc.
5. Each girl is allowed one assist to get the ball over the net on the serve.
6. A team is permitted three volleys, but for girls, one volley is defined as either one or two successive hits by the same girl.
7. Girls are required to handle the ball at least once in each series of volleys or before the ball is returned to the opposite side.

Administrative Suggestions

Representatives of the men's and women's intramural staff and other organizations interested in co-intramurals should be invited to the planning sessions. Attention should be given to selecting activities, establishing policies and procedures, arranging facilities and equipment, and providing supervision for the playing areas.

The most desirable type of program provides for daily co-participation opportunities. If facilities are available, participants should have a chance to recreate informally and co-intramurally throughout the day and evening. Another possibility is to schedule specific co-intramural sessions. These should be arranged at regular intervals so individuals can establish habits of participation. Sessions may be planned for the same days of each week such as Fridays and Saturdays. Weekend programs encourage students to remain on campus for their recreation and promote greater identification with the institution.

In addition to the informal participation, modified competitive tournaments may be arranged. These are usually more effective if scheduled during one or two evenings rather than over a period of several weeks. Competition may be encouraged by extending invitations to residence units and special interest clubs. "Quickie," on the spot tournaments are extremely successful in this type of programming.

For all co-intramural sessions, it is advisable to provide a congenial host and hostess to greet participants and make them feel they are most welcome. A first impression of an overly cautious guard at the door often leaves participants with an unwanted feeling and may cause them to seek recreation elsewhere.

Exhibitions in the pools or gymnasiums are excellent methods of exposing participants to new skills. Fencing, judo, karate, archery, badminton, tennis, gymnastic, and aquatic sports clubs have opportunities to exhibit bodily prowess and sports skills with the objective of entertaining participants and possibly gaining new members. Dancing and coke sessions may be scheduled to follow sporting activities.

Co-intramural activities may be scheduled in a men's or women's gymnasium or one accommodating both. Some older facilities may not be designed for co-intramurals, and special dressing room arrangements must be made. When participants play in a strange facility, men in a women's gym or vice versa, signs must be appropriately displayed to designate areas and to direct the flow of traffic from one to another. This procedure is particularly helpful when rotating groups at specified intervals to assure each participant an equal opportunity of using the various areas.

If volunteers assist in supervising and planning activities, there is very little cost involved in co-intramural programming. Publicity may be arranged through the usual intramural channels, and the same facilities and equipment are utilized. If community facilities are used, transportation costs may be provided through departmental funds, or each participant can be assessed a nominal fee.

Ideation sessions by program planners can produce numerous ideas for effective co-intramurals. The potential, as in all phases of intramural programming, is seemingly unlimited.

FACULTY PROGRAMS

Members of the faculty and/or staff of an educational or other institution have the same needs and desires for physical recreation as younger participants. Unfortunately, facilities and intramural staff are not always available to conduct these kinds of programs, and when such limitations exist, it is reasonable to establish priorities in favor of the students. However, the enthusiastic intramural director will find a time and a place to schedule faculty activities, even if it involves the use of community facilities such as public bowling lanes, golf courses, and parks.

Faculty members may organize their own teams and play in separate leagues. When the group is insufficiently large for this purpose, it may be possible to arrange challenge games with student groups and community teams. Size of the faculty is usually not a factor in arranging participation in individual and dual activities.

Scheduling faculty activities sometimes presents a problem due to the unpredictability of their professional commitments. Occasionally, they must attend local or out-of-town meetings on short notice. It is necessary to develop flexible scheduling patterns for faculty competition. As an example, substitution rules for bowling and golf teams must be lenient to allow for changes in team membership.

Types of Activities

Some of the most popular activities for the faculty are volleyball, bowling, slo pitch softball, basketball, water polo, tennis, golf, handball, paddleball, squash, badminton, swimming, jogging, and horseshoes. Basketball and touch football are too strenuous for older men and may only be successful where faculties include young instructors and teaching assistants.

The most effective means for faculty physical recreation is the informal, self-directed participation in which they engage leisurely in activities of their own choosing. However, some departments successfully conduct team competition on a league or tournament basis between the various colleges and departments. Point systems are used to create friendly rivalries between the various faculty groups. This type of competition is helpful in establishing rapport among members, particularly in large systems where opportunities for faculty interaction are limited.

Faculty members appreciate special dressing or locker room facilities. Ideal accommodations provide them with separate showers, steam rooms, and dressing and lounging areas for relaxation before and after participation. Another procedure which meets with faculty approval is reserving the swimming pool at specific times for their exclusive use.

Faculty sports clubs and faculty fitness forums are excellent methods of creating and maintaining interesting intramural participation. Instruction may be provided for members who wish to learn new skills, and competition can be arranged in the various activities. Newsletters can be distributed periodically to announce the winners of faculty competition and to inform them of the affairs of the club or forum. The group may elect officers and sponsor awards banquets and other social functions.

Faculty–Family Sessions

Faculty–family recreation sessions may be one of the most popular phases of the entire faculty intramural program. All facilities are reserved at specified times for use by members of the faculty, their wives, and children. These sessions are usually scheduled at times when students are least likely to use the facilities such as Friday evening, Saturday evening, or Sunday afternoon. The swimming pool, trampoline, and the gymnasium, where parents and children play badminton, volleyball, tennis, and basketball together, are favorite areas. When weather permits, outdoor areas may be utilized for family activities. Faculty–family picnics may be arranged to precede or terminate the day's activities.

A regulation which should be strictly enforced is that children should not be admitted unless accompanied by their parents. These sessions are designed for the entire family and parents should be encouraged to participate with their children. If youngsters are brought or sent to the session, the program loses its perspective. In addition to promoting family play, requiring parents to attend aids supervision because they can assume the responsibility for their own children. Additional intramural supervisors may be provided at the entrance, in the pool, and in the gymnasium area.

In some programs, parents are permitted to bring a limited number of guests, perhaps three or four. A boy may invite members of his Boy Scout troop or parents may celebrate their child's birthday by inviting neighborhood friends to a gymnasium play session followed by a birthday party at home.

Faculty–Student Sports Night

A faculty–student sports event is designed to promote fun, fellowship, and competition between faculty and student players. In this setting, students and instructors become better acquainted, and the mutual respect frequently generated provides for a better atmosphere in the classroom. This is particularly true in large school systems where classes are excessively large, limiting the opportunities for students and faculty to know each other.

Students usually welcome the challenge to play against and to defeat their instructors. They appreciate the teacher's willingness to "come down" to their level. Occasionally, students are shocked to hear their instructors complain about referees' decisions. They also note that many faculty members are as much concerned about recognition awards as students. The discovery is soon made that teachers are quite human, regardless of other impressions which may be received in the classroom.

Team, dual, and individual competition can be arranged once each year or during fall, winter, and spring seasons. Contests are scheduled for the afternoon and evening but usually not for more than one day. If events are scheduled over a period of several days, times and dates of the matches are often arranged by the contestants. Regular intramural activities are selected with emphasis on those which appear on the faculty program. This is not absolutely essential, but it is advantageous from the standpoint of maintaining relatively equal competition. If there is no faculty intramural program, it is usually possible to find some members who are reasonably proficient in performing the competitive skills of the activities selected.

In addition to offering a variety of sports, it is advisable to schedule several games or matches simultaneously. Three or four bowling matches, four or five volleyball games, several handball games and squash matches, all composed of different faculty–student teams and players, may be arranged. Championship I-M faculty teams can play student champions but not necessarily for the purpose of determining which team is better. The primary purpose of faculty–student programs is to expose students and faculty to social and sports experiences, regardless of their abilities.

For added interest, a simple point system can be utilized. One point is awarded to the faculty or student winner of each match or game. Three volleyball games equal three points; four handball games, four points; five bowling matches, five points; etc. A progressive point total is maintained with the final total determining the faculty–student winner. If there are twenty contests scheduled, the faculty or students could win by scores such as 11–9, 12–8, or 13–7.

A printed program listing team captains, players, officials, times, and courts serves as an effective method of administering and publicizing the faculty–student sports event. The printed program may instruct team captains to introduce their members to the opposition prior to playing and suggest that the losers treat the winners to coffee. Regardless of which group wins, participating in a faculty–student sports night can be a most enjoyable, meaningful experience.

SPECIAL EVENTS

Special events vary in name and content, but they have the same objectives of orientation, education, and entertainment. Exhibitions, festivals, circuses, carnivals, fairs, sportsoramas, clinics, and open houses attract large numbers of participants and spectators. Such functions stimulate interest in activities and publicize intramurals to the community. In some programs, limited intramural budgets are supplemented by charging small admission's fees to these events.

Separate exhibitions may be held in track, gymnastics, wrestling, fencing, diving, weight lifting, or all of these may be combined in one large demonstration. In some instances, championship intramural games in basketball, volleyball, and other indoor sports are played during these occasions. Novelty track and swimming events are sometimes included to add a humorous note.

Open Houses

The open house is an annual feature of many intramural programs. For this occasion, all facilities are used at the same time and spectators can observe a variety of activities. This type of program involves numerous minute details and requires careful planning and administration. Student managers and supervisors are extremely helpful in assisting with the coordination of these activities.

The annual open house offers an opportunity to play championship games before a large audience with the players gaining recognition for their participation and success. It is an excellent means of publicizing the intramural program to students, faculty, parents, participants, friends, and members of the community. The open house also serves as an educational opportunity to explain rules and sports techniques to the students and sports public.

Winter Sports Carnivals

Outdoor winter sports carnivals are popular where ice and snow are consistently available each winter. Activities include cross country skiing, cross country snow shoeing, ski relays, snow shoe dashes, ski jumping for distance, speed skating, and sled races. A point system is used to identify the winners.

Events may be combined with "snow week" celebrations. A student king and queen reign for the entire week and are honored guests at the ice show and snow week ball. When extensive carnivals are planned, they should provide activities for the highly skilled performer such as ice hockey, figure skating, and skiing for form and distance, as well as humorous events such as barrel stave races, broomball hockey with no skates, and dog sled races in which participants serve as the dogs.

Aquatic Festivals

Aquatic festivals or shows are staged indoors or outdoors, depending on available water facilities. Indoor productions are usually elaborate water pageants which portray a central theme. Many hours of practice are required to perform the synchronized swimming movements. An admission charge covers the cost of background material and costumes. These events are sometimes sponsored by girls or boys, but are usually more appealing if promoted on a co-intramural basis.

For the nonpageant-type festival, there is a wide variety of regulation and unusual aquatic events and contests from which to make selections. Swimming and diving events and canoe and boat races are of interest to spectators. For indoor and outdoor water exhibitions, life saving and boat safety are not only interesting but also educational.

Sports Clinics

The sports clinic may be staged at the beginning of the yearly intramural program to acquaint participants with the activities. At these sessions, beginners receive special instructions and more experienced players have opportunities to analyze and improve their skills. Instruction is given by varsity coaches, physical education teachers, and other experts. Demonstrations may be provided by varsity athletes and other skilled performers among the student body and faculty. Commercial establishments sometimes provide special services in the form of equipment loans and displays.

The clinic can be conducted in one afternoon or evening with each session emphasizing several different activities. Another method is to schedule several clinics throughout the year prior to the time various activities are offered in the program. This type of clinic publicizes intramurals and encourages individuals to participate who may not have done so previously on account of lack of ability or knowledge about the program.

PROGRAM EVALUATION

For effective programming, all phases of intramurals and extramurals must be continuously evaluated. The only thing that is constant is change, and intramural personnel should be totally aware of the changing patterns which affect participation. An analysis of the various aspects of the program not only aids in determining future directions, but also establishes soundings of the past.

Questions need to be answered such as: (1) To what degree does a program accomplish the predetermined objectives? (2) Is program quality sacrificed at the expense of quantity participation? (3) Are individuals satisfied to participate within the existing framework of operation? To answer these questions, points of reference must be established within the program for comparison with accepted standards and other programs. Suggestions for evaluating programs are presented in the following sections.

Statistical Records

Statistical records validly maintained and compared provide excellent criteria for program evaluation. However, they are primarily valuable for comparisons within a given program rather than between programs. Figures are sometimes misleading because directors apply different interpretations, and they are kept with varying degrees of accuracy. Consequently, a "participation" in one program may not have the same meaning in another program.

The form in Figure 14-1 identifies the kinds of information that are useful for evaluating intramural and extramural activities. Each activity

```
INTRAMURAL-EXTRAMURAL ACTIVITY EVALUATION

ACTIVITY_____INTRAMURAL_____EXTRAMURAL_____

BEGINNING DATE_____TERMINATION DATE_____

TYPE OF PARTICIPATION:  ORGANIZED COMPETITION_____SELF-DIRECTED, INFORMAL_____

                                         INDIVIDUAL_____DUAL_____TEAM_____

TYPE OF TOURNAMENT:_____

FACILITIES UTILIZED:_____

PUBLICITY MEDIA:_____

WINNER:_____RUNNER-UP:_____
```

- -

```
                          STATISTICAL SUMMARY
No. of potential participants  _____     No. of teams              _____

No. of participants            _____     No. of participations     _____

Percentage of participation    _____     Participations per team   _____

No. of games scheduled         _____     No. of officials          _____

No. of games forfeited         _____     No. of protests           _____

Percentage of games played     _____     No. of injuries           _____
```

- -

```
PROGRAMMING PROBLEMS:_____
_____
_____
_____

SUGGESTIONS FOR IMPROVEMENT:_____
_____
_____
_____

DATE OF EVALUATION:_____SUPERVISOR:_____
```

Fig. 14–1. Intramural–Extramural Activity Evaluation Form.

should be summarized on one of these forms for future reference. At the close of the intramural–extramural year, statistics from each form can be collated to provide participation totals for the entire year. Statistics from the previous year should be listed on the summary chart for purposes of comparison. Plotting these summaries on bar graphs presents a visual picture of participation cycles.

The following sections describe some of the statistical records utilized in the evaluative process.

Participants.   The term "participant" identifies the number of different individuals taking part in a program. The figure is particularly meaningful when related to the number of individuals enrolled in the institution. This comparison shows the percentage of the total enrollment participating in intramurals. When statistics are accurately recorded, avoiding duplication, they also indicate the number of times each individual participates.

In large programs, records of this type are cumbersome to maintain. As a substitute, the number of players per team is multiplied by the number of teams. This is not a valid figure in that it does not account for duplicate participation when totals of several activities are combined.

Participations.   A participation is intramurally defined as *each time* a player participates in an activity. If 12 team members from two teams play six basketball games, 72 participations are registered. However, two players playing five games in a single squash match are counted as two participations. These figures are found by totaling the number of players' names on all scorecards. Turnstiles or electric eye counters located at the entrance of participation areas may also be useful in determining the number of participations. Year-to-year comparisons show increases or decreases in overall program participation.

Number of Teams.   The number of teams in each activity is a valid figure to use in comparing year-to-year progress, particularly if tournament and other program procedures remain constant. It does not account for individual and dual competition, however, unless these activities are conducted on a team basis.

Number of Games.   Another valid evaluation figure is the number of games completed, if the count is made in the same manner each year. For example, a bowling match consists of three games and a volleyball match may involve five games. It is not proper to record one match for a particular year and the number of games per match the following year. A good principle to follow is to tabulate all games no matter how much playing time is involved, including games in matches for individual and dual activities such as handball, tennis, and table tennis.

Forfeits, Protests, and Ineligibles. Statistics on forfeits, drop-outs, game protests, and ineligible players provide an indication of student interest and responsibility as well as the effectiveness with which the program is administered. These items measure program "quality."

Ratings. The number of low sportsmanship ratings is another measure which reflects student cooperation and acceptance of the program. Officials' ratings are also valuable in evaluating the administration of game rules. A few isolated ratings may not be valid, but a percentage of high, average, or low ratings is meaningful, particularly when compared with previous records.

Check Lists and Rating Scales

Check lists containing statements of recommended program criteria may be developed for evaluating intramurals. These standards for reference can be located in professional literature, intramural textbooks, pamphlets, theses, and articles. An excellent example is the "Statement of Policies for Competition in Girls and Women's Sports," listed in Appendix B. Another method of developing a check list of program ingredients is to list the major headings and subheadings that appear in this textbook.

Evaluation check lists may be accompanied by scales that rate individual items according to the degree in which programs comply with the recommended standards. The scale may be equated on the basis of points such as 40, 30, 20, 10, 0, or word values—superior, excellent, average, fair, and poor.

An example of a check list is one developed by a National Conference on Intramural Sports for College Men and Women under the title "Criteria For Appraisal of Intramurals in Colleges and Universities." [1] Fifty-eight general operating principles are listed for intramural programs, and evaluators rate their presence in the program according to a scale of: (1) completely, (2) to a great degree, (3) to a moderate degree, (4) very little, and (5) not at all. No specific score is accumulated, but this comprehensive list identifies strong and weak points of programs.

Consultant Visitations

Intramural consultants may be invited to evaluate intramural programs. Although this procedure is extremely effective, consultant fees may be beyond the financial limitations of the budget. A similar evaluative procedure is to select a small group from the institution or community to visit successful intramural programs in institutions of comparable size. This

[1] American Association for Health, Physical Education, and Recreation, *Intramural Sports for College Men and Women* (Washington, D.C.: The Association, 1964), pp. 24–28.

visitation group compares other programs with the local program and makes suggestions for improvement. It should include professional and lay personnel from the community.

Evaluation by Participants

The reactions of participants provide an excellent barometer for determining the success of the program. Methods of soliciting their viewpoints are surveys, conferences, interviews, suggestion boxes, and council meetings. Information obtained reveals popularity of activities, effectiveness with which the program is administered, and suggestions for program improvement.

15

Scheduling and Tournament Aids

The scheduling and tournament forms, charts, and tables in this chapter provide invaluable assistance for intramural personnel and others charged with the responsibility of arranging competitive participation. These materials supplement the comprehensive tournament explanations in Chapter 9 and serve as ready references for administering some of the numerous organizational details involved in intramural programming. They can be utilized completely or partially in all programs, depending on the magnitude of the operation.

Experienced intramural directors realize the value of these aids as "short cuts" to repetitive office routines. A quick referral to the charts and tables produces an answer or presents a guide to tournament structuring and scheduling. If formulas, percentages, averages, seedings, byes, games, rounds, handicaps, and points are laboriously calculated with the long method each time competition is arranged, time is needlessly wasted and the margin for error increases. Secretaries, clerical assistants, and student managers can effectively arrange tournaments and other participation procedures by copying some of these forms, thereby freeing the director's attention for other administrative responsibilities.

Tournament Calculator

The tournament calculator in Figure 15–1 identifies the number of rounds, byes, and games for single elimination, double elimination, and

NO. OF EN- TRIES	SINGLE ELIMINATION				DOUBLE ELIMINATION				ROUND ROBIN		
	No. of Rounds	No. of Byes		No. of Games	No. of Rounds	No. of Byes		No. of Games	No. of Rounds	No. of Byes	No. of Games
		Top	Bot- tom			Top	Bot- tom				
3	2	0	1	2	4 or 5	0	1	4 or 5	3	3	3
4	2	0	0	3	4 or 5	0	0	6 or 7	3	0	6
5	3	1	2	4	6 or 7	1	2	8 or 9	5	5	10
6	3	1	1	5	6 or 7	1	1	10 or 11	5	0	15
7	3	0	1	6	6 or 7	0	1	12 or 13	7	7	21
8	3	0	0	7	6 or 7	0	0	14 or 15	7	0	28
9	4	3	4	8	8 or 9	3	4	16 or 17	9	9	36
10	4	3	3	9	8 or 9	3	3	18 or 19	9	0	45
11	4	2	3	10	8 or 9	2	3	20 or 21	11	11	55
12	4	2	2	11	8 or 9	2	2	22 or 23	11	0	66
13	4	1	2	12	8 or 9	1	2	24 or 25	13	13	78
14	4	1	1	13	8 or 9	1	1	26 or 27	13	0	91
15	4	0	1	14	8 or 9	0	1	28 or 29	15	15	105
16	4	0	0	15	8 or 9	0	0	30 or 31	15	0	120
17	5	7	8	16	10 or 11	7	8	32 or 33	17	17	136
18	5	7	7	17	10 or 11	7	7	34 or 35	17	0	153
19	5	6	7	18	10 or 11	6	7	36 or 37	19	19	171
20	5	6	6	19	10 or 11	6	6	38 or 39	19	0	190
21	5	5	6	20	10 or 11	5	6	40 or 41	21	21	210
22	5	5	5	21	10 or 11	5	5	42 or 43	21	0	231
23	5	4	5	22	10 or 11	4	5	44 or 45	23	23	253
24	5	4	4	23	10 or 11	4	4	46 or 47	23	0	276
25	5	3	4	24	10 or 11	3	4	48 or 49	25	25	300
26	5	3	3	25	10 or 11	3	3	50 or 51	25	0	325
27	5	2	3	26	10 or 11	2	3	52 or 53	27	27	351
28	5	2	2	27	10 or 11	2	2	54 or 55	27	0	378
29	5	1	2	28	10 or 11	1	2	56 or 57	29	29	406
30	5	1	1	29	10 or 11	1	1	58 or 59	29	0	435
31	5	0	1	30	10 or 11	0	1	60 or 61	31	31	465
32	5	0	0	31	10 or 11	0	0	62 or 63	31	0	496

Fig. 15–1. Tournament Calculator for Single Elimination, Double Elimination, and Round Robin Tournaments.

round robin tournaments involving three through thirty-two entries. For-mulas for determining this type of information are presented in Chapter 9. Since these are easily misunderstood or forgotten, this calculator lists the answers to the formulas for specific numbers of entries for the conven-ience of tournament designers.

A survey of this chart indicates which type of competition is best suited for a specific situation in terms of the numbers of entries to be organized and the time and facilities available. If there are 32 teams for a tournament and the director plans to use a round robin, the calculator shows that 496 games are required, a number which is highly impractical. The chart reveals the number of games when 32 teams are divided into eight 4-team leagues, four 8-team leagues, or two 16-team leagues. Four-team round robins require 6 games for each league; therefore, eight 4-team leagues total 48 games, considerably fewer than 496 games for a 32-team round robin.

When these 32 entries are arranged in four 8-team leagues, the total number of games is 112. The calculator indicates that 28 games must be played to complete each 8-team round robin, and 4 leagues times 28 games equal 112 games. The tournament director determines how many games can be played on the basis of available time, facilities, and equipment; and then, with the aid of the calculator, he selects eight 4-team leagues, four 8-team leagues, or another tournament plan.

If there are 13 entries for a tennis tournament and it seems best to run a single elimination tournament, the calculator shows that 3 byes, 4 rounds, and 12 games are necessary; for a double elimination tournament, 3 byes, 8 or 9 rounds, and 24 or 25 games.

Placement of Byes Chart

Correctly positioning byes on a draw sheet is a difficult task for many, particularly those of limited tournament construction experience. The chart in Figure 15–2 aids immeasurably in performing this assignment. This chart follows the "listed byes" technique of tournament structuring, but the "implied byes" method may be utilized by eliminating the word "bye" and advancing the entry to the second round in a bracket corresponding to a bye position.

Referring to this table, the intramural director can readily determine how many lines are needed for the draw sheet because they are directly related to the number of entries and byes. For example, the table shows a 16-line draw sheet is required for 14 entries, and byes are placed on lines 1 and 16. With 11 entries, 5 byes are positioned on lines 1, 8, 9, 13, and 16 of a 16-line draw sheet. For 8 entries, an 8-line draw sheet is used and there are no byes.

This chart conforms to the principles of positioning byes described in Chapter 9. All byes appear in the first round; when the number of byes is uneven the extra bye is placed in the bottom half of the tournament, and byes are positioned symmetrically throughout the draw sheet. To further simplify tournament structuring, printed tournament draw sheets are available from commercial sporting goods firms.

LINES

No. of Entries	No. of Byes	LINES		No. of Entries	No. of Byes	LINES
3	1	4		33	31	1,4,5,8,9,12,13,16,17,21,24,25,28,29,32,33,36,37,40,41,44,45,48,49,52,53,56,57,60,61,64
4	0	None		34	30	1,4,5,8,9,12,13,16,17,21,24,25,28,29,32,33,36,37,40,41,44,48,49,52,53,56,57,60,61,64
		Use 4-Line Draw Sheets		35	29	1,4,5,8,9,12,16,17,21,24,25,28,29,32,33,36,37,40,41,44,48,49,52,53,56,57,60,61,64
5	3	1,5,8		36	28	1,4,5,8,9,12,16,17,21,24,25,28,29,32,33,36,37,40,41,44,48,49,53,56,57,60,61,64
6	2	1,8		37	27	1,4,5,8,9,12,16,17,24,25,28,29,32,33,36,37,40,41,44,48,49,53,56,57,60,61,64
7	1	8		38	26	1,4,5,8,9,12,16,17,24,25,28,29,32,33,36,37,40,41,48,49,53,56,57,60,61,64
8	0	None		39	25	1,4,5,8,9,16,17,24,25,28,29,32,33,36,37,40,41,48,49,53,56,57,60,61,64
		Use 8-Line Draw Sheets		40	24	1,4,5,8,9,16,17,24,25,28,29,32,33,36,37,40,41,48,49,56,57,60,61,64
9	7	1,4,8,9,12,13,16		41	23	1,4,5,8,9,16,17,24,25,29,32,33,36,37,40,41,48,49,56,57,60,61,64
10	6	1,4,8,9,13,16		42	22	1,4,5,8,9,16,17,24,25,29,32,33,36,40,41,48,49,56,57,60,61,64
11	5	1,8,9,13,16		43	21	1,4,8,9,16,17,24,25,29,32,33,36,40,41,48,49,56,57,60,61,64
12	4	1,8,9,16		44	20	1,4,8,9,16,17,24,25,29,32,33,36,40,41,48,49,56,57,61,64
13	3	1,9,16		45	19	1,4,8,9,16,17,24,25,32,33,36,40,41,48,49,56,57,61,64
14	2	1,16		46	18	1,4,8,9,16,17,24,25,32,33,40,41,48,49,56,57,61,64
15	1	16		47	17	1,8,9,16,17,24,25,32,33,40,41,48,49,56,57,61,64
16	0	None		48	16	1,8,9,16,17,24,25,32,33,40,41,48,49,56,57,64
		Use 16-Line Draw Sheets		49	15	1,8,9,16,17,25,32,33,40,41,48,49,56,57,64
17	15	1,4,5,8,9,13,16,17,20,21,24,25,28,29,32		50	14	1,8,9,16,17,25,32,33,40,48,49,56,57,64
18	14	1,4,5,8,9,13,16,17,20,24,25,28,29,32		51	13	1,8,16,17,25,32,33,40,48,49,56,57,64
19	13	1,4,8,9,13,16,17,20,24,25,28,29,32		52	12	1,8,16,17,25,32,33,40,48,49,57,64
20	12	1,4,8,9,13,16,17,20,24,25,29,32		53	11	1,8,16,17,32,33,40,48,49,57,64
21	11	1,4,8,9,16,17,20,24,25,29,32		54	10	1,8,16,17,32,33,48,49,57,64
22	10	1,4,8,9,16,17,24,25,29,32		55	9	1,16,17,32,33,48,49,57,64
23	9	1,8,9,16,17,24,25,29,32		56	8	1,16,17,32,33,48,49,64
24	8	1,8,9,16,17,24,25,32		57	7	1,16,32,33,48,49,64
25	7	1,8,16,17,24,25,32		58	6	1,16,32,33,49,64
26	6	1,8,16,17,25,32		59	5	1,32,33,49,64
27	5	1,16,17,25,32		60	4	1,32,33,49,64
28	4	1,16,17,32		61	3	1,33,64
29	3	1,17,32		62	2	1,64
30	2	1,32		63	1	64
31	1	32		64	0	None
32	0	None				*Use 64-Line Draw Sheets*
		Use 32-Line Draw Sheets				

Fig. 15–2. Byes Placement Chart: 3 Through 64 Entries.

Fig. 15-3. Placement of Seedings On 4, 8, 16, and 32 Entry Draw Sheets.

Seeding Placement Chart

The proper placement of seeded players on a tournament draw sheet is an equally perplexing problem for some tournament directors. Although seeding is discussed in Chapter 9, Figure 15–3 resolves the placement problem by presenting the information in condensed form. The maximum number of seeded players for 4, 8, 16, and 32 entries is properly positioned in the first round of the respective draw sheets.

Usually no more than 2 players are seeded out of 4 entries, 4 players for 8 entries, 8 players for 16 entries, and 16 players for 32 entries. However, if sufficient information is known about the abilities of the participants, more of them may be seeded, and the numbers of these seeds are represented in parentheses. When the number of entries requires the use of byes, they should be given to the seeded players. The positioning of seeds in this chart conforms to the byes placement pattern established in Figure 15–2.

Elimination Tournament Work Sheet

The structuring of elimination tournaments can be greatly facilitated by utilizing the tournament work sheet in Figure 15–4. Each of the lines is numbered for 2-, 4-, 8-, 16-, and 32-entry draw sheets. This combination draw sheet may be used for any one of these tournaments. For example, when making a tournament with only 8 lines, the first 2 rounds (32- and 16-entry brackets) remain unused. After the byes, seedings, and players' names have been properly arranged, the tournament information can be mimeographed or transferred to a more permanent draw sheet reflecting only whatever portion of the work sheet is used.

When tournaments are originally designed, drawing them on graph paper expedites construction. Eighth-inch squares grouped in one-inch patterns eliminate the need for a ruler. This type of graph paper may also be placed under a sheet of vellum or other partially transparent white paper. The grid formed by the graph lines provides an excellent guide for equitably positioning the brackets throughout the draw sheet.

Single Elimination Tournament Draw Sheets

Single elimination tournament draw sheets for listed and implied byes are presented in Figure 15–5, a–f, for three through sixteen entries. Listed byes tournaments on the left side of each figure indicate entries by letters A, B, C, D, and so on. Implied byes are shown on the right side

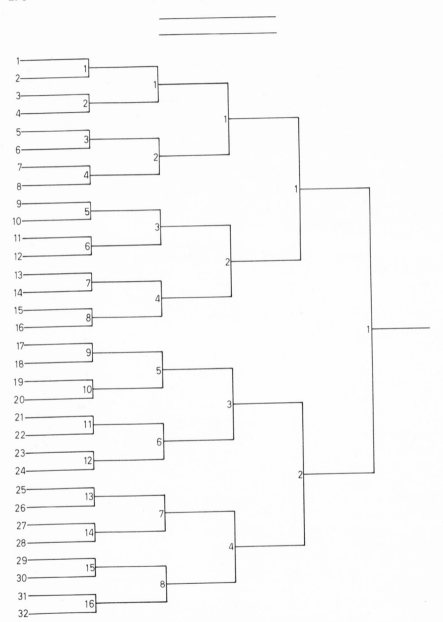

Fig. 15–4. Elimination Tournament Work Sheet.

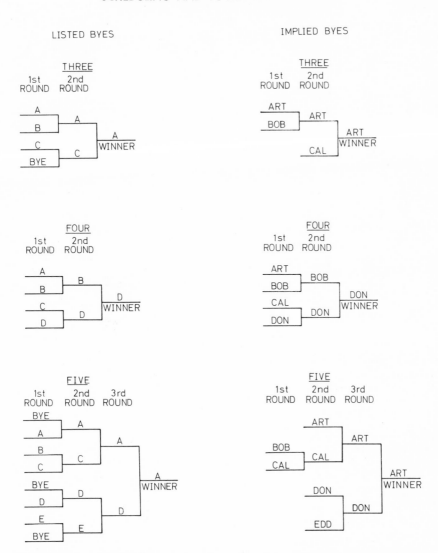

Fig. 15–5(a). Single Elimination Tournament Draw Sheets: 3 Through 16 Entries. (Left) Listed Byes. (Right) Implied Byes.

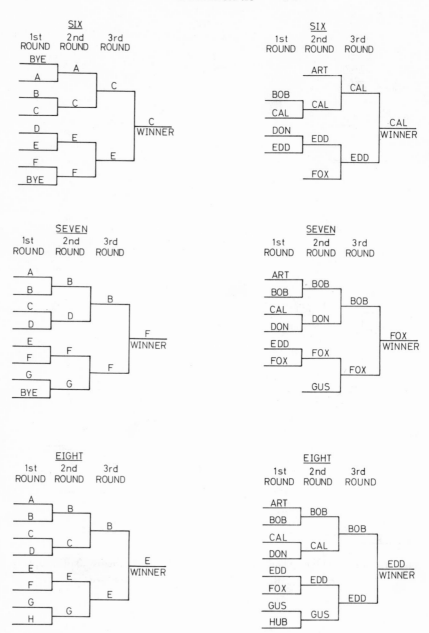

Fig. 15–5(b). (Continued.)

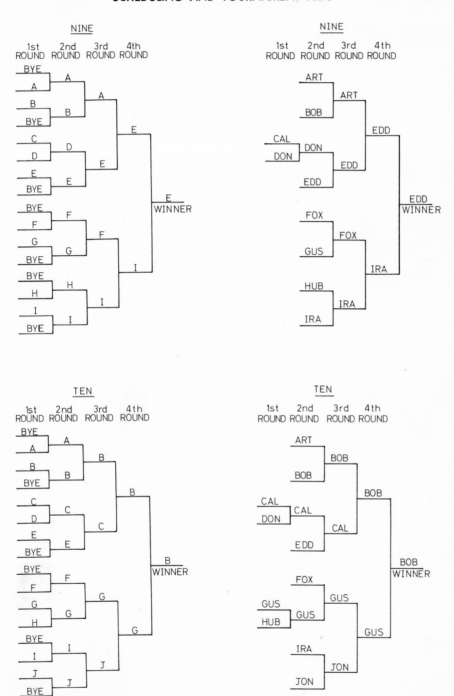

Fig. 15–5(c). (Continued.)

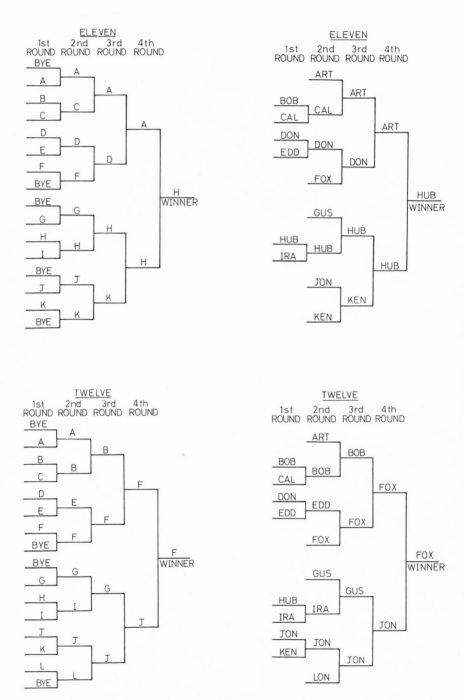

Fig. 15–5(d). (Continued.)

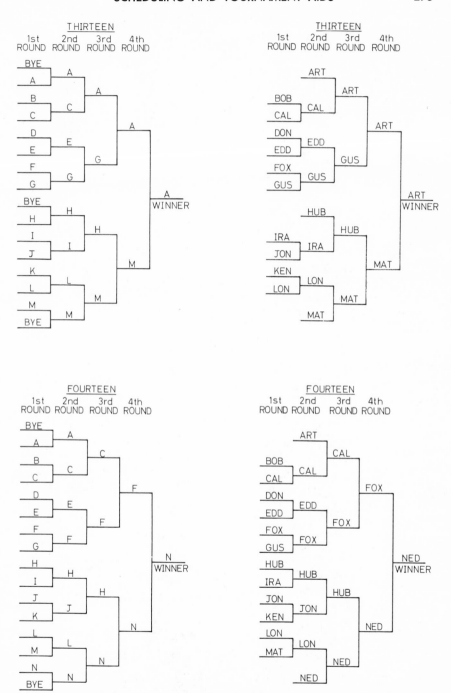

Fig. 15–5(e). (Continued.)

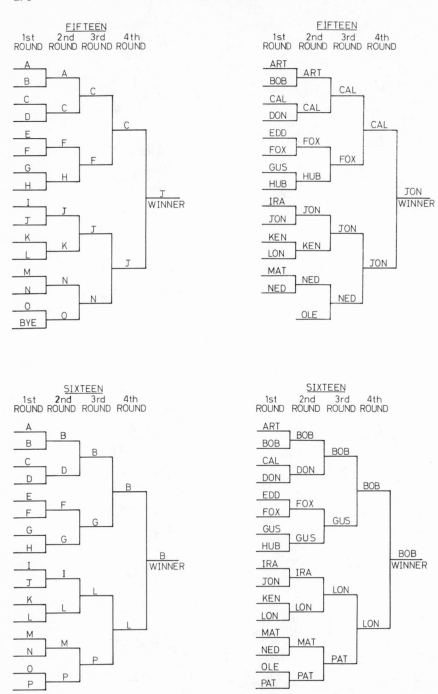

Fig. 15–5(f). (Concluded.)

with names for the entries. Byes on the draw sheets are positioned in accordance with the byes placement chart in Figure 15–2. After team or player names are substituted for the letters on the listed byes draw sheet and for the names on the implied byes brackets, the tournament is ready to be contested. Copies may be mimeographed or duplicated with some other process for distribution to the participants.

For larger numbers of entries, these draw sheets may be combined. For 27 entries, a 14-entry draw sheet is placed immediately above a 13-entry draw sheet, and the lines of the two finalists are connected. In a similar manner, two 27's, or two 14's and two 13's, can be combined for 54 entries. This arrangement will not produce properly positioned byes, but the number of byes will always be correct.

Double Elimination Tournament Draw Sheets

Double elimination draw sheets are more complicated to construct than single elimination tournaments primarily because byes exist beyond the first round in the losers' division, and it is difficult to bracket losing players in their proper order. Draw sheets for three through sixteen entries are presented as a guide for tournament supervisors in Figure 15–6, a–h.

The draw sheets are arranged according to the back-to-back method with implied byes. First names of individuals are used to identify the winners and losers readily. Names of teams or individual players can be substituted for those appearing in the brackets of the first round. The winners of the first round advance to the right, and the losers follow the broken lines and arrows to the left. The winners of these two tournaments play for the championship and unless one of them has two losses, an extra game is played. The bracket in the upper right-hand corner shows a final playoff game, if one is necessary. (See page 149 for an explanation.)

Mueller-Anderson Playback Draw Sheets

Mueller-Anderson playback tournament draw sheets for four through twelve entries are included in Figure 15–7, a–e. This type of playback conveniently ranks all of the players, and it is accomplished in approximately the same amount of time required for a single elimination of the same number of entries. In some of the designs, the winners are ranked from right to left, and in others, they are ranked partially from right to left with the remainder from left to right. Winners advance on solid lines and losers move on broken lines. It is also possible to structure these using the over-under method described in Chapter 9.

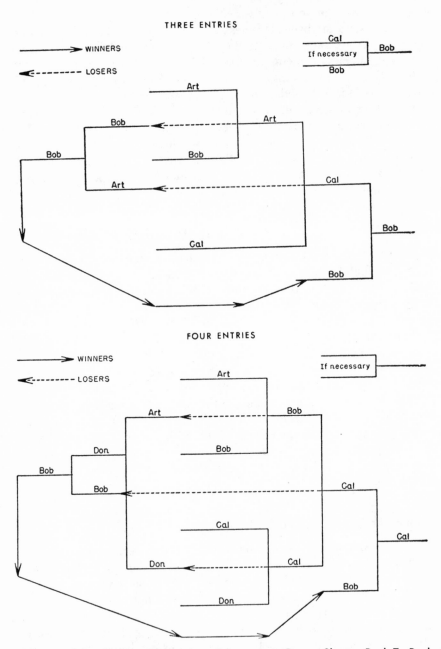

Fig. 15–6(a). Double Elimination Tournament Draw Sheet: Back-To-Back Method with Implied Byes; 3 Through 16 Entries.

FIVE ENTRIES

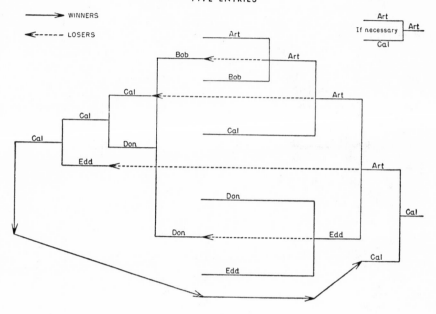

SIX ENTRIES

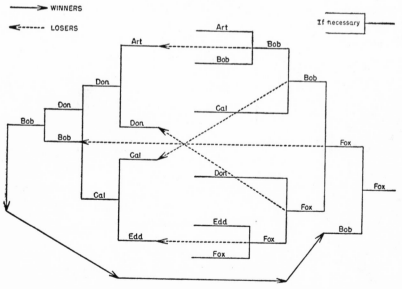

Fig. 15–6(b).   (Continued.)

SEVEN ENTRIES

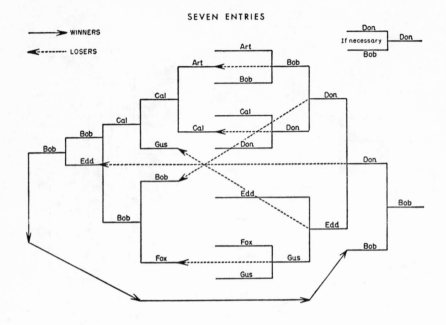

EIGHT ENTRIES

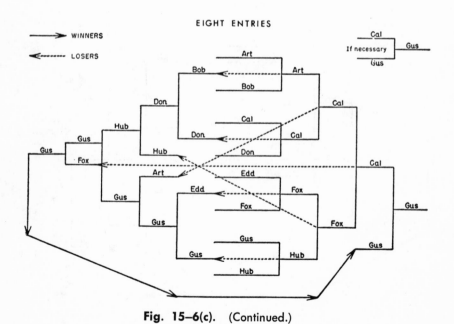

Fig. 15–6(c).   (Continued.)

NINE ENTRIES

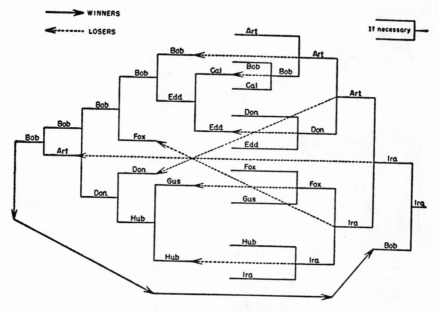

TEN ENTRIES

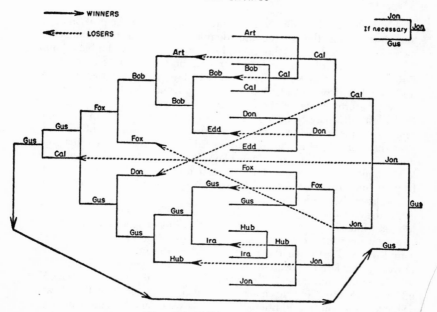

Fig. 15–6(d). (Continued.)

ELEVEN ENTRIES

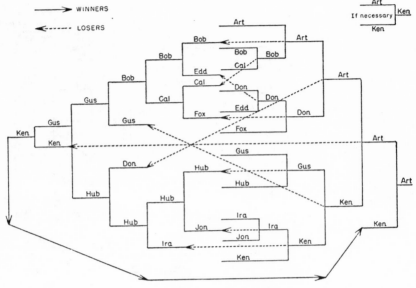

Fig. 15–6(e). (Continued.)

A detailed explanation of this draw sheet may be helpful since this tournament and the succeeding double elimination tournaments are more complicated than the preceding ones. With a double elimination tournament of eleven games or entrants, there are five byes—Art, Fox, Gus, Hub, and Ken. These do not play in the first round. In the first round Bob plays Cal; Bob wins and advances to the right and *Cal* follows the broken line to the left. Don plays Edd; *Edd* loses and moves to the left. Ira plays Jon; *Jon* loses and moves to the left. In the second round, Art plays Bob and wins; therefore moves to the right. *Bob* follows the broken line to the left to find Edd his partner for the first round of the "losers" tournament. Don plays *Fox* who loses and moves to the left to meet Cal. Gus and Hub meet; *Hub* loses and moves to the left to play Jon. *Ira* plays Ken and loses. Ira waits until the second round of the losers before he plays.

In the third round, Art and Don–Gus and Ken meet. *Don* and *Gus* lose and follow the broken line to the left to meet Hub and Bob respectively (winners of the second round of the losers tournament) in the third round of the losers. In the fourth round of the winners *Ken* loses and moves to the left to play Gus who has won his contest with Hub. Art wins the main tournament; Ken wins the second tournament. Now Ken advances to the right to meet Art for the play-off, which Art wins. (Should Ken win, an additional contest is necessary because this would be Art's first loss. The bracket in the upper right would obtain then— this shows Ken the winner of the over-all tourney.)

TWELVE ENTRIES

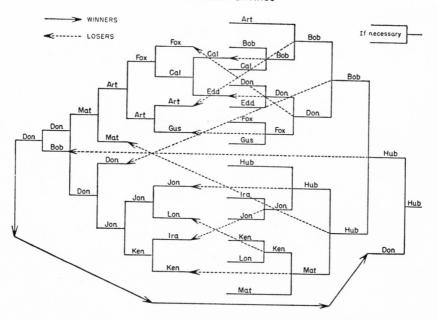

THIRTEEN ENTRIES

Fig. 15–6(f). (Continued.)

FOURTEEN ENTRIES

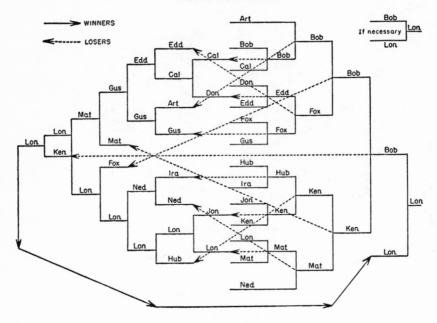

FIFTEEN ENTRIES

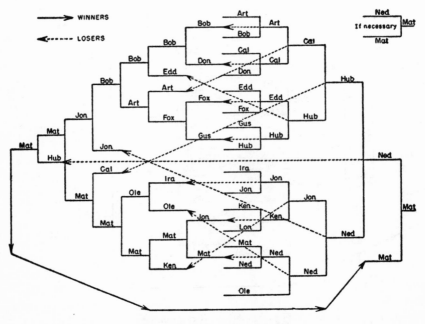

Fig. 15–6(g). (Continued.)

SIXTEEN ENTRIES

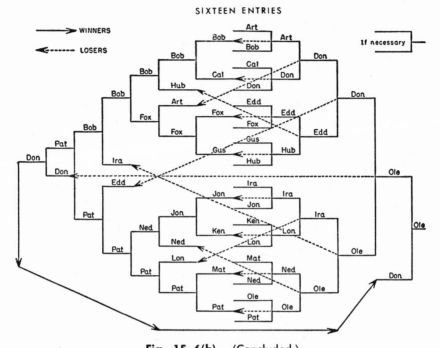

Fig. 15–6(h).   (Concluded.)

Tables of Round Robin Schedules

The round robin tables (Fig. 15–8, a and b) show the schedule for each date or round for three through sixteen entries. The numbers which appear for each date represent teams scheduled to play on a given day. For an uneven number of entries, the number receiving a bye is noted for each round. To schedule a complete round robin, the director simply substitutes names of entries for the numbers in the tables.

These tables designate the numbers of bowling lanes, courts, or fields, and are designed so participation is distributed as evenly as possible over each specifically numbered area. Some facilities may be such that it is distinctly advantageous or disadvantageous to play each round on the same location. This table accounts for this factor and distributes participation on a reasonably equitable basis. Some individuals responsible for scheduling are also concerned about playing half of the games at home and the other half away. The tables are constructed to reflect the home and visiting teams. Numbers in the first column in each round represent "home" games and those in the second column identify "away" games.

FOUR ENTRIES

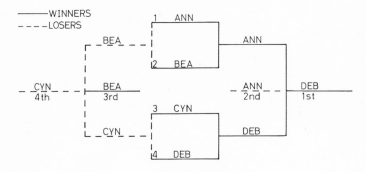

FIVE ENTRIES

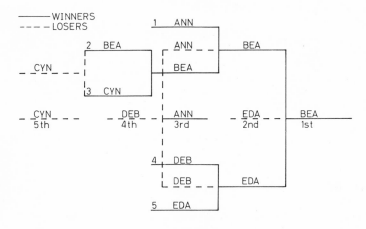

SIX ENTRIES

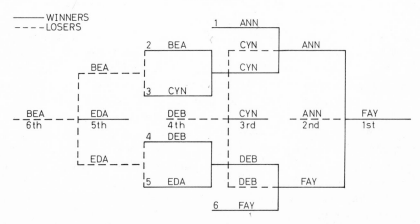

Fig. 15–7(a). Mueller-Anderson Playback Draw Sheets: Back-To-Back Method; 4 Through 12 Entries.

SEVEN ENTRIES

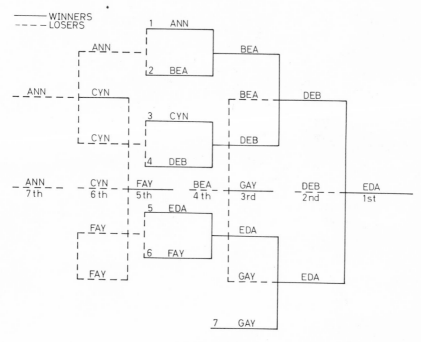

EIGHT ENTRIES

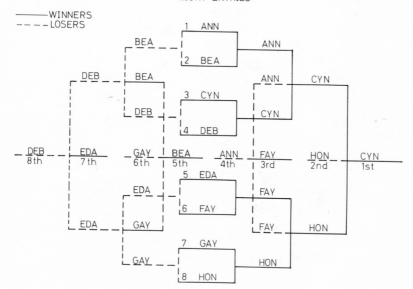

Fig. 15–7(b).   (Continued.)

NINE ENTRIES

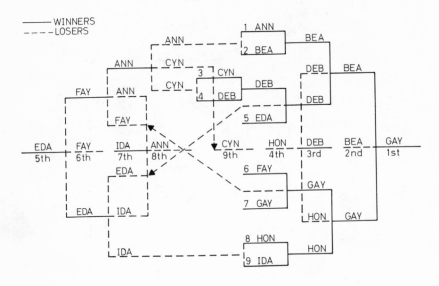

TEN ENTRIES

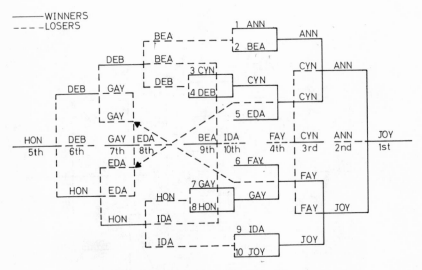

Fig. 15–7(c). (Continued.)

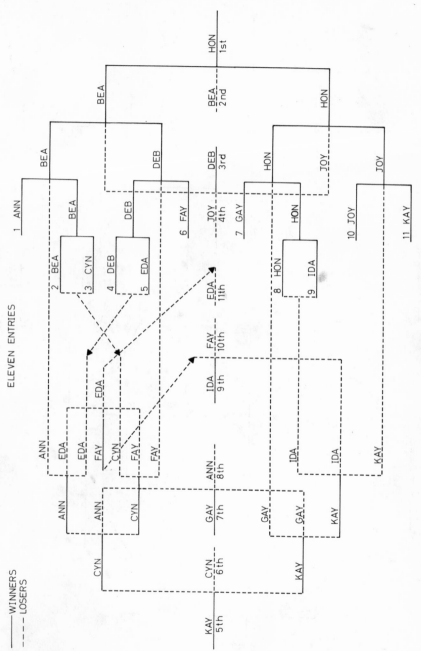

Fig. 15–7(d). (Continued.)

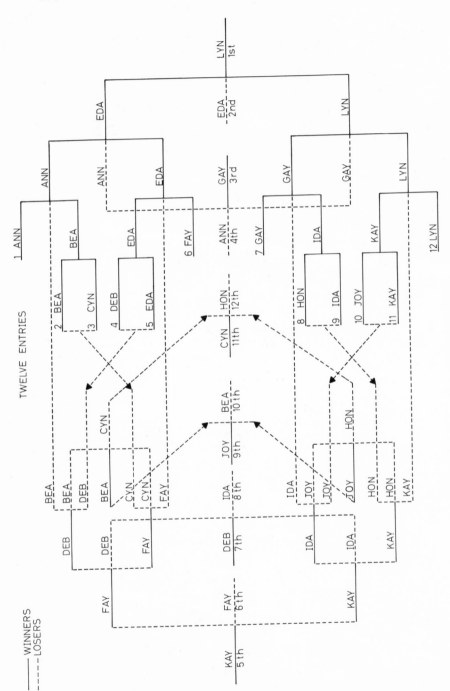

Fig. 15-7(e). (Concluded.)

No. of Entries	Lanes	Courts or Fields	1st Date H-A	2nd Date H-A	3rd Date H-A	4th Date H-A	5th Date H-A	6th Date H-A	7th Date H-A	8th Date H-A	9th Date H-A	10th Date H-A	11th Date H-A
3	1- 2	I	1- 2 3 bye	3- 1 2 bye	2- 3 1 bye	— —	— —	— —	— —	— —	— —	— —	— —
4	1- 2 3- 4	I II	1- 2 4- 3	3- 1 2- 4	3- 2 4- 1	— —	— —	— —	— —	— —	— —	— —	— —
5	1- 2 3- 4	I II	1- 5 4- 2 3 bye	5- 4 3- 1 2 bye	4- 3 2- 5 1 bye	3- 2 1- 4 5 bye	2- 1 5- 3 4 bye	— — —	— — —	— — —	— — —	— — —	— — —
6	1- 2 3- 4 5- 6	I II III	1- 2 4- 3 5- 6	6- 4 2- 5 3- 1	5- 3 4- 1 2- 6	3- 2 1- 6 4- 5	5- 1 6- 3 2- 4	— — —	— — —	— — —	— — —	— — —	— — —
7	1- 2 3- 4 5- 6	I II III	3- 6 1- 5 7- 2 4 bye	5- 7 4- 2 1- 3 6 bye	5- 4 7- 3 2- 6 1 bye	3- 4 2- 1 6- 5 7 bye	7- 1 4- 6 5- 2 3 bye	2- 3 6- 7 1- 4 5 bye	6- 1 3- 5 4- 7 2 bye	— — — —	— — — —	— — — —	— — — —
8	1- 2 3- 4 5- 6 7- 8	I II III IV	1- 2 3- 4 5- 6 7- 8	6- 8 5- 7 2- 4 1- 3	4- 5 8- 1 3- 7 2- 6	3- 6 7- 2 1- 5 4- 8	7- 1 6- 4 8- 3 5- 2	2- 3 8- 5 4- 1 6- 7	7- 4 1- 6 2- 8 3- 5	— — — —	— — — —	— — — —	— — — —
9	1- 2 3- 4 5- 6 7- 8	I II III IV	6- 5 3- 4 1- 2 7- 8 9 bye	4- 7 6- 9 8- 1 2- 5 3 bye	9- 8 5- 1 2- 6 7- 3 4 bye	7- 2 4- 9 8- 3 1- 6 5 bye	3- 5 6- 8 9- 7 2- 4 1 bye	8- 2 1- 7 5- 4 3- 9 6 bye	6- 3 5- 8 9- 2 4- 1 7 bye	8- 4 7- 6 3- 1 9- 5 2 bye	1- 9 2- 3 5- 7 4- 6 8 bye	— — — — —	— — — — —
10	1- 2 3- 4 5- 6 7- 8 9-10	I II III IV V	1-10 9- 2 3- 8 4- 7 5- 6	7- 2 6- 3 5- 4 10- 9 8- 1	8- 9 1- 7 2- 6 3- 5 4-10	4- 3 10- 8 9- 7 6- 1 5- 2	10- 6 7- 5 2- 1 8- 4 9- 3	5- 9 6- 8 7-10 3- 2 1- 4	3- 1 4- 9 8- 5 6- 7 10- 2	4- 6 5-10 9- 1 2- 8 7- 3	7- 8 2- 4 10- 3 1- 5 6- 9	— — — — —	— — — — —
11	1- 2 3- 4 5- 6 7- 8 9-10	I II III IV V	5- 6 3- 4 9-10 1- 2 7- 8 11 bye	10-11 8- 9 4- 5 2- 3 6- 7 1 bye	3- 5 4- 6 8-10 9- 7 11- 1 2 bye	7- 4 5- 1 6- 3 11- 8 10- 2 9 bye	2- 4 9-11 5- 7 6- 8 1- 3 10 bye	1-10 7- 2 6-11 4- 9 8- 5 3 bye	2- 8 10- 6 4- 1 11- 3 5- 9 7 bye	9- 1 3-10 7-11 8- 4 2- 5 6 bye	4-11 1- 8 6- 2 10- 7 3- 9 5 bye	9- 6 7- 1 8- 3 5-10 11- 2 4 bye	3- 7 11- 5 2- ,9 1- 6 10- 4 8 bye
12	1- 2 3- 4 5- 6 7- 8 9-10 11-12	I II III IV V VI	1- 2 3- 4 5- 6 7- 8 9-10 11-12	10-11 8- 9 12- 1 4- 5 6- 7 2- 3	3- 5 2-12 8-10 7- 9 1-11 4- 6	7- 4 5- 1 6- 3 10- 2 9-12 11- 8	8- 6 12-10 9-11 1- 3 2- 4 5- 7	3-12 4- 9 7- 2 6-11 8- 5 10- 1	2- 8 6-10 1- 4 5- 9 11- 3 12- 7	9- 1 7-11 3-10 12- 6 2- 5 4- 8	11- 4 6- 2 5-12 8- 1 10- 7 3- 9	9- 6 1- 7 2-11 4-12 8- 3 5-10	12- 8 11- 5 10- 4 7- 3 6- 1 9- 2

NOTE: Numbers in the 1st column of each round robin represent "home" games, and the 2nd column identifies "away" games.

Fig. 15–8(a). Tables of Round Robin Schedules: 3 Through 12 Entries.

No. of Entries	Lanes	Courts or Fields	1st Date H-A	2nd Date H-A	3rd Date H-A	4th Date H-A	5th Date H-A	6th Date H-A	7th Date H-A	8th Date H-A	9th Date H-A	10th Date H-A	11th Date H-A	12th Date H-A	13th Date H-A	14th Date H-A	15th Date H-A
13	1-2	I	3-4	8-11	5-10	4-9	6-13	5-8	12-2	1-3	6-7	7-11	5-9	1-13	6-12	—	—
	3-4	II	1-2	10-13	7-12	11-6	9-2	3-6	7-1	10-8	11-5	12-10	4-2	9-3	4-8	—	—
	5-6	III	6-5	12-1	11-2	13-8	4-11	10-7	8-9	2-6	3-13	5-3	13-12	11-10	5-1	—	—
	7-8	IV	7-8	6-9	8-3	1-10	12-5	2-13	3-11	7-9	10-1	6-4	11-1	12-4	13-7	—	—
	9-10	V	9-10	4-7	13-4	3-12	1-8	9-12	13-5	11-13	9-2	2-8	10-6	7-5	2-3	—	—
	11-12	VI	12-11	2-5	1-6	2-7	10-3	1-4	4-10	5-4	8-12	13-9	3-7	8-6	9-11	—	—
	—	—	13 bye	3 bye	9 bye	5 bye	7 bye	11 bye	6 bye	12 bye	4 bye	1 bye	8 bye	2 bye	10 bye	—	—
14	1-2	I	1-2	11-8	10-5	4-9	7-14	6-3	2-12	8-10	14-4	11-7	13-12	9-3	5-1	—	—
	3-4	II	3-4	13-10	7-12	11-6	9-2	8-5	6-14	1-3	10-2	14-1	5-9	12-4	13-7	—	—
	5-6	III	5-6	1-12	9-14	8-13	11-4	10-7	3-11	7-9	5-11	4-6	8-14	1-13	3-2	—	—
	7-8	IV	7-8	3-14	2-11	10-1	13-6	12-9	7-1	11-13	13-3	10-12	4-2	8-6	11-9	—	—
	9-10	V	9-10	5-2	13-4	12-3	1-8	14-11	10-4	2-6	6-7	3-5	6-10	2-14	6-12	—	—
	11-12	VI	12-11	4-7	6-1	14-5	3-10	13-2	9-8	12-14	12-9	9-13	1-7	7-5	14-10	—	—
	13-14	VII	14-13	6-9	8-3	2-7	5-12	4-1	5-13	5-4	1-8	2-8	3-11	10-11	4-8	—	—
15	1-2	I	7-8	15-12	9-2	14-8	6-12	11-1	1-8	8-2	4-5	4-9	9-3	3-13	10-6	5-14	13-15
	3-4	II	3-4	4-7	5-1	15-4	10-1	7-15	15-11	6-3	12-10	13-7	11-2	12-8	9-11	1-6	14-9
	5-6	III	5-6	8-11	3-7	2-13	8-9	8-6	14-7	9-12	11-3	3-5	5-13	10-1	14-2	9-15	4-1
	7-8	IV	1-2	9-6	12-14	7-1	15-3	4-10	6-4	14-11	8-9	15-10	7-15	11-5	12-4	11-13	8-3
	9-10	V	10-9	1-3	6-13	3-11	14-4	9-13	5-12	5-10	2-7	1-14	6-10	7-9	15-7	2-10	7-12
	11-12	VI	12-11	2-5	8-15	5-9	11-7	3-14	2-13	7-4	6-13	11-6	1-12	15-2	13-1	12-3	10-5
	13-14	VII	14-13	13-10	11-4	12-10	13-5	2-12	10-3	1-15	15-14	8-2	4-14	6-14	8-5	4-8	6-2
	—	—	15 bye	14 bye	10 bye	6 bye	2 bye	5 bye	9 bye	13 bye	1 bye	12 bye	8 bye	4 bye	3 bye	7 bye	11 bye
16	1-2	I	1-5	4-6	13-3	2-14	16-9	15-12	8-11	7-10	11-12	5-15	7-14	8-16	10-1	6-13	9-4
	3-4	II	6-2	7-1	14-4	3-15	13-10	9-8	10-16	11-16	8-1	13-7	15-6	4-10	3-12	5-14	13-16
	5-6	III	3-7	3-5	15-1	4-16	12-11	5-10	1-2	12-13	13-15	16-6	8-10	12-1	4-11	1-9	7-5
	7-8	IV	4-8	8-16	16-2	1-13	8-1	14-11	13-14	15-2	16-4	14-8	12-9	11-7	5-6	16-7	3-2
	9-10	V	13-9	9-14	5-11	6-10	7-2	4-7	12-15	5-1	2-3	10-3	11-2	15-9	7-8	12-4	14-15
	11-12	VI	10-14	15-10	6-12	7-11	3-6	1-16	9-4	3-4	6-7	1-9	1-4	13-5	2-9	11-3	8-6
	13-14	VII	11-15	11-13	7-9	8-12	5-14	6-13	3-5	14-8	14-9	12-2	5-16	2-6	14-13	15-8	10-11
	15-16	VIII	12-16	2-12	8-10	5-9	4-15	2-3	6-7	6-9	10-5	4-11	13-3	3-14	16-15	2-10	1-12

NOTE: Numbers in the 1st column of each round represent "home" games, and the 2nd column identifies "away" games.

Fig. 15-8(b). Tables of Round Robin Schedules: 13 Through 16 Entries.

Bowling Individual Handicap Chart

The bowling individual handicap chart (Fig. 15–9) may be used to determine handicaps of 66 2/3, 70, 75, and 80 per cent of the difference between the bowler's average and 180, 190, and 200 scratch. The term "scratch" represents the starting point or basis on which each player's handicap is figured. The scratch for each league may vary due to the scoring ability of the bowlers, but it should be approximately ten pins higher than the highest player average in the league.

After figuring each bowler's average, the chart is used to determine handicaps. For example, averages for five members of a bowling team in a 75 per cent handicap, 180 scratch league are 140, 145, 160, 164, and 172. The 180 scratch chart indicates handicaps of 30, 26, 15, 12, and 6 for a total handicap of 89. This handicap is added to the team's actual pinfall for each game. Refer to Chapter 9 for additional information on bowling handicaps.

Round Robin Schedule Forms

Figure 15–10, a–f, includes round robin schedule forms for three through sixteen teams. Although the headings refer to teams, they may also be used for individual and dual competition. Team names are placed in the spaces at the top of the form and are subsequently listed below on the lines of the corresponding numbers in each round. The schedule is completed by filling in the sites, dates, and times for the games. After the games have been played, scores may be recorded in the appropriate columns. Each form can be used for an uneven number of teams by substituting the word bye for one of the numbers, preferably the highest number. These forms may be used as a work sheet from which the schedule can be reproduced, or they may be posted on the bulletin board as the final schedule.

Golf Handicap Charts

The United States Golf Association Handicap Differential Chart for 18 holes is illustrated in Figure 15–11. Differentials at the top of the chart are used for golfers with 20 scores, and those with less than this number but with 5 or more use the supplementary table at the bottom of the chart. An explanation of this system is found on page 179.

Figure 15–12 contains a 9-hole handicap chart which is an adaptation of the USGA 18-hole system. It is designed for 9-hole intramural golf tournaments and is not intended to be official in any way. Essentially, the pattern of operation is the same except that it applies to 9-hole scores and as few as two rounds may be used for establishing a handicap.

180 SCRATCH

Per Cent					Per Cent					Per Cent					Per Cent					Per Cent				
Ave	66⅔	70	75	80	Ave	66⅔	70	75	80	Ave	66⅔	70	75	80	Ave	66⅔	70	75	80	Ave	66⅔	70	75	80
180	–	–	–	–	164	10	11	12	12	148	21	22	24	25	132	32	33	36	38	116	42	44	48	51
179	–	–	–	–	163	11	11	12	13	147	22	23	24	26	131	32	34	36	39	115	43	45	48	52
178	1	1	1	1	162	12	12	13	14	146	22	23	25	27	130	33	35	37	40	114	44	46	49	52
177	2	2	2	2	161	12	13	14	15	145	23	24	26	28	129	34	35	38	40	113	44	46	50	53
176	2	2	3	3	160	13	14	15	16	144	24	25	27	28	128	34	36	39	41	112	45	47	51	54
175	3	3	3	3	159	14	14	15	16	143	24	25	27	29	127	35	37	39	42	111	46	48	51	55
174	4	4	4	4	158	14	15	16	17	142	25	26	28	30	126	36	37	40	43	110	46	49	52	56
173	4	4	5	5	157	15	16	17	18	141	26	27	29	31	125	36	38	41	44	109	47	49	53	56
172	5	5	6	6	156	16	16	18	19	140	26	28	30	32	124	37	39	42	44	108	48	50	54	57
171	6	6	6	7	155	16	17	18	20	139	27	28	30	32	123	38	39	42	45	107	48	51	54	58
170	6	7	7	8	154	17	18	19	20	138	28	29	31	33	122	38	40	43	46	106	49	51	55	59
169	7	7	8	8	153	18	18	20	21	137	28	30	32	34	121	39	41	44	47	105	50	52	56	60
168	8	8	9	9	152	18	19	21	22	136	29	30	33	35	120	40	42	45	48	104	50	53	57	60
167	8	9	9	10	151	19	20	21	23	135	30	31	33	36	119	40	42	45	48	103	51	53	57	61
166	9	9	10	11	150	20	21	22	24	134	30	32	34	36	118	41	43	46	49	102	52	54	58	62
165	10	10	11	12	149	20	21	23	24	133	31	32	35	37	117	42	44	47	50	101	52	55	59	63

190 SCRATCH

Per Cent					Per Cent					Per Cent					Per Cent					Per Cent				
Ave	66⅔	70	75	80	Ave	66⅔	70	75	80	Ave	66⅔	70	75	80	Ave	66⅔	70	75	80	Ave	66⅔	70	75	80
190	–	–	–	–	172	12	12	13	14	154	24	25	27	28	136	36	37	40	43	118	48	50	54	57
189	–	–	–	–	171	12	13	14	15	153	24	25	27	29	135	36	38	41	44	117	48	51	54	58
188	1	1	1	1	170	13	14	15	16	152	25	26	28	30	134	37	39	42	44	116	49	51	55	59
187	2	2	2	2	169	14	14	15	16	151	26	27	29	31	133	38	39	42	45	115	50	52	56	60
186	2	2	3	3	168	14	15	16	17	150	26	28	30	32	132	38	40	43	46	114	50	53	57	60
185	3	3	3	4	167	15	16	17	18	149	27	28	30	32	131	39	41	44	47	113	51	53	57	61
184	4	4	4	4	166	16	16	18	19	148	28	29	31	33	130	40	42	45	48	112	52	54	58	62
183	4	4	5	5	165	16	17	18	20	147	28	30	32	34	129	40	42	45	48	111	52	55	59	63
182	5	5	6	6	164	17	18	19	20	146	29	30	33	35	128	41	43	46	49	110	53	56	60	64
181	6	6	6	7	163	18	18	20	21	145	30	31	33	36	127	42	44	47	50	109	54	56	60	64
180	6	7	7	8	162	18	19	21	22	144	30	32	34	36	126	42	44	48	51	108	54	57	61	65
179	7	7	8	8	161	19	20	21	23	143	31	32	35	37	125	43	45	48	52	107	55	58	62	66
178	8	8	9	9	160	20	21	24	24	142	32	33	36	38	124	44	46	49	52	106	56	58	63	67
177	8	9	9	10	159	20	21	23	24	141	32	34	36	39	123	44	46	50	53	105	56	59	63	68
176	9	9	10	11	158	21	22	24	25	140	33	35	37	40	122	45	47	51	54	104	57	60	64	68
175	10	10	11	12	157	22	23	24	26	139	34	35	38	40	121	46	48	51	55	103	58	60	65	69
174	10	11	12	12	156	22	23	25	27	138	34	36	39	41	120	46	49	52	56	102	58	61	66	70
173	11	11	12	13	155	23	24	26	28	137	35	37	39	42	119	47	49	53	56	101	59	62	66	71

200 SCRATCH

Per Cent					Per Cent					Per Cent					Per Cent					Per Cent				
Ave	66⅔	70	75	80	Ave	66⅔	70	75	80	Ave	66⅔	70	75	80	Ave	66⅔	70	75	80	Ave	66⅔	70	75	80
200	–	–	–	–	180	13	14	15	16	160	26	28	30	32	140	40	42	45	48	120	53	56	60	64
199	–	–	–	–	179	14	14	15	16	159	27	28	30	32	139	40	42	45	48	119	54	56	60	64
198	1	1	1	1	178	14	15	16	17	158	28	29	31	33	138	41	43	46	49	118	54	57	61	65
197	2	2	2	2	177	15	16	17	18	157	28	30	32	34	137	42	44	47	50	117	55	58	62	66
196	2	2	3	3	176	16	16	18	19	156	29	30	33	35	136	42	44	48	51	116	56	58	63	67
195	3	3	3	4	175	16	17	18	20	155	30	31	33	36	135	43	45	48	52	115	56	59	63	68
194	4	4	4	4	174	17	18	19	20	154	30	32	34	36	134	44	46	49	52	114	57	60	64	68
193	4	4	5	5	173	18	18	20	21	153	31	32	35	37	133	44	46	50	53	113	58	60	65	69
192	5	5	6	6	172	18	19	21	22	152	32	33	36	38	132	45	47	51	54	112	58	61	66	70
191	6	6	6	7	171	19	20	21	23	151	32	34	36	39	131	46	48	51	55	111	59	62	66	71
190	6	7	7	8	170	20	21	22	24	150	33	35	37	40	130	46	49	52	56	110	60	63	67	72
189	7	7	8	8	169	20	21	23	24	149	34	35	38	40	129	47	49	53	56	109	60	63	68	72
188	8	8	9	9	168	21	22	24	24	148	34	36	39	41	128	48	50	54	57	108	61	64	69	73
187	8	9	9	10	167	22	23	24	26	147	35	37	39	42	127	48	51	54	58	107	62	65	69	74
186	9	9	10	11	166	22	23	25	27	146	36	37	40	43	126	49	51	55	59	106	62	65	70	75
185	10	10	11	12	165	23	24	26	28	145	36	38	41	44	125	50	52	56	60	105	63	66	71	76
184	10	11	12	12	164	24	25	27	28	144	37	39	42	44	124	50	53	57	60	104	64	67	72	76
183	11	11	12	13	163	24	25	27	29	143	38	39	42	45	123	51	53	57	61	103	64	67	72	77
182	12	12	13	14	162	25	26	28	30	142	38	40	43	46	122	52	54	58	62	102	65	68	73	78
181	12	13	14	15	161	26	27	29	31	141	39	41	44	47	121	52	55	59	63	101	66	69	74	79

Fig. 15–9. Bowling Individual Handicap Chart—Single Game: 180, 190, and 200 Scratch. (Courtesy American Bowling Congress.)

FOUR OR THREE TEAM ROUND ROBIN

SPORT _____ DIVISION _____ DATE _____

1 _____ 2 _____ 3 _____ 4 _____

ROUND 1 TEAM*	SCORE		TEAM	SITE	DATE	TIME
1	vs	2				
4	vs	3				

ROUND 3

	TEAM		
3			
4			

ROUND 2 TEAM*		SITE	DATE	TIME			
3	vs	2					
2	vs	1					

SCORE		TEAM	SITE	DATE	TIME
1	vs				
4	vs				

* RECORD TEAM NAMES IN SPACES THAT CORRESPOND WITH TEAM NUMBERS ABOVE.

NOTE: FOR 3 TEAMS SUBSTITUTE THE WORD "BYE" FOR NUMBER 4.

SIX OR FIVE TEAM ROUND ROBIN

SPORT _____ DIVISION _____ DATE _____

1 _____ 2 _____ 3 _____ 4 _____
5 _____ 6 _____

ROUND 1 TEAM*	SCORE		TEAM	SITE	DATE	TIME
1	vs	2				
4	vs	3				
5	vs	6				

ROUND 3

	SCORE		TEAM			
5	vs	3				
4	vs	1				
2	vs	6				

ROUND 5

5	vs	1				
6	vs	3				
2	vs	4				

ROUND 2 TEAM*		SITE	DATE	TIME	SCORE		TEAM
6	vs				4		
2	vs				5		
3	vs				1		

ROUND 4

3					2		
1					6		
4					5		

* RECORD TEAM NAMES IN SPACES THAT CORRESPOND WITH TEAM NUMBERS ABOVE.

NOTE: FOR 5 TEAMS SUBSTITUTE THE WORD "BYE" FOR NUMBER 6.

Fig. 15–10(a). Round Robin Schedule Forms: (Top) 4 or 3 Teams. (Bottom) 6 or 5 Teams.

EIGHT OR SEVEN TEAM ROUND ROBIN

SPORT _____ DIVISION _____ DATE _____

1 _____ 2 _____ 3 _____ 4 _____
5 _____ 6 _____ 7 _____ 8 _____

ROUND 1	TEAM*	SCORE		TEAM	SITE	DATE	TIME	ROUND 2	TEAM*	SCORE		TEAM	SITE	DATE	TIME
1		vs	2					6		vs	8				
3		vs	4					5		vs	7				
5		vs	6					2		vs	4				
7		vs	8					1		vs	3				

ROUND 3								ROUND 4							
4		vs	5					3		vs	6				
8		vs	1					7		vs	2				
3		vs	7					1		vs	5				
2		vs	6					4		vs	8				

ROUND 5								ROUND 6							
7		vs	1					2		vs	3				
6		vs	4					8		vs	5				
8		vs	3					4		vs	1				
5		vs	2					6		vs	7				

ROUND 7							
7		vs	4				
1		vs	6				
2		vs	8				
3		vs	5				

*RECORD TEAM NAMES IN SPACES THAT CORRESPOND WITH TEAM NUMBERS ABOVE.

NOTE: FOR 7 TEAMS SUBSTITUTE THE WORD "BYE" FOR NUMBER 8.

Fig. 15-10(b). Round Robin Schedule Form: 8 or 7 Teams.

TEN OR NINE TEAM ROUND ROBIN

SPORT _____ DIVISION _____ DATE _____

1 ____ 2 ____ 3 ____ 4 ____ 5 ____
6 ____ 7 ____ 8 ____ 9 ____ 10 ____

ROUND 1 TEAM*	SCORE	vs		TEAM	SITE	DATE	TIME
1		vs	10				
9		vs	2				
3		vs	8				
4		vs	7				
5		vs	6				

ROUND 2 TEAM*	SCORE	vs		TEAM	SITE	DATE	TIME
7		vs	2				
6		vs	3				
5		vs	4				
10		vs	9				
8		vs	1				

ROUND 3	SCORE	vs		TEAM	SITE	DATE	TIME
8		vs	9				
1		vs	7				
2		vs	6				
3		vs	5				
4		vs	10				

ROUND 4	SCORE	vs		TEAM	SITE	DATE	TIME
4		vs	3				
10		vs	8				
9		vs	7				
6		vs	1				
5		vs	2				

ROUND 5	SCORE	vs		TEAM	SITE	DATE	TIME
10		vs	6				
7		vs	5				
2		vs	1				
8		vs	4				
9		vs	3				

ROUND 6	SCORE	vs		TEAM	SITE	DATE	TIME
5		vs	9				
6		vs	8				
7		vs	10				
3		vs	2				
1		vs	4				

ROUND 7	SCORE	vs		TEAM	SITE	DATE	TIME
3		vs	1				
4		vs	9				
8		vs	5				
6		vs	7				
10		vs	2				

ROUND 8	SCORE	vs		TEAM	SITE	DATE	TIME
4		vs	6				
5		vs	10				
9		vs	1				
2		vs	8				
7		vs	3				

ROUND 9	SCORE	vs		TEAM	SITE	DATE	TIME
7		vs	8				
2		vs	4				
10		vs	3				
1		vs	5				
6		vs	9				

*RECORD TEAM NAMES IN SPACES THAT CORRESPOND WITH TEAM NUMBERS ABOVE.

NOTE: FOR 9 TEAMS SUBSTITUTE THE WORD "BYE" FOR NUMBER 10.

Fig. 15–10(c). Round Robin Schedule Form: 10 or 9 Teams.

TWELVE OR ELEVEN TEAM ROUND ROBIN

SPORT _____ DIVISION _____ DATE _____

1 _____ 2 _____ 3 _____ 4 _____
5 _____ 6 _____ 7 _____ 8 _____
9 _____ 10 _____ 11 _____ 12 _____

ROUND 1

TEAM*	SCORE		SCORE	TEAM	SITE	DATE	TIME
1		vs	2				
3		vs	4				
5		vs	6				
7		vs	8				
9		vs	10				
11		vs	12				

ROUND 2

TEAM*	SCORE		SCORE	TEAM	SITE	DATE	TIME
10		vs	11				
8		vs	9				
12		vs	1				
4		vs	5				
6		vs	7				
2		vs	3				

ROUND 3

TEAM	SCORE		SCORE	TEAM	SITE	DATE	TIME
3		vs	5				
2		vs	12				
8		vs	10				
7		vs	9				
1		vs	11				
4		vs	6				

ROUND 4

TEAM	SCORE		SCORE	TEAM	SITE	DATE	TIME
7		vs	4				
5		vs	1				
6		vs	3				
10		vs	2				
9		vs	12				
11		vs	8				

ROUND 5

TEAM	SCORE		SCORE	TEAM	SITE	DATE	TIME
8		vs	6				
12		vs	10				
9		vs	11				
1		vs	3				
2		vs	4				
5		vs	7				

ROUND 6

TEAM	SCORE		SCORE	TEAM	SITE	DATE	TIME
3		vs	12				
4		vs	9				
7		vs	2				
6		vs	11				
8		vs	5				
10		vs	1				

ROUND 7		
2	vs	8
6	vs	10
1	vs	4
5	vs	9
11	vs	3
12	vs	7

ROUND 8		
9	vs	1
7	vs	11
3	vs	10
12	vs	6
2	vs	5
4	vs	8

ROUND 9		
11	vs	4
6	vs	2
5	vs	12
8	vs	1
10	vs	7
3	vs	9

ROUND 10		
9	vs	6
1	vs	7
2	vs	11
4	vs	12
8	vs	3
5	vs	10

ROUND 11		
12	vs	8
11	vs	5
10	vs	4
7	vs	3
6	vs	1
9	vs	2

NOTE: FOR 11 TEAMS SUBSTITUTE THE WORD "BYE" FOR NUMBER 12.

* RECORD TEAM NAMES IN SPACES THAT CORRESPOND WITH TEAM NUMBERS ABOVE.

Fig. 15—10(d). Round Robin Schedule Form: 12 or 11 Teams.

FOURTEEN OR THIRTEEN TEAM ROUND ROBIN

SPORT _____

DIVISION _____

DATE _____

1 _____	2 _____	3 _____	4 _____
5 _____	6 _____	7 _____	8 _____
9 _____	10 _____	11 _____	12 _____
	13 _____	14 _____	

ROUND 1   TEAM*

	SCORE		TEAM	SITE	DATE	TIME
1		vs 2				
3		vs 4				
5		vs 6				
7		vs 8				
9		vs 10				
12		vs 11				
14		vs 13				

ROUND 2   TEAM*

	SCORE		TEAM	SITE	DATE	TIME
11		vs 8				
13		vs 10				
1		vs 12				
3		vs 14				
5		vs 2				
4		vs 7				
6		vs 9				

ROUND 3

	SCORE		TEAM	SITE	DATE	TIME
10		vs 5				
7		vs 12				
9		vs 14				
2		vs 11				
13		vs 4				
6		vs 1				
8		vs 3				

ROUND 4

	SCORE		TEAM	SITE	DATE	TIME
4		vs 9				
11		vs 6				
8		vs 13				
10		vs 1				
12		vs 3				
14		vs 5				
2		vs 7				

ROUND 5

	SCORE		TEAM	SITE	DATE	TIME
7		vs 14				
9		vs 2				
11		vs 4				
13		vs 6				
1		vs 8				
3		vs 10				
5		vs 12				

ROUND 6

	SCORE		TEAM	SITE	DATE	TIME
6		vs 3				
8		vs 5				
10		vs 7				
12		vs 9				
14		vs 11				
13		vs 2				
4		vs 1				

Fig. 15–10(e). Round Robin Schedule Form: 14 or 13 Teams.

ROUND 7		ROUND 8		ROUND 9		ROUND 10	
2	vs 12	8	vs 10	14	vs 4	11	vs 7
6	vs 14	1	vs 3	10	vs 2	14	vs 1
3	vs 11	7	vs 9	5	vs 11	4	vs 6
7	vs 1	4	vs 5	13	vs 3	10	vs 12
10	vs 4	11	vs 13	6	vs 7	3	vs 5
9	vs 8	2	vs 6	12	vs 8	9	vs 13
5	vs 13	12	vs 14	1	vs 9	2	vs 8

ROUND 11		ROUND 12		ROUND 13	
13	vs 12	9	vs 3	5	vs 1
5	vs 9	12	vs 4	13	vs 7
8	vs 14	1	vs 13	3	vs 2
4	vs 2	8	vs 6	11	vs 9
6	vs 10	2	vs 14	6	vs 12
11	vs 1	7	vs 5	14	vs 10
7	vs 3	10	vs 11	4	vs 8

NOTE: FOR 13 TEAMS SUBSTITUTE THE WORD "BYE" FOR NUMBER 14.

* RECORD TEAM NAMES IN SPACES THAT CORRESPOND WITH TEAM NUMBERS ABOVE.

SIXTEEN OR FIFTEEN TEAM ROUND ROBIN

SPORT_____ DIVISION_____ DATE_____

1 _____ 2 _____ 3 _____ 4
5 _____ 6 _____ 7 _____ 8
9 _____ 10 _____ 11 _____ 12
13 _____ 14 _____ 15 _____ 16

ROUND 1 TEAM*

	SCORE		TEAM	SITE	DATE	TIME
1		vs 5				
6		vs 2				
3		vs 7				
4		vs 8				
13		vs 9				
10		vs 14				
11		vs 15				
12		vs 16				

ROUND 3

	SCORE		TEAM	SITE	DATE	TIME
13		vs 3				
14		vs 4				
15		vs 1				
16		vs 2				
5		vs 11				
6		vs 12				
7		vs 9				
8		vs 10				

ROUND 5

	SCORE		TEAM	SITE	DATE	TIME
16		vs 9				
10		vs 13				
11		vs 6				
12		vs 7				
8		vs 1				
5		vs 2				
14		vs 3				
15		vs 4				

ROUND 2 TEAM*

	SCORE		TEAM	SITE	DATE	TIME
4		vs 6				
1		vs 7				
2		vs 8				
3		vs 5				
14		vs 12				
9		vs 15				
10		vs 16				
11		vs 13				

ROUND 4

	SCORE		TEAM	SITE	DATE	TIME
2		vs 14				
3		vs 15				
4		vs 16				
1		vs 13				
6		vs 10				
7		vs 11				
12		vs 8				
9		vs 5				

ROUND 6

	SCORE		TEAM	SITE	DATE	TIME
15		vs 12				
9		vs 8				
5		vs 10				
14		vs 11				
7		vs 4				
16		vs 1				
13		vs 2				
6		vs 3				

ROUND 7
8 vs 11
12 vs 5
9 vs 14
10 vs 15
3 vs 16
4 vs 13
1 vs 6
2 vs 7

ROUND 8
7 vs 10
11 vs 16
12 vs 13
6 vs 9
15 vs 2
3 vs 8
5 vs 4
14 vs 1

ROUND 9
11 vs 12
2 vs 1
8 vs 5
13 vs 15
10 vs 9
16 vs 14
6 vs 7
4 vs 3

ROUND 10
5 vs 15
13 vs 7
16 vs 6
14 vs 8
1 vs 3
10 vs 12
2 vs 4
9 vs 11

ROUND 11
7 vs 14
15 vs 6
3 vs 10
12 vs 9
11 vs 2
1 vs 4
5 vs 16
8 vs 13

ROUND 12
8 vs 16
4 vs 10
12 vs 2
11 vs 1
13 vs 5
15 vs 7
9 vs 3
6 vs 14

ROUND 13
10 vs 1
3 vs 12
4 vs 11
5 vs 6
7 vs 8
2 vs 9
14 vs 13
16 vs 15

ROUND 14
6 vs 13
5 vs 14
1 vs 9
16 vs 7
12 vs 4
11 vs 3
15 vs 8
2 vs 10

ROUND 15
9 vs 4
13 vs 16
7 vs 5
3 vs 2
14 vs 15
8 vs 6
10 vs 11
1 vs 12

NOTE: FOR 15 TEAMS SUBSTITUTE THE WORD "BYE" FOR NUMBER 16.

* RECORD TEAM NAMES IN SPACES THAT CORRESPOND WITH TEAM NUMBERS ABOVE.

Fig. 15–10(f). Round Robin Schedule Form: 16 or 15 Teams.

USGA HANDICAP DIFFERENTIAL CHART

TOTAL OF LOWEST 10 HANDICAP DIFFERENTIALS			TOTAL OF LOWEST 10 HANDICAP DIFFERENTIALS		
FROM	TO	HANDICAP	FROM	TO	HANDICAP
− 41.1	− 29.5	+ 3	182.4	194.1	16
− 29.4	− 17.7	+ 2	194.2	205.8	17
− 17.6	− 5.9	+ 1	205.9	217.6	18
− 5.8	+ 5.8	0	217.7	229.4	19
			229.5	241.1	20
+ 5.9	+ 17.6	1	241.2	252.9	21
17.7	29.4	2	253.0	264.7	22
29.5	41.1	3	264.8	276.4	23
41.2	52.9	4	276.5	288.2	24
53.0	64.7	5	288.3	299.9	25
64.8	76.4	6	300.0	311.7	26
76.5	88.2	7	311.8	323.5	27
88.3	99.9	8	323.6	335.2	28
100.0	111.7	9	335.3	347.0	29
111.8	123.5	10	347.1	358.8	30
123.6	135.2	11	358.9	370.5	31
135.3	147.0	12	370.6	382.3	32
147.1	158.8	13	382.4	394.1	33
158.9	170.5	14	394.2	405.8	34
170.6	182.3	15	405.9	417.6	35
			417.7	AND OVER	36

Total the lowest 10 differentials (scores minus the course rating) of the last 20 rounds and apply this sum to the above chart.

5 THROUGH 19 DIFFERENTIALS

1) If fewer than 20 but at least 5 differentials are available, determine the number of differentials to be used from the following table:

DIFFERENTIALS AVAILABLE	DIFFERENTIALS TO BE USED
5	Lowest 1
6	Lowest 2
7	Lowest 3
8 or 9	Lowest 4
10 or 11	Lowest 5
12 or 13	Lowest 6
14 or 15	Lowest 7
16 or 17	Lowest 8
18 or 19	Lowest 9

2) Compute the average differential, multiply it by 10 and apply the result to the USGA Handicap Differential Chart.

3) Fewer than 5 scores: no handicap. A USGA Handicap shall not be issued to a player who has returned fewer than 5 socres.

Fig. 15–11. USGA Golf Handicap Differential Chart. Eighteen Holes. (Copyright 1966 by United States Golf Association, reproduced by courtesy of the copyright owner. Full text of the USGA Golf Handicap System may be obtained from the United States Golf Association.)

9-HOLE GOLF HANDICAP CHART

TOTAL OF LOWEST 10 HANDICAP DIFFERENTIALS		HANDICAP	TOTAL OF LOWEST 10 HANDICAP DIFFERENTIALS		HANDICAP
− 41.1 to	− 29.5	+ 3	135.3 to	147.0	12
− 29.4 to	− 17.7	+ 2	147.1 to	158.8	13
− 17.6 to	− 5.9	+ 1	158.9 to	170.5	14
− 5.8 to	+ 5.8	0	170.6 to	182.3	15
+ 5.9 to	+ 17.6	1	182.4 to	194.1	16
17.7 to	29.4	2	194.2 to	205.8	17
29.5 to	41.1	3	205.9 to	217.6	18
41.2 to	52.9	4	217.7 to	229.4	19
53.0 to	64.7	5	229.5 to	241.1	20
64.8 to	76.4	6	241.2 to	252.9	21
76.5 to	88.2	7	253.0 to	264.7	22
88.3 to	99.9	8	264.8 to	276.4	23
100.0 to	111.7	9	276.5 to	288.2	24
111.8 to	123.5	10	288.3 to and up		25
123.6 to	135.2	11			

COMPUTATION INSTRUCTIONS

1) The handicap is computed from the lowest 10 handicap differentials (score for 9 holes minus the course rating for 9 holes) of the player's last 20 rounds.

   a. Total the lowest 10 differentials.

   b. Locate the range within which the total falls in the above chart. The handicap is listed to the right of the same line.

2) For fewer than 20 differentials, the following method is used:

   a. Supplementary table.

DIFFERENTIALS AVAILABLE	DIFFERENTIALS TO BE UTILIZED
2 or 3	Lowest 1
4 or 5	Lowest 2
6 or 7	Lowest 3
8 or 9	Lowest 4
10 or 11	Lowest 5
12 or 13	Lowest 6
14 or 15	Lowest 7
16 or 17	Lowest 8
18 or 19	Lowest 9

   b. Determine the average of the differentials to be used, multiply the average by 10 and apply this number to the handicap chart.

Fig. 15–12. A 9-Hole Golf Handicap Chart: An Unofficial Adaptation of the USGA 18-Hole Handicap System.

A one-round golf handicap chart known as the Callaway system appears in Figure 15–13. This method is used for golfers who do not have handicaps. Based on a player's gross score, the table indicates the number of highest holes, always excluding holes 17 and 18, to be deducted, plus or minus an adjustment. No hole may be scored at more than twice par. If a golfer's gross score is 87 and the two highest scores are 7 and 8 among holes 1 through 16, the net score is 71, after deducting 1 stroke for the adjustment.

Participation—Performance Point Tables

Three participation–performance point tables are shown in Figures 15–14, 15–15, and 15-16. These tables simplify calculations for those who use the participation–performance point system described in Chapter 10. Each table provides distributions for 35 places. Figure 15–14 represents a major division activity scale with a minimum of 50 points and a maximum of 150. Thus, if a director allocates points for 16 places, the scale indicates the winner receives 150 points; next highest, 143; third place, 137; and so on down the scale with 50 points awarded to last place. When teams tie for a place in the standings, points allotted for each position are added and the sum is divided by the number of teams tied. Example: If two teams are tied for first place in an 11-team league, each of the two receives 145 points ($150 + 140 \div 2 = 145$).

Figure 15–15 lists points scaled from 35 through 100 for participation and performance in activities allocated to the intermediate division. If four places are allotted points for an activity in this category, first place receives 100 points; second place, 78; third place, 57; and last place, 35.

The number of entries participating in a particular league or the number of places to be allotted points determines the size of the point spread between places. In some instances, two whole number intervals are used to eliminate decimals or fractions. In the 50–150 participation–performance point range, the interval for 11 places is 10, whereas the intervals for 25 places are 4 and 5. The intervals for 11 places in the intermediate range (35–100) are 6 and 7, and for the same number of places in the minor range (25–75) the interval is 5.

In Figure 15–16, points are distributed from 25 through 75 for participation and performance in those activities considered minor in relation to the number of players per team, tournament methods, number of games, etc. Use of these tables eliminates the time-consuming task of figuring point distributions each time a tournament is conducted and assures calculation and assignment of points according to a consistent pattern.

CALLAWAY ONE-ROUND GOLF HANDICAP SYSTEM

GROSS SCORES						HANDICAP DEDUCTION
–	–	70	71	72	–	SCRATCH AND NO ADJUSTMENT
73	74	75	–	–	–	½ HIGHEST HOLE AND ADJUSTMENT
76	77	78	79	80	–	1 HIGHEST HOLE AND ADJUSTMENT
81	82	83	84	85	–	1½ HIGHEST HOLES AND ADJUSTMENT
86	87	88	89	90	–	2 HIGHEST HOLES AND ADJUSTMENT
91	92	93	94	95	–	2½ HIGHEST HOLES AND ADJUSTMENT
96	97	98	99	100	–	3 HIGHEST HOLES AND ADJUSTMENT
101	102	103	104	105	–	3½ HIGHEST HOLES AND ADJUSTMENT
106	107	108	109	110	–	4 HIGHEST HOLES AND ADJUSTMENT
111	112	113	114	115	–	4½ HIGHEST HOLES AND ADJUSTMENT
116	117	118	119	120	–	5 HIGHEST HOLES AND ADJUSTMENT
121	122	123	124	125	–	5½ HIGHEST HOLES AND ADJUSTMENT
126	127	128	129	130	–	6 HIGHEST HOLES AND ADJUSTMENT

						ADJUSTMENT
– 2	– 1	0	+ 1	+ 2	–	ADD TO OR DEDUCT FROM HANDICAP

NOTE: 1. NO HOLE CAN BE SCORED AT MORE THAN TWICE ITS PAR.
2. HALF STROKES COUNT AS A WHOLE.
3. THE **SEVENTEENTH** AND **EIGHTEENTH** HOLES ARE NEVER DEDUCTED.
4. IN CASE OF TIES LOWER HANDICAP OR ADJUSTMENT SHOULD BE GIVEN PREFERENCE.

Fig. 15–13. Callaway One-Round Golf Handicap Chart. ((Courtesy National Golf Foundation.)

Percentages and Averages

Statistical records involving percentages and averages of individual and team performances add considerable interest to intramural participation. These include percentage of games won and averages for batting, fielding, pitching, and scoring. Office clerical assistants can maintain these records, or team managers may be encouraged to do so with the aid of mimeographed reference tables and explanations as to how they are calculated.

Figure 15–17 lists percentages of games won for one through thirty games. The table can be expanded beyond this number by dividing the

PLACES	1	2	3	4	5	6	7	8	9	10	11	12	13	14	15	16	17	18	19	20	21	22	23	24	25	26	27	28	29	30	31	32	33	34	35
1	150	150	150	150	150	150	150	150	150	150	150	150	150	150	150	150	150	150	150	150	150	150	150	150	150	150	150	150	150	150	150	150	150	150	150
2	.	50	100	117	125	130	133	135	137	139	140	141	141	142	143	143	144	144	144	145	145	145	145	146	146	146	146	146	146	147	147	147	147	147	147
3	.	.	50	83	100	110	116	121	125	128	130	132	133	134	136	137	138	138	139	140	140	140	141	141	142	142	142	142	143	143	144	144	144	144	144
4	.	.	.	50	75	90	100	107	112	117	120	123	125	127	129	130	131	132	133	135	135	135	136	137	138	138	139	139	139	140	140	141	141	141	141
5	.	.	.	.	50	70	84	93	100	106	110	114	116	119	121	123	125	126	128	129	130	131	132	133	133	134	135	135	136	136	137	137	138	138	138
6	.	.	.	.	.	50	67	79	88	94	100	105	108	112	114	117	119	121	122	124	125	126	127	128	129	130	131	131	132	133	134	134	135	135	135
7	.	.	.	.	.	.	50	65	75	83	90	95	100	104	107	110	112	115	117	119	120	121	123	124	125	126	127	128	129	129	130	131	132	132	132
8	.	.	.	.	.	.	.	50	63	72	80	86	92	96	100	103	106	109	111	113	115	116	118	120	121	122	123	124	125	126	127	128	128	129	129
9	.	.	.	.	.	.	.	.	50	61	70	77	84	88	93	97	100	103	106	108	110	111	114	115	117	118	119	120	121	122	124	124	125	126	126
10	.	.	.	.	.	.	.	.	.	50	60	68	75	81	86	90	94	97	100	103	105	107	109	111	112	114	115	117	118	119	120	121	122	123	123
11	.	.	.	.	.	.	.	.	.	.	50	59	67	73	79	83	88	91	94	97	100	102	105	107	108	110	112	113	114	115	117	118	119	120	120
12	.	.	.	.	.	.	.	.	.	.	.	50	59	66	71	77	81	85	89	92	95	98	100	102	104	106	108	109	111	112	114	115	116	117	117
13	.	.	.	.	.	.	.	.	.	.	.	.	50	58	64	70	75	79	83	87	90	93	95	98	100	102	104	106	107	108	110	112	113	114	115
14	.	.	.	.	.	.	.	.	.	.	.	.	.	50	57	63	69	74	78	81	85	88	91	93	96	98	100	102	104	105	107	108	109	111	112
15	.	.	.	.	.	.	.	.	.	.	.	.	.	.	50	57	62	68	72	76	80	84	86	89	92	94	96	98	100	102	104	105	106	108	109
16	.	.	.	.	.	.	.	.	.	.	.	.	.	.	.	50	56	62	67	71	75	79	82	85	88	90	92	94	96	98	100	102	103	105	106
17	.	.	.	.	.	.	.	.	.	.	.	.	.	.	.	.	50	56	61	65	70	74	77	80	83	86	88	91	93	95	97	98	100	102	103
18	.	.	.	.	.	.	.	.	.	.	.	.	.	.	.	.	.	50	56	60	65	69	73	76	79	82	85	87	89	91	93	95	97	98	100
19	.	.	.	.	.	.	.	.	.	.	.	.	.	.	.	.	.	.	50	55	60	65	68	72	75	78	81	83	86	88	90	92	94	95	97
20	.	.	.	.	.	.	.	.	.	.	.	.	.	.	.	.	.	.	.	50	55	60	64	67	71	74	77	80	82	85	86	89	91	92	94
21	.	.	.	.	.	.	.	.	.	.	.	.	.	.	.	.	.	.	.	.	50	55	59	63	67	70	73	76	79	81	83	85	88	89	91
22	.	.	.	.	.	.	.	.	.	.	.	.	.	.	.	.	.	.	.	.	.	50	55	59	62	66	69	72	75	78	80	82	84	86	88
23	.	.	.	.	.	.	.	.	.	.	.	.	.	.	.	.	.	.	.	.	.	.	50	54	58	62	65	69	71	74	76	79	81	83	85
24	.	.	.	.	.	.	.	.	.	.	.	.	.	.	.	.	.	.	.	.	.	.	.	50	54	58	62	65	68	71	73	76	78	80	83
25	.	.	.	.	.	.	.	.	.	.	.	.	.	.	.	.	.	.	.	.	.	.	.	.	50	54	58	61	64	67	70	72	75	77	80
26	.	.	.	.	.	.	.	.	.	.	.	.	.	.	.	.	.	.	.	.	.	.	.	.	.	50	54	58	61	64	66	69	72	74	77
27	.	.	.	.	.	.	.	.	.	.	.	.	.	.	.	.	.	.	.	.	.	.	.	.	.	.	50	54	57	60	63	66	68	71	74
28	.	.	.	.	.	.	.	.	.	.	.	.	.	.	.	.	.	.	.	.	.	.	.	.	.	.	.	50	54	57	60	63	65	68	71
29	.	.	.	.	.	.	.	.	.	.	.	.	.	.	.	.	.	.	.	.	.	.	.	.	.	.	.	.	50	53	56	59	62	65	68
30	.	.	.	.	.	.	.	.	.	.	.	.	.	.	.	.	.	.	.	.	.	.	.	.	.	.	.	.	.	50	53	56	59	62	65
31	.	.	.	.	.	.	.	.	.	.	.	.	.	.	.	.	.	.	.	.	.	.	.	.	.	.	.	.	.	.	50	53	56	59	62
32	.	.	.	.	.	.	.	.	.	.	.	.	.	.	.	.	.	.	.	.	.	.	.	.	.	.	.	.	.	.	.	50	53	56	59
33	.	.	.	.	.	.	.	.	.	.	.	.	.	.	.	.	.	.	.	.	.	.	.	.	.	.	.	.	.	.	.	.	50	53	56
34	.	.	.	.	.	.	.	.	.	.	.	.	.	.	.	.	.	.	.	.	.	.	.	.	.	.	.	.	.	.	.	.	.	50	53
35	.	.	.	.	.	.	.	.	.	.	.	.	.	.	.	.	.	.	.	.	.	.	.	.	.	.	.	.	.	.	.	.	.	.	50

Fig. 15–14. Participation–Performance Point Table: Major, 50–150.

Games Lost

Games Won	1	2	3	4	5	6	7	8	9	10	11	12	13	14	15	16	17	18	19	20	21	22	23	24	25	26	27	28	29	30
1	.500	.333	.250	.200	.167	.143	.125	.111	.100	.091	.083	.077	.071	.067	.063	.059	.056	.053												
2	.667	.500	.400	.333	.286	.250	.222	.200	.182	.167	.154	.143	.133	.125	.118	.111	.105	.100												
3	.750	.600	.500	.429	.375	.333	.300	.273	.250	.231	.214	.200	.188	.176	.167	.158	.150	.143	.136	.130	.125	.120	.115	.111	.107	.103	.100			
4	.800	.667	.571	.500	.444	.400	.364	.333	.308	.286	.267	.250	.235	.222	.211	.200	.190	.182	.174	.167	.160	.154	.148	.143	.138	.133	.129	.125	.121	.118
5	.833	.714	.625	.556	.500	.455	.417	.385	.357	.333	.313	.294	.278	.263	.250	.238	.227	.217	.208	.200	.192	.185	.179	.172	.167	.161	.156	.152	.147	.143
6	.857	.750	.667	.600	.545	.500	.462	.429	.400	.375	.353	.333	.316	.300	.286	.273	.261	.250	.240	.231	.222	.214	.207	.200	.194	.188	.182	.176	.171	.167
7	.875	.778	.700	.636	.583	.538	.500	.467	.438	.412	.389	.368	.350	.333	.318	.304	.292	.280	.269	.259	.250	.241	.233	.226	.219	.212	.206	.200	.194	.189
8	.889	.800	.727	.667	.615	.571	.533	.500	.471	.444	.421	.400	.381	.364	.348	.333	.320	.308	.296	.286	.276	.267	.258	.250	.242	.235	.229	.222	.216	.211
9	.900	.818	.750	.692	.643	.600	.563	.529	.500	.474	.450	.429	.409	.391	.375	.360	.346	.333	.321	.310	.300	.290	.281	.273	.265	.257	.250	.243	.237	.231
10	.909	.833	.769	.714	.667	.625	.588	.556	.526	.500	.476	.455	.435	.417	.400	.385	.370	.357	.345	.333	.323	.313	.303	.294	.286	.278	.270	.263	.256	.250
11	.917	.846	.786	.733	.688	.647	.611	.579	.550	.524	.500	.478	.458	.440	.423	.407	.393	.379	.367	.355	.344	.333	.324	.314	.306	.297	.289	.282	.275	.268
12	.923	.857	.800	.750	.706	.667	.632	.600	.571	.545	.522	.500	.480	.462	.444	.429	.414	.400	.387	.375	.364	.353	.343	.333	.324	.316	.308	.300	.293	.286
13	.929	.867	.813	.765	.722	.684	.650	.619	.591	.565	.542	.520	.500	.481	.464	.448	.433	.419	.406	.394	.382	.371	.361	.351	.342	.333	.325	.317	.310	.302
14	.933	.875	.824	.778	.737	.700	.667	.636	.609	.583	.560	.538	.519	.500	.483	.467	.452	.438	.424	.412	.400	.389	.378	.368	.359	.350	.341	.333	.326	.318
15	.938	.882	.833	.789	.750	.714	.682	.652	.625	.600	.577	.556	.536	.517	.500	.484	.469	.455	.441	.429	.417	.405	.395	.385	.375	.366	.357	.349	.341	.333
16	.941	.889	.842	.800	.762	.727	.696	.667	.640	.615	.593	.571	.552	.533	.516	.500	.485	.471	.457	.444	.432	.421	.410	.400	.390	.381	.372	.364	.356	.348
17	.944	.895	.850	.810	.773	.739	.708	.680	.654	.630	.607	.586	.567	.548	.531	.515	.500	.486	.472	.459	.447	.436	.425	.415	.405	.395	.386	.378	.370	.362
18	.947	.900	.857	.818	.783	.750	.720	.692	.667	.643	.621	.600	.581	.563	.545	.529	.514	.500	.486	.474	.462	.450	.439	.429	.419	.409	.400	.391	.383	.375
19	.950	.904	.864	.826	.792	.760	.731	.704	.679	.655	.633	.613	.594	.576	.559	.543	.528	.514	.500	.487	.475	.463	.452	.442	.432	.422	.413	.404	.396	.388
20	.952	.909	.870	.833	.800	.769	.741	.714	.690	.667	.645	.625	.606	.588	.571	.556	.541	.526	.513	.500	.488	.476	.465	.455	.444	.435	.426	.417	.408	.400
21	.955	.913	.875	.840	.808	.778	.750	.724	.700	.677	.656	.636	.618	.600	.583	.568	.553	.538	.525	.512	.500	.488	.477	.467	.457	.447	.438	.429	.420	.412
22	.957	.917	.880	.846	.815	.786	.759	.733	.710	.688	.667	.647	.629	.611	.595	.579	.564	.550	.537	.524	.512	.500	.489	.478	.468	.458	.449	.440	.431	.423
23	.958	.920	.885	.852	.821	.793	.767	.742	.719	.697	.676	.657	.639	.622	.605	.590	.575	.561	.548	.535	.523	.511	.500	.489	.479	.469	.460	.451	.442	.434
24	.960	.923	.889	.857	.828	.800	.775	.750	.727	.706	.686	.667	.649	.632	.615	.600	.585	.571	.558	.545	.533	.522	.511	.500	.490	.480	.471	.462	.453	.444
25	.962	.926	.893	.862	.833	.806	.781	.758	.735	.714	.694	.676	.658	.641	.625	.610	.595	.581	.568	.556	.543	.532	.521	.510	.500	.490	.481	.472	.463	.455
26	.963	.929	.897	.867	.839	.813	.788	.765	.743	.722	.703	.684	.667	.650	.634	.619	.605	.591	.578	.565	.553	.542	.531	.520	.510	.500	.491	.481	.473	.464
27	.964	.931	.900	.871	.844	.818	.794	.771	.750	.730	.711	.692	.675	.659	.643	.628	.614	.600	.587	.574	.563	.551	.540	.529	.519	.509	.500	.491	.482	.474
28	.966	.933	.903	.875	.848	.824	.800	.778	.757	.737	.718	.700	.683	.667	.651	.636	.622	.609	.596	.583	.571	.560	.549	.538	.528	.519	.509	.500	.491	.483
29	.967	.935	.906	.879	.853	.829	.806	.784	.763	.744	.725	.707	.690	.674	.659	.644	.630	.617	.604	.592	.580	.569	.558	.547	.537	.527	.518	.509	.500	.492
30	.968	.938	.909	.882	.857	.833	.811	.789	.769	.750	.732	.714	.698	.682	.667	.652	.638	.625	.612	.600	.588	.577	.566	.556	.545	.536	.526	.517	.508	.500

Fig. 15–17. Percentage Table.

number of games won by the number of games played with the division carried three places to the right of the decimal point.

$$\text{Example:} \quad \frac{\text{Games won}}{\text{Games played}} = \frac{24}{47} = .511$$

On the table, the percentage figure of .511 is obtained by matching the 24-games-won line with the 23-games-lost column. Games won are listed vertically along the left margin, and games lost are shown horizontally at the top of the table.

Batting, fielding, earned run, and scoring averages are figured as follows:

1. Batting averages for baseball or softball are determined by dividing the number of hits by the total number of times at bat.
2. Fielding averages are figured by dividing the total number of put-outs, assists, and errors into the total number of put-outs and assists.
3. Pitchers' earned run averages are calculated by multiplying the number of earned runs by 9 and dividing this product by the total number of innings pitched. For 7-inning games, the number of earned runs is multiplied by 7.
4. A scoring average in basketball or any other sport is determined by dividing the number of games played into the total points scored.

Appendix A

Suggested Course Outline for Intramurals

I. Title: Programming Intramurals

II. Course Description: Study of the basic ingredients required for administering successful intramural programs

III. Credits: Three

IV. Objectives:

A. To develop an understanding of the framework within which intramural programs exist.

B. To develop an awareness of the fundamental actions and reactions which guarantee successful programming.

C. To develop the technique of ideation as it relates to producing new ideas for solving program problems.

D. To demonstrate that basic program ingredients are identical and applicable at all levels and for all programs: boys and girls, men and women, military units, industrial firms, community recreation centers, elementary schools, junior high schools, senior high schools, colleges, and universities.

V. References:

American Association for Health, Physical Education, and Recreation. *Campus Recreation.* Washington, D.C.: The Association, 1968, p. 90.

———. *Desirable Athletic Competition for Children of Elementary School Age.* Washington, D.C.: The Association, 1968, p. 28.

———. *Intramural Sports for College Men and Women,* rev. ed. Washington, D.C.: The Association, 1964, p. 28.

Anton, Thomas, and Toschi, Louis. *A Practical Approach to Intramural Sports.* Portland, Maine: J. Weston Walch, 1964, p. 133.

Beeman, Harris F., and Humphrey, James H. *Intramural Sports—A Text and Study Guide.* Dubuque, Iowa: Wm. C. Brown Company, 1960, p. 101.

Boyden, E. Douglas, and Burton, Roger G. *Staging Successful Tournaments.* New York: Association Press, 1957, p. 169.

California Association for Supervision and Curriculum Development. *Organizing and Conducting Intramural Programs, Play Days, Sports Days, Field Days, Grades 4–8.* Sacramento: The Association, 1964, p. 75.

Dade County Public Schools. *Elementary After School Intramural Handbook.* Miami: Dade County Public Schools, 1961, p. 60.

Department of the Army. *Intramural Sports for the Army.* Washington, D.C.: Department of the Army, 1965, p. 47.

Division of Girls and Women's Sports. *Standards in Sports for Girls and Women.* rev. ed. Washington, D.C.: American Association for Health, Physical Education, and Recreation, 1964, p. 56.

Hall, J. Tillman. *School Recreation: Its Organization, Supervision, and Administration.* Dubuque, Iowa: Wm. C. Brown Company, 1966, p. 157.

Hurst-Euless-Bedford Public Schools. *Intramural Activities Guide.* Hurst, Texas: Hurst-Euless-Bedford Public Schools, 1967, p. 37.

Kleindienst, Viola K., and Weston, Arthur. *Intramural and Recreation Programs for Schools and Colleges.* New York: Appleton-Century-Crofts, 1964, p. 559.

Leavitt, Norma M., and Price, Hartley D. *Intramural and Recreational Sports for High School and College.* New York: The Ronald Press Company, 1958, p. 309.

Matthews, David O., ed. *Intramurals for Elementary School Children.* The Athletic Institute, 1964, p. 50.

———. *Intramurals for the Junior High School.* The Athletic Institute, 1964, p. 45.

———. *Intramurals for the Senior High School.* The Athletic Institute, 1964, p. 53.

Means, Louis A. *Intramurals: Their Organization and Administration.* Englewood Cliffs, N.J.: Prentice-Hall, Inc., 1963, p. 381.

Mueller, C. E., and McGurie, Raymond. *Directory of References for Intramurals.* Washington, D.C.: American Association for Health, Physical Education, and Recreation. In press.

National Industrial Recreation Association. *How to Organize and Manage Tournaments.* Chicago: The Association, 1945, p. 32.

Werner, George I. *After-School Games and Sports, Grades 4, 5, 6.* Washington, D.C.: American Association for Health, Physical Education, and Recreation, 1964, p. 55.

VI. Course Procedures:

A. Classes meet three times weekly and consist of lectures, audio visual presentations, and buzz sessions.

B. Written summaries of assigned intramural readings are required.

C. Students must prepare a comprehensive written report on some phase of intramural programming. This project emphasizes ideation concepts, creating a method for resolving an existing problem or evolving a totally new program idea, regardless of its apparent practical application.

D. Study quizzes and examinations are based on supplementary readings, lectures, and discussions.

E. Evaluation
1. Participation in class discussions
2. Written reports of reading assignments
3. Class project
4. Written study quizzes and examinations

VII. Topical Outline:

A. Intramurals: What and Why
1. The meaning of intramurals
   a. Evolution of intramural terminology
   b. Related terminology
2. Scope of intramurals
   a. Phases of intramurals
      (1) Highly organized, competitive
      (2) Self-directed, impromptu, informal
   b. Intramurals as recreation
   c. Intramurals as physical education
   d. Intramurals and varsity sports
3. Values of intramural participation
   a. Historical references
   b. Success and failure experiences
   c. Physical fitness
   d. Mental and emotional health
   e. Social contacts
   f. Use of leisure time
   g. Esprit de corps
   h. Permanent participator–spectator interests

B. Intramurals: Past, Present, and Future
1. Development of intramurals in America
   a. Student organization
   b. Departmental control
   c. Early programs for women
2. Formation of professional intramural groups
   a. National Intramural Association
   b. National Intramural Sports Council
3. Summary of historical dates
4. Present status and future trends

C. Administrative Organization and Personnel
1. Organizational patterns
   a. Military units
   b. Industrial firms
   c. Elementary, junior high, and senior high schools
   d. Colleges and universities
   e. Campus recreation coordination
   f. Organizational associations

2. Student versus faculty administration
3. Combined student and faculty administration
4. Program personnel
5. Administrative considerations

D. Ideas for Intramurals
1. Power of an idea
2. Process of producing ideas
3. Individual and group ideation
4. Examples of ideas for intramurals

E. Finances, Facilities, and Equipment
1. Finances
   a. Sources of income
   b. Budgetary considerations
   c. Budget outline
2. Facilities
   a. Indoor facilities
   b. Outdoor facilities
   c. Cooperative use of facilities
3. Equipment
   a. General policies
   b. Purchase of equipment
   c. Care of equipment
   d. Issuing equipment
4. Future facilities and equipment concepts

F. Units of Participation
1. Athletic club units
2. Boarding club units
3. Boy and Girl Scout units
4. Co-intramural units
5. Departmental or divisional units
6. Dormitory units
7. Faculty-staff units
8. Foreign students' units
9. Fraternities' and sororities' units
10. Geographical or residential units
11. Grade or class units
12. Graduate student units
13. Home room or advisory units
14. Military units
15. Physical education section units
16. Religious units
17. Special interest units
18. Sports club units
19. Unaffiliated units
20. Unstructured participation

G. Program of Activities
1. Criteria for selection
2. Seasonal activities
3. Summaries of selected activities

H. Scheduling: When and How
1. Time periods
   a. Early mornings, middays, late afternoons
   b. Evenings and weekends
   c. Activity periods and gym classes
   d. Vacation and special intramural days
2. Scheduling procedures
   a. Scheduling considerations
   b. Entry blanks
   c. Scheduling forms
   d. Postponements and rescheduling
   e. Forfeits

I. Structuring Tournaments
1. Meets
   a. Track and field
   b. Swimming
   c. Gymnastics
2. Round robin tournaments
   a. Round robin calculations
      (1) Rotation methods
      (2) Graph methods
   b. Round robin variations
      (1) Continuous round robin
      (2) Play-til-you-win method
      (3) Lombard tournament
3. Elimination tournaments
   a. Single elimination tournaments
   b. Double elimination tournaments
      (1) Over-and-under method
      (2) Back-to-back method
   c. Semi-double elimination tournaments
   d. Consolation tournaments
      (1) Simple elimination
      (2) Second place
      (3) Mueller-Anderson playback
      (4) Bagnall-Wild
4. Challenge tournaments
   a. Ladder, pyramid, and open pyramid
   b. King or crown
   c. Funnel and upside-down funnel
   d. Round-the-clock and spider web
   e. Record bump board

5. Informal-type tournaments
   a. Marker and ringer
   b. Rotation and detour
   c. Telephonic, telegraphic, and postal
6. Classification and equalization methods
   a. Combination tournaments
      (1) Round robin-elimination
      (2) Mueller-Anderson playback-elimination
      (3) Mueller-Anderson playback-round robin
   b. Qualifying rounds or heats
   c. Age, height, weight classifications
   d. Seeding participants
   e. Handicap procedures

J. Point Systems: Group and Individual
1. Pros and cons of point systems
2. Types of systems and distribution methods
3. Selection of a point system
4. Participation–performance point system
   a. Minimum–maximum scale
   b. Point distribution
   c. Application of points for competition
   d. Point totals and tables
5. Individual point systems
   a. Team scoring
   b. Individual scoring
   c. Combination scoring

K. Program Rules and Regulations
1. Game rules
   a. Modifications of rules
   b. Officiating game rules
      (1) Selection of officials
      (2) Payment of officials
      (3) Rating of officials
      (4) Sportsmanship rating of teams
   c. Conduct of participants
2. Eligibility rules
   a. Individual eligibility
      (1) Scholarship
      (2) Participation limitations
      (3) Letter winners
      (4) Varsity and freshman squads
      (5) Professional athletes
   b. Organizational eligibility
      (1) Dormitory units
      (2) Fraternities'–sororities' units
      (3) Independent units
      (4) League classifications

       c. Eligibility forms
          (1) Eligibility lists and cards
          (2) Parental approval
   3. Violations and disciplinary procedures
       a. Protests
       b. Role of unit managers
   4. Health and safety
       a. Medical examinations
       b. Safety procedures

L. Publicity and Recognition
   1. Publicity
       a. Principles of advertising
       b. Communications media
   2. Symbols of recognition
       a. Awards considerations
       b. Types of awards
       c. Presentation of awards
       d. Other forms of recognition

M. Extramurals and Sports Clubs
   1. Extramurals
       a. Types of extramural participation
          (1) Sports days
          (2) Play days
       b. Pros and cons of extramurals
       c. Administrative considerations
          (1) Management
          (2) Finances
          (3) Transportation
          (4) Liability and insurance
   2. Sports clubs
       a. Organization
       b. Competition
       c. Types of clubs

N. Co-Intramurals, Special Programs, and Evaluation
   1. Co-intramurals
       a. Types of activities
       b. Administrative suggestions
   2. Faculty programs
       a. Types of activities
       b. Faculty–family sessions
       c. Faculty–student sports nights
   3. Special events
       a. Open houses
       b. Winter sports carnivals
       c. Aquatic festivals
       d. Sports clinics

4. Program evaluation
   a. Statistical records
   b. Check lists and rating scales
   c. Consultant visitations
   d. Evaluation by participants

Appendix B

Statement of Policies for Competition in Girls and Women's Sports [1,2]

Approved May 1963 by Division for Girls and Women's Sports Executive Council and American Association for Health, Physical Education, and Recreation Board of Directors

The Division for Girls and Women's Sports of the American Association for Health, Physical Education, and Recreation believes the competitive element in sports activities can be used constructively for achievement of desirable educational and recreational objectives. When favorable con-

[1] This is a revision of the "Statement of Policies and Procedures for Competition in Girls and Women's Sports," which was published in the September 1957 *Journal of Health, Physical Education, Recreation* and later in 1958 and 1961 editions of *Standards in Sports for Girls and Women,* published by AAHPER. This revised statement is an outgrowth of recent DGWS discussions of major issues, one of which dealt with the needs and interests of the highly skilled girl.

[2] Division for Girls and Women's Sports, *Standards in Sports for Girls and Women* (rev. ed.; Washington, D.C.: American Association for Health, Physical Education, and Recreation, 1964), pp. 46–50. (Courtesy AAHPER.)

ditions are present, competitive experiences may be wholesome and beneficial and result in acceptable conduct and attitudes. Competition in and of itself does not automatically result in desirable or undesirable outcomes.

The adoption of practices best suited for the attainment of desirable outcomes is the responsibility of all associated with competitive events. Sponsoring agencies, players, teachers, coaches, officials, and spectators must share responsibility for valid practices in competitive sports.

DGWS believes participation in sports competition is the privilege of all girls and women. Sound instructional and well-organized intramural programs will answer the needs and desires of the majority of young women. For the college woman and high school girl who seek and need additional challenges in competition and skills, a sound, carefully planned, and well-directed program of extramural sports is recommended. The provisions for extramural sports opportunities should be broad, including such events as sports days, leagues, meets, and tournaments. Development of all participants toward higher competencies and advanced skills should be a major objective in all sports programs.

DGWS advocates the following policies through which desirable outcomes in competition may be achieved.

Definition of Competition

Competition is defined as the participation in a sport activity by two or more persons, in which a winner can result. The educational values of competition are determined by the quality of leadership and of the participation. For the best results, there should be comprehensive physical education, intramural, and extramural programs. The organized competitive programs should offer opportunities in terms of individual ability and should be adapted to the needs and interests of the participants.

Forms of Competition

Intramural competition is sports competition in which all participants are identified with the same school, community center, club, organization, institution, or industry, or are residents of a designated small neighborhood or community. This form of competition stresses the participation of "the many." A good intramural program which offers a variety of activities, at various skill levels, including corecreational activities, frequently is sufficient to meet the needs and desires of the majority of girls and women.

It is the responsibility of the school or agency sponsoring the intramural program to provide the time, facilities, and competent leadership, with preference given to professional, qualified women. Intramural programs should be an outgrowth of and a complement to the school physical education program or the organized community recreation program.

Extramural competition is a plan of sports competition in which participants from two or more schools, community centers, clubs, organizations, institutions, industries, or neighborhoods compete. The forms of extramural competition include:

1. Sport days—school or sport group participates as a unit.
2. Telegraphic meets—results are compared by wire or mail.
3. Invitational events—symposiums, games, or matches, for which a school or sport group invites one or more teams to participate.
4. Interscholastic, intercollegiate, or interagency programs—groups which are trained and coached play a series of scheduled games and/or tournaments with teams from other schools, cities, or organizations.

The extramural program is planned and carried out to complement the intramural and instructional programs. For the best welfare of the participants, it is essential that the program be conducted by qualified leaders, be supported by budgeted funds, and be representative of approved objectives and standards for girls and women's sports, including acceptable conditions of travel, protective insurance, appropriate facilities, proper equipment, and desirable practices in the conduct of the events. When the program affords group participation as a team in a series of games on appropriate tournament or schedule basis, additional coaching by qualified staff members must be provided.

It is assumed that the sponsoring organization recognizes its obligation to delegate responsibility for this program to the supervisor or specialist in charge of the girls and women's sports programs. When admission charges are made, the proceeds should be used for furthering the sports programs for girls (instructional, intramural, and extramural).

Adaptation of Competitive Sports for Age-Level Groupings in School Prgrams

In junior high school, it is desirable that intramural programs of competitive activities be closely integrated with the basic physical education program. Appropriate competition at this level should be comprised of intramural and informal extramural events consistent with social needs and recreational interests. A well-organized and well-conducted sports program should take into account the various skill levels and thus meet the needs of the more highly skilled.

In senior high school, a program of intramural and extramural participation should be arranged to augment a sound and inclusive instructional program in physical education. It should be recognized that an interscholastic program will require professional leadership, time, and funds in addition to those provided for the intramural programs. Facilities should be such that the intramural and instructional programs need not be eliminated or seriously curtailed if an interscholastic program is offered.

Specifically, the following standards should prevail:

1. The medical status of the player is ascertained by a physician and the health of the players is carefully supervised.
2. Activities for girls and women are planned to meet their needs, not for the personal glorification of coaches and/or sponsoring organizations.
3. The salary, retention, and promotion of an instructor are not dependent upon the outcome of the games.
4. Qualified women teach, coach, and officiate wherever and whenever possible, and in all cases the professional background and experience of the leader meet established standards.
5. Rules approved by DGWS are used.
6. Schedules do not exceed the ability and endurance relative to the maturity and physiological conditioning of the participants. Standards for specific sports are defined by DGWS and appear in sports guides, published by the American Association for Health, Physical Education, and Recreation, 1201 Sixteenth Street, N.W., Washington, D. C. 20036.
7. Sports activities for girls and women are scheduled independently from boys and men's sports. Exceptions will occur when the activities and/or time and facilities are appropriate for both.
8. Girls and women may participate in appropriate corecreational activities or teams. Girls and women may not participate as members of boys and men's teams.
9. The program, including health insurance for players, is financed by budgeted school or organization funds rather than entirely by admission charges.
10. Provision is made by the school or organization for safe transportation by bonded carriers, with chaperones who are responsible to the sponsoring group.

In colleges and universities, it is desirable that opportunities be provided for the highly skilled beyond the intramural program. Regulations for the conduct of collegiate competition have been developed by the National Joint Committee on Extramural Sports for College Women [3] and are available from the committee for any specific sport activity. While

[3] Composed of representatives of the Division for Girls and Women's Sports, Athletic and Recreation Federation of College Women, and National Association for Physical Education of College Women. Write to American Association for Health, Physical Education, and Recreation, 1201 Sixteenth Street, N.W., Washington, D. C. 20036.

the statements of NJCESCW apply to approval for state-wide or wider geographical tournaments, the principles may also be applicable to or guide the conduct of local and district tournaments.

In addition to the standards previously listed, other standards pertinent to the colleges are:

1. The amount and kind of intercollegiate competition should be determined by the women's physical education department.
2. The financial arrangements relative to all intercollegiate sports events should be administered with the approval of the women's physical education department.
3. The time involved in relation to intercollegiate competition should not interfere with the academic program of the institution sponsoring the event and should not make excessive demands upon the participants' academic schedules.
4. All housing arrangements relative to visiting participants should be approved by the women's physical education department.

Adaptations of Competitive Sports for Age-Level Groupings in Public and Private Recreation Agency Programs

DGWS recognizes that the sports programs of public and private recreation agencies make a valuable contribution to girls and women. The aims and objectives of community recreation agencies in their conduct of sports programs are similar to those of the schools. By using common rules and applying basic standards in organizing competition, many girls and women can be given the opportunity to develop skills and to enjoy a desirable type of competition.

Students should be informed of the opportunities for participation in the sports activities of these agencies. If a student contemplates entering events which appear to jeopardize her welfare, she should be given guidance which will help her to make wise decisions.

If individuals are grouped according to age and skill ability, the statements of policy outlined above can be applied by these agencies in organizing desirable forms of competition. The formation of leagues is often the organizational structure through which many recreation programs are conducted. The definitions of intramural and extramural competition, as previously stated, may be interpreted to apply to programs provided by public and private agencies.

Modifications will be required in planning policies for competition depending upon the age level involved:

1. For girls under senior high school age, competition may be provided in intramural games, that is, games with teams of the same age and

ability from the same neighborhood, playground, recreation center, or league. Extramural events consistent with social needs and recreational interests of junior high school age groups may be arranged with similar teams from other playgrounds, centers, or leagues.

2. For girls of senior high school age, it is recommended that all standards listed for senior high school be used for intramural and extramural competition. A player should affiliate with only one team in one sport.

3. For girls over senior high school age, it is recommended that the intercollegiate standards be followed for competition at this age level.

Sponsorship by recreational agencies of the participation of women in tournaments and meets organized at successively higher levels (local, sectional, national) should be governed by the best practices for safeguarding the welfare of the participants. The organization, administration, and leadership of such competitive events should be conducted so that the basic policies of DGWS are upheld.

Appendix C

Sigma Delta Psi
Requirements and
Scoring Tables

Sigma Delta Psi is a national honorary athletic fraternity with chapters in many colleges and universities. To become a member, a student must pass certain sports tests. The requirements and scoring tables are presented for the convenience of personnel responsible for these activities. Member schools may use them for national and local competition, and others can utilize the requirements for a self-testing program and apply the point tables to local team and individual participation.

Ten students with the highest total points, as determined by the tables on the basis of individual performances for each test, comprise each team for national competition. The same pattern can be followed for competition between local intramural organizations, with a possible modification of using less than ten team members.

Individual records indicating best times, distances, and most points earned can be maintained. Additional information about receiving charters and participating in national competition can be obtained by writing to college and university intramural departments.

SIGMA DELTA PSI REQUIREMENTS *

TEST NO.   REQUIREMENT

1. 100-yard dash .... 11⅗ seconds
2. 120-yard low hurdles .... 16 seconds
3. Running high jump .... Height, weight classification
4. Running broad jump .... 17 feet
5. 16-pound shot put .... 30 feet
6. 20-foot rope climb .... 12 seconds
   or golf .... 4 of 5 shots
7. Baseball throw .... 250 feet
   or javelin throw .... 130 feet
8. Football punt .... 120 feet
9. 100-yard swim .... 1 minute, 45 seconds
10. 1-mile run .... 6 minutes
11. Front handspring, landing on feet .... ———
12. Handstand .... 10 seconds
    or bowling .... 160 average for 3 games
13. Bar vault .... Chin high
14. Good posture .... Standard B (H.B.M.)
15. Scholarship .... Eligible for varsity competition

* Reproduced by permission from Sigma Delta Psi.

TEST NO. 2. Five standard low hurdles, placed twenty yards apart, shall be used to a flight. The test to be valid necessitates that all hurdles must remain upright from their bases.

TEST NO. 3. The high jump requirement is based on a graduated scale that considers the height and weight of each individual.

TEST NO. 5. Thirty feet is the requirement for a man of 160 pounds or over, the requirement to be scaled down in accordance with the following proportion for candidates of less weight:

160 pounds is to the candidate's weight as 30 feet is to the requirement.

TEST NO. 6. *Rope Climb.* The candidate shall start from a sitting position on the floor and climb rope without use of legs. Legs may be used in the descent.

Golf. 4 out of 5 shots must land on the fly in a circle (10 ft. radius) from a distance of 75 feet.

TEST NO. 12. *Handstand.* The candidate shall not be compelled to remain stationary during the test, neither shall he be allowed to advance or retreat more than three feet in any direction.

Bowling. The candidate must average 160 for 3 games. Only 3 games may be bowled in any one day.

TEST NO. 14. The candidate shall be required to pass the B standard of the Harvard Body Mechanics Posture Chart. These charts will be furnished all local chapters. The Director or Committee on Certification should observe the candidate's posture when he is not aware of the fact.

TEST NUMBERS 1, 2, 5, 7, and 8 shall be attempted crosswise or into the wind to be accepted by the Director or Committee on Certification.

The national collegiate rules for the various activities of the tests are the accepted standards.

Sigma Delta Psi

This certifies that

Glenn Miller

*has been elected a member of Sigma Delta Psi
by Intramural University, Iota Mu Chapter,
December 4, 1975*

E. E. Mueller
National President

J. S. Picard
National Secretary Treasurer

SIGMA DELTA PSI
SHOT PUT
WEIGHT AND DISTANCE SCALE

WEIGHT	DISTANCE	WEIGHT	DISTANCE
160 LBS. AND OVER	30' 0"	139 LBS.	26' 3/4"
159 LBS.	29' 9 3/4"	138 LBS.	25'10 1/2"
158 LBS.	29' 7 1/2"	137 LBS.	25' 8 1/4"
157 LBS.	29' 5 1/4"	136 LBS.	25' 6"
156 LBS.	29' 3"	135 LBS.	25' 3 3/4"
155 LBS.	29' 3/4"	134 LBS.	25' 1 1/2"
154 LBS.	28'10 1/2"	133 LBS.	24'11 1/4"
153 LBS.	28' 8 1/4"	132 LBS.	24' 9"
152 LBS.	28' 6"	131 LBS.	24' 6 3/4"
151 LBS.	28' 3 3/4"	130 LBS.	24' 4 1/2"
150 LBS.	28' 1 1/2"	129 LBS.	24' 2 1/4"
149 LBS.	27'11 1/4"	128 LBS.	24' 0"
148 LBS.	27' 9"	127 LBS.	23' 9 3/4"
147 LBS.	27' 6 3/4"	126 LBS.	23' 7 1/2"
146 LBS.	27' 4 1/2"	125 LBS.	23' 5 1/4"
145 LBS.	27' 2 1/4"	124 LBS.	23' 3"
144 LBS.	27' 0"	123 LBS.	23' 3/4"
143 LBS.	26' 9 3/4"	122 LBS.	22'10 1/2"
142 LBS.	26' 7 1/2"	121 LBS.	22' 8 1/4"
141 LBS.	26' 5 1/4"	120 LBS.	22' 6"
140 LBS.	26' 3"		

SIGMA DELTA PSI HIGH JUMP REQUIREMENTS

CANDIDATE	WEIGHT-CLASS	JUMP	CANDIDATE	WEIGHT-CLASS	JUMP
6' 4"	BELOW 159	5' 4"	5' 9"	BELOW 149	4' 9"
	160 to 169	5' 3"		150 to 159	4' 8"
	170 to 179	5' 2"		160 to 169	4' 7"
	180 to 189	5' 1"		170 to 179	4' 6"
	190 AND OVER	5' 0"		180 AND OVER	4' 5"
6' 3"	BELOW 159	5' 3"	5' 8"	BELOW 139	4' 8"
	160 to 169	5' 2"		140 to 149	4' 7"
	170 to 179	5' 1"		150 to 159	4' 6"
	180 to 189	5' 0"		160 to 169	4' 5"
	190 AND OVER	4' 11"		170 AND OVER	4' 4"
6' 2"	BELOW 159	5' 2"	5' 7"	BELOW 139	4' 7"
	160 to 169	5' 1"		140 to 149	4' 6"
	170 to 179	5' 0"		150 to 159	4' 5"
	180 to 189	4' 11"		160 to 169	4' 4"
	190 AND OVER	4' 10"		170 AND OVER	4' 3"
6' 1"	BELOW 159	5' 1"	5' 6"	BELOW 139	4' 6"
	160 to 169	5' 0"		140 to 149	4' 5"
	170 to 179	4' 11"		150 to 159	4' 4"
	180 to 189	4' 10"		160 to 169	4' 3"
	190 AND OVER	4' 9"		170 AND OVER	4' 2"
6' 0"	BELOW 149	5' 0"	5' 5"	BELOW 139	4' 5"
	150 to 159	4' 11"		140 to 149	4' 4"
	160 to 169	4' 10"		150 to 159	4' 3"
	170 to 179	4' 9"		160 to 169	4' 2"
	180 AND OVER	4' 8"		170 AND OVER	4' 1"
5' 11"	BELOW 149	4' 11"	5' 4"	BELOW 129	4' 4"
	150 to 159	4' 10"		130 to 139	4' 3"
	160 to 169	4' 9"		140 to 149	4' 2"
	170 to 179	4' 8"		150 to 159	4' 1"
	180 AND OVER	4' 7"		160 AND OVER	4' 0"
5' 10"	BELOW 149	4' 10"	5' 3"	BELOW 129	4' 3"
	150 to 159	4' 9"		130 to 139	4' 2"
	160 to 169	4' 8"		140 to 149	4' 1"
	170 to 179	4' 7"		150 to 159	4' 0"
	180 AND OVER	4' 6"		160 AND OVER	3' 11"

FOOTBALL PUNT

Distance	Points
210'	100*
205'	96.2
200'	92.4
195'	88.6
190'	84.8
185'	81.0
180'	77.2
175'	73.4
170'	69.6
165'	65.8
160'	62.0
155'	58.2
150'	54.4
145'	50.6
140'	46.8
135'	43.0
130'	39.2
125'	35.4
120'	31.6
115'	27.6
110'	23.6
105'	19.6
100'	15.6
95'	11.6
90'	7.6
85'	3.6

120 YARD LOW HURDLES

Time	Points	Time	Points
12.4	100*	15.1	48.7
12.5	98.1	15.2	46.8
12.6	96.2	15.3	44.9
12.7	94.3	15.4	43.0
12.8	92.4	15.5	41.1
12.9	90.5	15.6	39.2
13.0	88.6	15.7	37.3
13.1	86.7	15.8	35.4
13.2	84.8	15.9	33.5
13.3	82.9	16.0	31.6
13.4	81.0	16.1	29.7
13.5	79.1	16.2	27.8
13.6	77.2	16.3	25.9
13.7	75.3	16.4	24.0
13.8	73.4	16.5	22.1
13.9	71.5	16.6	20.2
14.0	69.6	16.7	18.3
14.1	67.7	16.8	16.4
14.2	65.8	16.9	14.5
14.3	63.9	17.0	12.6
14.4	62.0	17.1	10.7
14.5	60.1	17.2	8.8
14.6	58.2	17.3	6.9
14.7	56.3	17.4	5.0
14.8	54.4	17.5	3.1
14.9	52.5	17.6	1.2
15.0	50.6		

RUNNING HIGH JUMP

Height	Points
6' 6"	100*
6' 5"	96.2
6' 4"	92.4
6' 3"	88.6
6' 2"	84.8
6' 1"	81.0
6' 0"	77.2
5'11"	73.4
5'10"	69.6
5' 9"	65.8
5' 8"	62.0
5' 7"	58.2
5' 6"	54.4
5' 5"	50.6
5' 4"	46.8
5' 3"	43.0
5' 2"	39.2
5' 1"	35.4
5' 0"	31.6
4'11"	27.8
4'10"	24.0
4' 9"	20.2
4' 8"	16.4
4' 7"	12.6
4' 6"	8.8
4' 5"	5.0
4' 4"	1.2

BASEBALL THROW

Dist.	Pts.	Dist.	Pts.
350'	100*	268'	43.3
346'	97.9	265'	41.2
343'	95.8	262'	39.1
340'	93.7	259'	37.0
337'	91.6	256'	34.9
334'	89.5	253'	32.8
331'	87.4	250'	30.7
328'	85.3	247'	29.2
325'	83.2	244'	27.7
322'	81.1	241'	26.2
319'	79.0	238'	24.7
316'	76.9	235'	23.2
313'	74.8	232'	21.7
310'	72.7	229'	20.2
307'	70.6	226'	18.7
304'	68.5	223'	17.2
301'	66.4	220'	15.7
298'	64.3	217'	14.2
295'	62.2	214'	12.7
292'	60.1	211'	11.2
289'	58.0	208'	9.7
286'	55.9	205'	8.2
283'	53.8	202'	6.7
280'	51.7	199'	5.2
277'	49.6	196'	3.7
274'	47.5	193'	2.2
271'	45.4	190'	1.1

16- LB. SHOT PUT

Dist.	Pts.	Dist.	Pts.
49'	100*	35' 6"	51.4
48' 6"	98.2	35'	49.6
48'	96.4	34' 6"	47.8
47' 6"	94.6	34'	46.0
47'	92.8	33' 6"	44.2
46' 6"	91.0	33'	42.4
46'	89.2	32' 6"	40.6
45' 6"	87.4	32'	38.8
45'	85.6	31' 6"	37.0
44' 6"	83.8	31'	35.2
44'	82.0	30' 6"	33.4
43' 6"	80.2	30'	31.6
43'	78.4	29' 6"	29.6
42' 6"	76.6	29'	27.6
42'	74.8	28' 6"	25.6
41' 6"	73.0	28'	23.6
41'	71.2	27' 6"	21.6
40' 6"	69.4	27'	19.6
40'	67.6	26' 6"	17.6
39' 6"	65.8	26'	15.6
39'	64.0	25' 6"	13.6
38' 6"	62.2	25'	11.6
38'	60.4	24' 6"	9.6
37' 6"	58.6	24'	7.6
37'	56.8	23' 6"	5.6
36' 6"	55.0	23'	3.6
36'	53.2	22' 6"	1.6

		100-YARD							
BAR VAULT		**DASH**		**ONE-MILE RUN**					

Ht.	Pts.
7' 0"	100*
6'11"	97.1
6'10"	94.2
6' 9"	91.3
6' 8"	88.4
6' 7"	85.5
6' 6"	82.6
6' 5"	79.7
6' 4"	76.8
6' 3"	73.9
6' 2"	71.0
6' 1"	68.1
6' 0"	65.2
5'11"	62.3
5'10"	59.4
5' 9"	56.5
5' 8"	53.6
5' 7"	50.7
5' 6"	47.8
5' 5"	44.9
5' 4"	42.0
5' 3"	39.1
5' 2"	36.2
5' 1"	33.3
5' 0"	30.4
4'11"	27.4
4'10"	24.4
4' 9"	21.4
4' 8"	18.4
4' 7"	15.4
4' 6"	12.4
4' 5"	9.4
4' 4"	6.4
4' 3"	3.4

Time	Pts.
9.8	100*
9.9	96.2
10.0	92.4
10.1	88.6
10.2	84.8
10.3	81.0
10.4	77.2
10.5	73.4
10.6	69.6
10.7	65.8
10.8	62.0
10.9	58.2
11.0	54.4
11.1	50.6
11.2	46.8
11.3	43.0
11.4	39.2
11.5	35.4
11.6	31.6
11.7	28.6
11.8	25.6
11.9	22.6
12.0	19.6
12.1	16.6
12.2	13.6
12.3	10.6
12.4	7.6
12.5	4.6
12.6	2.6

Time	Pts.	Time	Pts.	Time	Pts.	Time	Pts.
4:15	100*	4:49	77.9	5:23	55.8	5:57	33.7
4:16	99.4	4:50	77.3	5:24	55.2	5:58	33.1
4:17	98.7	4:51	76.6	5:25	54.5	5:59	32.4
4:18	98.1	4:52	76.0	5:26	53.9	6:00	31.8
4:19	97.4	4:53	75.3	5:27	53.2	6:01	30.8
4:20	96.8	4:54	74.7	5:28	52.6	6:02	29.8
4:21	96.1	4:55	74.0	5:29	51.9	6:03	28.8
4:22	95.5	4:56	73.4	5:30	51.3	6:04	27.8
4:23	94.8	4:57	72.7	5:31	50.6	6:05	26.8
4:24	94.2	4:58	72.1	5:32	50.0	6:06	25.8
4:25	93.5	4:59	71.4	5:33	49.3	6:07	24.8
4:26	92.9	5:00	70.8	5:34	48.7	6:08	23.8
4:27	92.2	5:01	70.1	5:35	48.0	6:09	22.8
4:28	91.6	5:02	69.5	5:36	47.4	6:10	21.8
4:29	90.9	5:03	68.8	5:37	46.7	6:11	20.8
4:30	90.3	5:04	68.2	5:38	46.1	6:12	19.8
4:31	89.6	5:05	67.5	5:39	45.4	6:13	18.8
4:32	89.0	5:06	66.9	5:40	44.8	6:14	17.8
4:33	88.3	5:07	66.2	5:41	44.1	6:15	16.8
4:34	87.7	5:08	65.6	5:42	43.5	6:16	15.8
4:35	87.0	5:09	64.9	5:43	42.8	6:17	14.8
4:36	86.4	5:10	64.3	5:44	42.2	6:18	13.8
4:37	85.7	5:11	63.6	5:45	41.5	6:19	12.8
4:38	85.1	5:12	63.0	5:46	40.9	6:20	11.8
4:39	84.4	5:13	62.3	5:47	40.2	6:21	10.8
4:40	83.8	5:14	61.7	5:48	39.6	6:22	9.8
4:41	83.1	5:15	61.0	5:49	38.9	6:23	8.8
4:42	82.5	5:16	60.4	5:50	38.3	6:24	7.8
4:43	81.8	5:17	59.7	5:51	37.6	6:25	6.8
4:44	81.2	5:18	59.1	5:52	37.0	6:26	5.8
4:45	80.5	5:19	58.4	5:53	36.3	6:27	4.8
4:46	79.9	5:20	57.8	5:54	35.7	6:28	3.8
4:47	79.2	5:21	57.1	5:55	35.0	6:29	2.8
4:48	78.6	5:22	56.5	5:56	34.4	6:30	1.8

RUNNING BROAD JUMP

Distance	Pts.	Distance	Pts.	Distance	Pts.	Distance	Pts.
25' 0"	100*	22' 3"	76.9	19' 6"	53.8	16' 9"	30.1
24'11"	99.3	22' 2"	76.2	19' 5"	53.1	16' 8"	29.2
24'10"	98.6	22' 1"	75.5	19' 4"	52.4	16' 7"	28.3
24' 9"	97.9	22' 0"	74.8	19' 3"	51.7	16' 6"	27.4
24' 8"	97.2	21'11"	74.1	19' 2"	51.0	16' 5"	26.5
24' 7"	96.5	21'10"	73.4	19' 1"	50.3	16' 4"	25.6
24' 6"	95.8	21' 9"	72.7	19' 0"	49.6	16' 3"	24.7
24' 5"	95.1	21' 8"	72.0	18'11"	48.9	16' 2"	23.8
24' 4"	94.4	21' 7"	71.3	18'10"	48.2	16' 1"	22.9
24' 3"	93.7	21' 6"	70.6	18' 9"	47.5	16' 0"	22.0
24' 2"	93.0	21' 5"	69.9	18' 8"	46.8	15'11"	21.1
24' 1"	92.3	21' 4"	69.2	18' 7"	46.1	15'10"	20.2
24' 0"	91.6	21' 3"	68.5	18' 6"	45.4	15' 9"	19.3
23'11"	90.9	21' 2"	67.8	18' 5"	44.7	15' 8"	18.4
23'10"	90.2	21' 1"	67.1	18' 4"	44.0	15' 7"	17.5
23' 9"	89.5	21' 0"	66.4	18' 3"	43.3	15' 6"	16.6
23' 8"	88.8	20'11"	65.7	18' 2"	42.6	15' 5"	15.7
23' 7"	88.1	20'10"	65.0	18' 1"	41.9	15' 4"	14.8
23' 6"	87.4	20' 9"	64.3	18' 0"	41.2	15' 3"	13.9
23' 5"	86.7	20' 8"	63.6	17'11"	40.5	15' 2"	13.0
23' 4"	86.0	20' 7"	62.9	17'10"	39.8	15' 1"	12.1
23' 3"	85.3	20' 6"	62.2	17' 9"	39.1	15' 0"	11.2
23' 2"	84.6	20' 5"	61.5	17' 8"	38.4	14'11"	10.3
23' 1"	83.9	20' 4"	60.8	17' 7"	37.7	14'10"	9.4
23' 0"	83.2	20' 3"	60.1	17' 6"	37.0	14' 9"	8.5
22'11"	82.5	20' 2"	59.4	17' 5"	36.3	14' 8"	7.6
22'10"	81.8	20' 1"	58.7	17' 4"	35.6	14' 7"	6.7
22' 9"	81.1	20' 0"	58.0	17' 3"	34.9	14' 6"	5.8
22' 8"	80.4	19'11"	57.3	17' 2"	34.2	14' 5"	4.9
22' 7"	79.7	19'10"	56.6	17' 1"	33.5	14' 4"	4.0
22' 6"	79.0	19' 9"	55.9	17' 0"	32.8	14' 3"	3.1
22' 5"	78.3	19' 8"	55.2	16'11"	31.9	14' 2"	2.2
22' 4"	77.6	19' 7"	54.5	16'10"	31.0	14' 1"	1.3

JAVELIN THROW

Dist.	Pts.	Dist.	Pts.	Dist.	Pts.
200'	100*	167'	67	134'	34
199'	99	166'	66	133'	33
198'	98	165'	65	132'	32
197'	97	164'	64	131'	31
196'	96	163'	63	130'	30
195'	95	162'	62	129'	29
194'	94	161'	61	128'	28
193'	93	160'	60	127'	27
192'	92	159'	59	126'	26
191'	91	158'	58	125'	25
190'	90	157'	57	124'	24
189'	89	156'	56	123'	23
188'	88	155'	55	122'	22
187'	87	154'	54	121'	21
186'	86	153'	53	120'	20
185'	85	152'	52	119'	19
184'	84	151'	51	118'	18
183'	83	150'	50	117'	17
182'	82	149'	49	116'	16
181'	81	148'	48	115'	15
180'	80	147'	47	114'	14
179'	79	146'	46	113'	13
178'	78	145'	45	112'	12
177'	77	144'	44	111'	11
176'	76	143'	43	110'	10
175'	75	142'	42	109'	9
174'	74	141'	41	108'	8
173'	73	140'	40	107'	7
172'	72	139'	39	106'	6
171'	71	138'	38	105'	5
170'	70	137'	37	104'	4
169'	69	136'	36	103'	3
168'	68	135'	35	102'	2
				101'	1

100-YARD SWIM

Time	Pts.	Time	Pts.	Time	Pts.
:56	100*	1:23	62.2	1:50	26.4
:57	98.6	1:24	60.8	1:51	25.4
:58	97.2	1:25	59.4	1:52	24.4
:59	95.8	1:26	58.0	1:53	23.4
1:00	94.4	1:27	56.6	1:54	22.4
1:01	93.0	1:28	55.2	1:55	21.4
1:02	91.6	1:29	53.8	1:56	20.4
1:03	90.2	1:30	52.4	1:57	19.4
1:04	88.8	1:31	51.0	1:58	18.4
1:05	87.4	1:32	49.6	1:59	17.4
1:06	86.0	1:33	48.2	2:00	16.4
1:07	84.6	1:34	46.8	2:01	15.4
1:08	83.2	1:35	45.4	2:02	14.4
1:09	81.8	1:36	44.0	2:03	13.4
1:10	80.4	1:37	42.6	2:04	12.4
1:11	79.0	1:38	41.2	2:05	11.4
1:12	77.6	1:39	39.8	2:06	10.4
1:13	76.2	1:40	38.4	2:07	9.4
1:14	74.8	1:41	37.0	2:08	8.4
1:15	73.4	1:42	35.6	2:09	7.4
1:16	72.0	1:43	34.2	2:10	6.4
1:17	70.6	1:44	32.8	2:11	5.4
1:18	69.2	1:45	31.4	2:12	4.4
1:19	67.8	1:46	30.4	2:13	3.4
1:20	66.4	1:47	29.4	2:14	2.4
1:21	65.0	1:48	28.4	2:15	1.4
1:22	63.6	1:49	27.4		

20-FOOT ROPE CLIMB

Time	Pts.	Time	Pts.	Time	Pts.
4.0	100*	7.8	67.7	11.6	35.4
4.1	99.2	7.9	66.9	11.7	34.6
4.2	98.3	8.0	66.0	11.8	33.7
4.3	97.5	8.1	65.2	11.9	32.9
4.4	96.6	8.2	64.3	12.0	32.0
4.5	95.8	8.3	63.5	12.1	31
4.6	94.9	8.4	62.6	12.2	30
4.7	94.1	8.5	61.8	12.3	29
4.8	93.2	8.6	60.9	12.4	28
4.9	92.4	8.7	60.1	12.5	27
5.0	91.5	8.8	59.2	12.6	26
5.1	90.7	8.9	58.4	12.7	25
5.2	89.8	9.0	57.5	12.8	24
5.3	89.0	9.1	56.7	12.9	23
5.4	88.1	9.2	55.8	13.0	22
5.5	87.3	9.3	55.0	13.1	21
5.6	86.4	9.4	54.1	13.2	20
5.7	85.6	9.5	53.3	13.3	19
5.8	84.7	9.6	52.4	13.4	18
5.9	83.9	9.7	51.6	13.5	17
6.0	83.0	9.8	50.7	13.6	16
6.1	82.2	9.9	49.9	13.7	15
6.2	81.3	10.0	49.0	13.8	14
6.3	80.5	10.1	48.2	13.9	13
6.4	79.6	10.2	47.3	14.0	12
6.5	78.8	10.3	46.5	14.1	11
6.6	77.9	10.4	45.6	14.2	10
6.7	77.1	10.5	44.8	14.3	9
6.8	76.2	10.6	43.9	14.4	8
6.9	75.4	10.7	43.1	14.5	7
7.0	74.5	10.8	42.2	14.6	6
7.1	73.7	10.9	41.4	14.7	5
7.2	72.8	11.0	40.5	14.8	4
7.3	72.0	11.1	39.7	14.9	3
7.4	71.1	11.2	38.8	15.0	2
7.5	70.3	11.3	38.0	15.1	1
7.6	69.4	11.4	37.1		
7.7	68.6	11.5	36.3		

HAND STAND

Time	Pts.	Time	Pts.	Time	Pts.
60.0	100*	38.0	69.2	16.0	38.4
59.5	99.3	37.5	68.5	15.5	37.7
59.0	98.6	37.0	67.8	15.0	37.0
58.5	97.9	36.5	67.1	14.5	36.3
58.0	97.2	36.0	66.4	14.0	35.6
57.5	96.5	35.5	65.7	13.5	34.9
57.0	95.8	35.0	65.0	13.0	34.2
56.5	95.1	34.5	64.3	12.5	33.5
56.0	94.4	34.0	63.6	12.0	32.8
55.5	93.7	33.5	62.9	11.5	32.1
55.0	93.0	33.0	62.2	11.0	31.4
54.5	92.3	32.5	61.5	10.5	30.7
54.0	91.6	32.0	60.8	10.0	30.0
53.5	90.9	31.5	60.1	9.9	29
53.0	90.2	31.0	59.4	9.8	28
52.5	89.5	30.5	58.7	9.7	27
52.0	88.8	30.0	58.0	9.6	26
51.5	88.1	29.5	57.3	9.5	25
51.0	87.4	29.0	56.6	9.4	24
50.5	86.7	28.5	55.9	9.3	23
50.0	86.0	28.0	55.2	9.2	22
49.5	85.3	27.5	54.5	9.1	21
49.0	84.6	27.0	53.8	9.0	20
48.5	83.9	26.5	53.1	8.9	19
48.0	83.2	26.0	52.4	8.8	18
47.5	82.5	25.5	51.7	8.7	17
47.0	81.8	25.0	51.0	8.6	16
46.5	81.1	24.5	50.3	8.5	15
46.0	80.4	24.0	49.6	8.4	14
45.5	79.7	23.5	48.9	8.3	13
45.0	79.0	23.0	48.2	8.2	12
44.5	78.3	22.5	47.5	8.1	11
44.0	77.6	22.0	46.8	8.0	10
43.5	76.9	21.5	46.1	7.9	9
43.0	76.2	21.0	45.4	7.8	8
42.5	75.5	20.5	44.7	7.7	7
42.0	74.8	20.0	44.0	7.6	6
41.5	74.1	19.5	43.3	7.5	5
41.0	73.4	19.0	42.6	7.4	4
40.5	72.7	18.5	41.9	7.3	3
40.0	72.0	18.0	41.2	7.2	2
39.5	71.3	17.5	40.5	7.1	1
39.0	70.6	17.0	39.8		
38.5	69.9	16.5	39.1		

BOWLING

3 Game Ave.	Pts.	3 Game Ave.	Pts.	3 Game Ave.	Pts.	3 Game Ave.	Pts.
230	100*	205	75	180	50	155	25
229	99	204	74	179	49	154	24
228	98	203	73	178	48	153	23
227	97	202	72	177	47	152	22
226	96	201	71	176	46	151	21
225	95	200	70	175	45	150	20
224	94	199	69	174	44	149	19
223	93	198	68	173	43	148	18
222	92	197	67	172	42	147	17
221	91	196	66	171	41	146	16
220	90	195	65	170	40	145	15
219	89	194	64	169	39	144	14
218	88	193	63	168	38	143	13
217	87	192	62	167	37	142	12
216	86	191	61	166	36	141	11
215	85	190	60	165	35	140	10
214	84	189	59	164	34	139	9
213	83	188	58	163	33	138	8
212	82	187	57	162	32	137	7
211	81	186	56	161	31	136	6
210	80	185	55	160	30	135	5
209	79	184	54	159	29	134	4
208	78	183	53	158	28	133	3
207	77	182	52	157	27	132	2
206	76	181	51	156	26	131	1

GOLF

Successful Attempts		Maximum Attempts	Points
15	out of	15	100*
14	out of	15	93
13	out of	14	86
12	out of	13	80
11	out of	12	74
10	out of	11	68
9	out of	10	62
8	out of	9	56
7	out of	8	50
6	out of	7	44
5	out of	6	38
4	out of	5	32
3	out of	5	24
2	out of	5	16
1	out of	5	8

Index